CLYDESIDE CAPITAL

For Janne

CLYDESIDE CAPITAL, 1870–1920:

A Social History of Employers

Ronald Johnston

TUCKWELL PRESS

First published in Great Britain by
Tuckwell Press
The Mill House
Phantassie
East Linton
East Lothian EH40 3DG
Scotland

Copyright © Ronald Johnston, 2000

ISBN 1 86232 102 7

Typeset by Carnegie Publishing, Lancaster
Printed by The Cromwell Press, Trowbridge, Wilts

Contents

Acknowledgements

I would like to thank several people for making the writing of this book an easier and more enjoyable task than it might have been. Firstly, Arthur McIvor of Strathclyde University – my one-time supervisor and now friend and colleague – who got me interested in employers' organisations in the first place, and whose knowledge, enthusiasm and advice have greatly assisted me in taking this project from Ph.D. thesis to monograph. The helpful comments of Professors Rick Trainor and Hamish Fraser are also much appreciated. The task of locating the various records of collective employer activity would have been even more demanding without the help of the staff in the various archives that I visited, and those who allowed me access to records kept in private collections deserve my warmest thanks too. Finally, and most importantly, the book would not have been written at all without the long-suffering support of my partner Janne. No value can be placed on her patience over the last four years.

Illustrations

Abbreviations

AEMIA	Ayrshire Employers' Mutual Insurance Association
ASE	Amalgamated Society of Engineers
CSA	Clyde Shipbuilders' Association
CSOA	Clyde Steamship Owners' Association
CSSOA	Clyde Sailing Ship Owners' Association
EEF	Engineering Employers' Federation
FBI	Federation of British Industry
FSA	Farmers' Supply Association
GBRA	Glasgow Boot Retailers' Association
GCVC	Glasgow City Vigilance Committee
GCU	Glasgow Citizens' Union
GCC	Glasgow Chamber of Commerce
GH	*Glasgow Herald*
GLTDA	Glasgow Licensed Trade Defence Association
GMBA	Glasgow Master Bakers' Association
GMMA	Glasgow Master Masons' Association
GMWA	Glasgow Master Wrights' Association
GTA	Glasgow Typographical Association
GWSEC	Glasgow and West of Scotland Employers' Council
GWSLGA	Glasgow and West of Scotland Licensed Grocers' Association
GWSMMA	Glasgow and West of Scotland Metal Merchants' Association
GWSMPA	Glasgow and West of Scotland Master Plumbers' Association
LCA	Lanarkshire Coalmasters' Association
LPDL	Liberty and Property Defence League
MAGB	Mining Association of Great Britain
MCU	Middle Class Union
NCEO	National Confederation of Employers' Organisations
NFUS	National Farmers' Union of Scotland
NWETEA	North West Engineering Trades Employers' Association
SAMP	Scottish Alliance of Master Printers
SAO	Scottish Agricultural Organisation
SBTA	Scottish Building Trades' Association

SMBA	Scottish Master Builders' Association
SCEA	Scottish Coal Exporters' Association
SCMA	Scottish Coal Merchants' Association
SCWS	Scottish Co-operative Wholesale Society
SEFISF	Scottish Employers' Federation of Iron and Steel Founders
SFMA	Scottish Furniture Manufacturers' Association
SFSU	Scottish Farm Servants' Union
SGF	Scottish Grocers' Federation
SIMA	Steel Ingot Makers' Association
SLMA	Scottish Lead Manufacturers' Association
SMBA	Scottish Master Bakers' Association
SMSA	Scottish Master Slaters' Association
SNBTF	Scottish National Building Trades' Federation
STUC	Scottish Trade Union Congress
TDA	Traders' Defence Association
TMA	Tapestry Manufacturers' Association
TUC	Trade Union Congress
UCBS	United Co-operative Baking Society
WSCA	West of Scotland Confectioners' Association
WSISFA	West of Scotland Iron and Steel Founders' Association
WSRDA	West of Scotland Retail Drapers' Association
WSTA	West of Scotland Textile Association

CHAPTER ONE

Introduction and Historiography

Clydeside – which for the purpose of this study encompasses the counties of Lanarkshire, Dunbartonshire, Renfrewshire, and Ayrshire – has a long tradition of internationally renowned industrial excellence. Here, despite the demise of heavy engineering over the last 20 years, the expression 'Clyde-built' still survives as a declaration of craft pride, while the phrase 'Red Clydeside' is embedded deep within the region's folklore and recalls a proud radical past. Many parts of the region were heavily dependent on volatile capital goods markets, and this rendered the area susceptible to a turbulent business cycle. Although the cyclical nature of the market tended to directly affect the engineering and shipbuilding firms, ultimately most of the Clydeside labour force was affected by economic downturns and many workers in the area had to endure frequent bouts of unemployment. The processes of industrialisation and urbanisation occurred much faster here than in any other comparable British region, and Clydeside was further characterised by having high levels of Irish and Highland migration – producing religious sectarianism which unfortunately continues to the present day.

However, although much has been written about Clydeside workers, little has been said about those who employed them. In general, research on Clydeside employers tends to concentrate upon individual 'captains of industry' and the industrial elite, or focuses on specific industries.[1] This is a characteristic of the literature on employers in general, and it has only been comparatively recently that detailed research has been conducted on employer collective action. McIvor's study of the northwest of England finds that employer associations in engineering, the building trade, and cotton textiles were significant and at times powerful organisations in the sphere of labour relations as well as in the regulation of trade.[2] To date, though, with the exception of McIvor's work and unpublished work on woollen manufacturers in Yorkshire, the issue of

---

1. For example A. Slaven and S. Checkland, *Directory of Business Biography 1860–1960*, Vols 1 and 2 (Aberdeen, 1986 and 1990); M. Moss and J. R. Hume, *Workshop of the British Empire: Engineering and Shipbuilding in the West of Scotland* (London, 1977).

2. A. J. McIvor, *Organised Capital* (London, 1996).

employer combination has remained relatively neglected by labour and business historians.[3]

This study attempts to redress the balance by examining the collective action of employers in the Clydeside region over the 1870–1920 period when many employers in the West of Scotland – like British capitalists in general – faced new challenges in the shape of intensifying competition from both British and overseas competitors; from increased state intervention in free-market capitalism; and from a strengthening labour movement. As a consequence of these powerful forces many employers turned to collective action, and the number of employers' associations in the region grew. However, it will be shown that employer combination frequently entailed more than just a defensive collectivism for the purpose of regulating industrial relations, as many associations also became important forums for the propagation of a collective employer consciousness.

As well as illustrating the importance of employers' organisations in the West of Scotland in a range of industries during this period, this regional study will also investigate some theories of business management strategy in general. There are several approaches to the question of what determines labour management policy. Some business theorists argue that the structure of a firm is dictated by its size, and that managers have no real control over its future shape – although the current orthodoxy holds that managers have the power to exercise strategic choices over company structural policy.[4] This argument has filtered into labour history too. Gospel, for example, holds that managerial strategy – and hence the form of a company's labour relations – is, to a great extent, determined by the market in which the firm operates.[5] For Gospel, companies which were able to deal with industrial relations at plant level normally operated in large homogeneous markets, operated continuous-process technology, and lent themsleves to an increased division of labour.[6] Such stable product markets meant that workers in these firms enjoyed relative security of employment, and this made the propagation of company loyalty an effective managerial tactic. Companies such as these, then, did not need the help of their fellow employers to deal with industrial relations. We can briefly relate this model to Clydeside where the shipbuilding companies depended

3. I. M. Magrath, 'Wool Textile Employers' Organisations, Bradford *c.* 1914–1945', Ph.D. thesis, University of Bradford, 1991.

4. See L. Donaldson, *For Positivist Organizational Theory* (London, 1996).

5. H. Gospel, *Markets, Firms and the Management of Labour in Modern Britain* (London, 1992) p. 6.

6. *Ibid.*, p. 17.

upon highly organised skilled labour to produce bespoke capital goods for a volatile market. The short-term employment pattern dictated by this market – and the shifting character of the workforce – prevented the establishment of internal labour control systems, and compelled the shipbuilders to delegate industrial relations issues to employers' associations. In contrast, Singers' sewing machine factory at Clydebank manufactured for a relatively stable 'white goods' market, and this allowed the company to build up a long-term workforce. Singers, therefore – which utilised poorly organised semi-skilled workers under a strict division of labour system – was able to successfully internalise all its labour relations problems.[7]

This approach to labour relations is neo-classical, as it echoes Adam Smith's contention that the division of labour is dictated by the peculiarities of the market. Marxist writers on the other hand take a different perspective – although, like Gospel, their approach is still quite deterministic. In *Capital*, Marx argued that employers could only purchase the *potential* labour power of a workforce. Consequently, in order to ensure the realisation of maximum surplus value, capital must secure control of the point of production.[8] A prerequisite for this authority, though, was the dismantling of the craft autonomy enjoyed by skilled workers – a deskilling dynamic which, Marx believed, became stronger once machinery was extensively utilised.[9] Control, therefore, is the keynote of Marxist approaches to labour management, and within such a model employers' associations are seen primarily as extensions of the capitalists' compulsion to maintain such control. Burawoy argues that the very method of factory production adopted by capitalists – and hence the method of labour control selected – is decreed by the nature of competition and the extent of state intervention. Similarly, Edwards sees capitalist power over labour as essential to profit maximisation.[10]

7. Recent research has found that the propagation of company loyalty by this firm involved a strict anti-trade union policy, and that the firm utilised its flow production technology to increase the pace of production to the detriment of the workers' health and safety. See Glasgow Labour History Workshop, 'A Clash of Work Regimes 'Americanisation' and the Strike at the Singer Sewing Machine Company 1911', W. Kenefick and A. J. McIvor (eds), *Roots of Red Clydeside 1910–1914?* (Edinburgh, 1996), pp. 175–193.

8. Marx argued that the capitalist's eventual seizure of control of the point of production was 'as inevitable as a general taking command of a field of battle'. K. Marx, *Capital Vol. 1* (London, 1976) footnote 34, p. 475.

9. *Ibid.*, p. 536.

10. M. Burawoy, *The Politics of Production: Factory Regimes under Capitalism and Socialism* (1985); R. Edwards, *Contested Terrain: the Transformation of the Workplace in the 20th Century* (New York, 1979).

Offe and Weisenthal argue that employer organisation is inherently stronger than labour organisation – for the simple reason that capitalists are already organised within the firm whereas labour has first to build its collective strength.[11]

There is also a middle-road approach to labour management that lies somewhere between the neo-classical and the Marxist models. Friedman agrees that labour management policy was motivated by capital's need to control labour, but argues that the cyclical nature of capitalism compels industrialists to resort to more subtle forms of control – such as the granting of responsible autonomy to key groups of workers.[12] Fitzgerald, too, argues that industrial relations are all about power struggle, but stresses that co-operation could be as important a management tactic as coercion.[13] To some extent this echoes Gramsci's emphasis on the importance of consensus as a tool of capitalist hegemony, and other writers have seized upon this theory.[14] Kirk, for example, has recently argued that in Britain over the 1850–1920 period 'workplace relations were characterised by the complex interplay of forces of conflict and compromise' – while McIvor's assessment of employers' associations in the north-west of England finds their effectiveness lay in their neutralising of industrial conflict *within* collective bargaining agreements.[15]

There is also what could be classed as a revisionist perspective on management strategy. This stream of historical writing has attacked the idea that managerial strategy was predominantly shaped by the influences of markets or technology – whatever the degree of control. Tolliday and Zeitlin emphasise the diversity of management strategies between employers, regions, and sectors, and believe that it is unwise to try and impose national models as these only obscure the patchiness of British economic development, ignore the persistence of rule-of-thumb

11. C. Offe, *Disorganised Capitalism* (Cambridge, 1985).
12. A. L. Friedman, *Industry and Labour: Class Struggle at Work and Monopoly Capitalism* (London, 1977). For an appraisal of Friedman's theory, see C. R. Littler and G. Salaman, 'Recent theories of the labour process', *Sociology* 16 (1982), pp. 261–263.
13. R. Fitzgerald, *British Labour Management and Industrial Welfare 1846–1939* (London, 1988), p. 13.
14. Gramsci's sharpest example is drawn from the USA. Here, he argued that in order to propagate new methods of production, the American state colluded in the destruction of trade unions. However, this hard line was tempered by employers – such as Ford – conceding high wages so that the 'trained gorillas' of the assembly line were distracted from radical thoughts. E. Morera, *Gramsci's Historicism* (London, 1990), pp. 144–145.
15. N. Kirk, *Change, Continuity and Class: Labour in British Society 1880–1920* (Manchester, 1998), p. 160; A. J. McIvor, *Organised Capital*, pp. 16, 120.

management, and marginalise the resilience of craft labour in being able to resist managerial encroachment at the point of production.[16] More importantly, the idea that a class-based analysis can enhance our understanding of employer behaviour is also rejected.

Throughout *The Power To Manage?* (1991), the resilience of craft labour is emphasised, and capital's weakness and disunity are constantly stressed. Consequently, employers' organisations are depicted as being generally weak and ineffective. Zeitlin, for example, argues that, despite a resounding victory against the Amalgamated Society of Engineers in 1897–98, the heterogeneous nature of the engineering industry prevented employers from sustaining a united front and bringing about substantial changes to the engineering production process.[17] Reid presents a similar case for shipbuilders, and concludes that in this industry workers retained high levels of skill, and that the employers made little effort to increase their control over production processes.[18]

Other historians have emphasised the weakness of employer collective action. In his exploration of the inter-war Clyde shipbuilding industry McKinlay argues that employer organisation was difficult to achieve and limited in its effectiveness.[19] Yarmie's exploration of employers' associations in mid-Victorian Britain draws similar conclusions. Employer organisations, according to this writer, were characterised by internal conflicts of interests, and by intense competition between members – this was especially the case with small employers who were hampered by an inability to enforce lock-outs. It was, according to Yarmie, only when whole industries were threatened that large employers effectively combined to form organisations.[20] Another historian has noted that employer organisation in the British coal industry was fairly ineffectual in the pre-First World War period – a weakness attributed to differing geological and marketing conditions prevailing throughout the industry.[21] Internal conflicts of interest did make

16. S. Tolliday, and J. Zeitlin (eds), *The Power To Manage?* (London, 1991), p. 273.
17. J. Zeitlin, 'The Internal Politics of Employer Organisation, The Engineering Employers' Federation 1896–1939', in *Power to Manage?*, pp. 52–80.
18. A. J. Reid, 'Employers' Strategies and Craft Production', in *Power to Manage?*, p. 48.
19. A. McKinlay, 'Employers and skilled workers in the interwar depression: engineering and shipbuilding on Clydeside, 1919–1939', DPhil thesis, Oxford (1986), p. 28. McKinlay adopts a more balanced view than some writers, though, and argues that employer behaviour was constrained by a need to accommodate labour. Ibid., p. 4.
20. A. H. Yarmie, 'Employers' Organisations in Mid-Victorian Britain', *International Review of Social History*, 25 (1980), pp. 209–235.
21. R. Church, *The History of the British Coal Industry Volume 3, 1830–1913* (Oxford, 1986), pp. 654–681.

employer organisation hard to sustain at times. For example, it would appear that the National Farmers' Union of Scotland was susceptible to such pressures.[22] However, as the evidence from Clydeside will show, it is wrong to tar all employer associations with the same brush. More importantly, it would be equally wrong to argue from such evidence that employers in general were incapable of effective combination. This is a view held by Phelps Brown, who argues – like Zeitlin – that engineering employers failed to capitalise on their 1897 victory.[23] Moreover, for Phelps Brown the individualism which he believes characterised the engineering employers was indicative of a fatal flaw running through the structure of British capital. It was primarily due to this flaw that British employers failed to close ranks and shake off trade union interference in the post-Second World War period.[24]

As we shall see throughout this book, the Clydeside evidence suggests that employer organisation was stronger than several writers allow, and that the recent emphasis upon individualism and strategic choice regarding management strategy has gone too far.[25] Other historians have come to similar conclusions. Recently Kirk has added support to the notion that British employers responded to the challenge of intensifying competition and a militant labour movement by embarking on effective class-based collective action.[26] Also, as noted earlier, McIvor's evidence from the north-west of England suggests that too much stress has been placed on British employers' inability to draw together and organise effectively against a labour threat.[27] Magrath's Yorkshire study of employer organisation draws a similar conclusion. Here, again, it is the effectiveness of employer association which is stressed.[28] Like McIvor's, Magrath's work illustrates how employers worked together for a variety of reasons – and not just through a defensive need to combat the labour threat. Magrath also emphasises the role of chambers of commerce as vehicles of employer collective identity, and this is a theme taken up in Chapter 3 when we look at the orientation of Clydeside's two chambers.[29]

This study also looks at the thorny issue of class. It is difficult –

22. R. Anthony, *Herds and Hinds* (East Linton, 1997), pp. 111–118.
23. H. Phelps Brown, *The Origins of Trade Union Power* (Oxford, 1986), p. 135.
24. *Ibid.*, p. 115.
25. There has recently been a turning away from strategic choice within business theory. See L. Donaldson, *For Positivist Organizational Theory* (London, 1996).
26. N. Kirk, *Change, Continuity and Class*, pp. 164–179.
27. A. J. McIvor, *Organised Capital*, p. 25.
28. I. M. Magrath, 'Wool Textile Employers' Organisations, Bradford *c.* 1914–1945', Ph.D. thesis, University of Bradford (1991).
29. Ibid., pp. 30–33.

if not impossible – to embark on a study of employer collectivism without being drawn to the notion of class consciousness. The whole idea of class has undergone a fading fortune recently, and, as Knox says, 'class has been dethroned as historians look elsewhere for explanatory categories in order to understand the processes of social and political change.[30]' Many researchers now emphasise factors which divided classes internally – such as skill, income, and cultural differences.[31] This is a commendable development, as several important fields of social history – notably women's history – can only benefit from being freed from the shackles of male-centred class-based approaches. However, the dethronement process has led several writers to the point of denying that the concept of class has any validity at all.[32]

The main debate revolves around the issue of working-class consciousness – and in particular the tendency for capitalism to deskill workers. The notion of employer class consciousness has been given little attention. Some writers, mostly of the left, do allow that British employers have at times shown signs of class consciousness.[33] Looking at the West of Scotland, Foster follows Hinton by arguing that employers there were much more opposed to collective bargaining than those in comparable industrial regions.[34] This is broadly the view of

30. W. Knox, *Industrial Nation* (Edinburgh, 1999), p. 4.
31. See, for example, A. J. Reid, 'The Division of Labour and Politics in Britain 1880–1920', in W. Mommeson and H. G. Husung (eds), *The Development of Trade Unionism in Great Britain and Germany 1880–1914* (London, 1985). Also E. F. Biagini and A. J. Reid (eds), *Currents of Radicalism: Popular Radicalism, Organised Labour and Party Politics in Britain 1850–1914* (Cambridge, 1991).
32. See G. S. Jones, *The Language of Class: Studies of English Working Class History 1832–1986* (Cambridge, 1983); P. Joyce, *Visions of the People: Industrial England and the Question of Class 1848–1914* (Cambridge, 1991), Chapter 5. For a reaction to the postmodernist attack on class see J. Belchem, 'Reconstructing Labour History', *Labour History Review*, 62, 3, Winter (1997), pp. 318–323. Also, D. Howell, 'Reading Alistair Reid: A Future for Labour History?', in N. Kirk (ed.), *Social Class and Marxism* (Aldershot, 1996), pp. 214–237; M. Savage and A. Miles, *The Remaking of the British Working Class 1840–1940* (London, 1994), *passim*. See also N. Kirk, *Change, Continuity and Class* (Manchester, 1998).
33. See, for example, K. Burgess, *The Challenge of Labour* (London, 1980); R. Price, *Masters, Unions and Men* (London, 1980).
34. J. Hinton, *The First Shop Stewards' Movement* (London, 1973); J. Foster, 'A Proletarian Nation? Occupation and Class Since 1914', in T. Dickson and J. Treble (eds), *People and Society in Scotland 1914–1990* (Edinburgh, 1992). See also J. Foster, 'Strike Action and Working Class Politics on Clydeside 1914–1919', *International Review of Social History* 35 (1990). And, more recently, his chapter on class in A. Cooke *et al.* (eds), *Modern Scottish History* (East Linton, 1998), pp. 210–235. T. Dickson (ed.), *'Scottish Capitalism'* (London, 1980), complements this Marxist stream of research, although the subject of employers is given sparse attention.

Melling, who suggests that much industrial welfarism in the West of
Scotland was created primarily to destroy trade unionism; and that
technological innovations were initiated by employers to facilitate
greater labour control.[35] However, although it is implicit in these
Marxist accounts that capitalists acted at times out of class consciousness, no real attempt has been made to determine how significant class
identity was to those who employed labour – probably reflecting Marx's
own marginalisation of the bourgeoisie in his theorising.

The issue of middle-class identity has generally been left to those
who utilise the theories of Max Weber. Nenadic, for example, puts such
a methodology to good effect in her exploration of Glasgow's middle
classes between 1800 and 1870.[36] And Trainor adopts a similar approach
in his research on the social elites of the English Midlands.[37] The main
shortcoming here, though, is that these writers tend to concentrate their
attention on industrial and commercial elites, and little attention is
given to smaller-scale capitalists – a recurrent fault with those who
look at trade regulation practices too, and at business management in
general. The historiography of Clydeside industrial relations, then –
Marxist and non-Marxist – fails to devote sufficient attention to the
significance of employer organisations for labour relations purposes or
to capitalist collectivism *per se*.

According to Knox 'the working class is not a static economic
category. It is re-made and makes itself in a dialectical interplay as
changes which occur in the economic and social structure of capitalism
elicit political responses'.[38] This notion of a class being made and
re-made can equally be applied to the employers classes too. It will be
argued throughout this book, then, that, although we cannot speak of
a homogeneous capitalist class on the Clyde, the notion of a class
consciousness at play at certain times cannot be ruled out.

The regional case study which follows investigates the extent of

35. J. Melling, '"Non-Commissioned Officers': British Employers and their Supervisory
    Workers, 1880–1920', *Social History* 5 (1980), pp. 183–221. See also J. Melling,
    'Scottish Industrialists', in T. Dickson (ed.), *Capital and Class in Scotland* (Edinburgh,
    1982).
36. S. Nenadic, 'The Structure, Values and Influence of the Scottish Urban Middle
    Class, Glasgow 1800–1870' Ph.D. thesis, Glasgow (1986), p. 10.
37. R. Trainor, *Black Country Elites* (Oxford, 1993), p. 17. This research illustrates that
    industrialists played a much more influential role in the nineteenth century social
    order of the English Midlands than has been previously assumed. Moreover,
    Trainor and Morgan arrive at a similar conclusion for the West of Scotland too.
    M. Morgan and R. Trainor, 'The Dominant Classes', in W. H. Fraser and
    R. J. Morris (eds), *People and Society in Scotland Vol. 2, 1830–1914* (1989).
38. W. Knox, *Industrial Nation*, p. 17.

employer collectivism in the Clydeside region – both at the economic and the social levels – amongst large and small capitalists, and for trade regulatory as well as labour regulatory reasons. This study will not adhere to any one specific theory. The main rationale for this approach is more pragmatic than doctrinaire, as the spectrum of capitalist collectivism examined in the regional case study cannot be adequately squeezed into one rigid model. However, throughout the book, the collective action of Clydeside employers will be tested against several theories. As well as Marxist and Weberian notions of class and status consciousness, the strength of corporatism as a model of collective action will be assessed. During the First World War, according to one commentator, the state maintained its authority through compromise, and this successful strategy ensured a political stability which lasted until the mid-1960s – with the trade unions and the employers' associations becoming 'estates of the realm' by the 1920s.[39] However, it will be shown that when we try to apply such a model to Clydeside, there are problems. The number of employers' organisations in the region increased during this period as Clydeside capitalists responded to a growing trade union movement and a more interventionist state. However, this growth was not just restricted to large-scale capital, but occurred in industries as diverse as carting and shipbuilding. At this level employer combination cannot be explained solely by reference to the state's willingness to form estates of the realm. Despite important caveats, though, certain aspects of corporatist theory are useful in explaining the formation of some large employer groupings: such as the Federation of British Industry (FBI) in 1916, and the National Confederation of Employers' Organisations (NCEO) in 1919 – although one writer stresses the sectional interests of these organisations, and argues that they were unsuccessful in pushing the British state towards corporatism in the post-war period.[40]

It has also been argued that corporatist models alone cannot explain the formation of trade associations; and although corporatism's 'top-down' approach is useful for explaining how some associations functioned, it is fairly unhelpful in explaining how and why they were formed. Van Waarden, in his work on Dutch trade associations, utilises a corporatist model combined with the theory of collective action propounded by Olson.[41] Individual interest, according to Olson, is best

39. K. Middlemas, *Politics in Industrial Society* (London, 1979), pp. 14, 21.
40. J. Turner (ed.), *Businessmen and Politics* (London, 1984), pp. 37–48.
41. F. Van Waarden, 'Orgaizational Emergence and Developments of Business Interest Associations: An Example from the Netherlands'. Unpublished paper presented at Rijks University Leiden, 1991.

served by individual action – there being no point in 'forming an organisation simply to play solitaire'.[42] However, it is equally irrational
for an individual to take part in collective action for the pursuit of a
collective good which will be shared by non-group members. This 'free
rider' problem implies that class-based collective action cannot be explained rationally, and there must be some other reason for its popularity
– other than a class dynamic. Olson deals with this by arguing that
organisations provide *selective incentives* to their members over and above
any lobbying role which they perform, and that this is the main
attraction of group action.[43] Once again it is possible to test Olson's
theory against evidence from Clydeside – although it should be noted
that this theory has already been attacked for its lack of empirical
grounding.[44]

While British employers are portrayed as incapable of collective action
by some historians, others argue that they had little influence at the
political level.[45] Once again this is a hypothesis that can be tested against
evidence from Clydeside. In Chapter 4, examination of how influential
Clydeside employers were as regional and national politicians suggests
that this is another hypothesis in need of modification.

This is also the case with the notion, propounded by the likes of
Foster and Melling, that Clydeside employers were more authoritarian
than employers in other parts of the British Isles.[46] Within this school
of thought Clydeside's rapid industrialisation, and the fact that the
region's employers were blessed with an over-abundant labour pool,
made capital in this area much more hostile to collective bargaining
than in other parts of the country. This hypothesis is also put to the
test in Chapter 7.

42. M. Olson Jnr., *The Logic of Collective Action* (Oxford, 1965), p. 5.
43. *Ibid.*, p. 132.
44. D. Marsh, 'On Joining Interest Groups: An Empirical Consideration of the Work
   of Mancur Olson Jnr.', *British Journal of Political Science* 6 (1976), pp. 257–271.
   Moe argues that business people sometimes join interest groups out of a sense
   of duty. See T. M. Moe, *The Organisation of Interests* (Chicago, 1980).
45. J. Turner (ed.), *Businessmen and Politics*; K. Middlemas, *Politics in Industrial Society.*
46. J. Melling, 'Employers, Industrial Housing and the Evolution of Company Welfare
   Policies in Britain's Heavy Industries', *International Review of Social History* 26
   (1981). Also 'Scottish Industrialists and the Changing Character of Class Relations
   in the Clyde Region *c.* 1880–1918.', in Dickson, T. (ed.), *Capital and Class in Scotland*
   (Edinburgh, 1982); J. Foster, 'A Proletarian Nation? Occupation and Class Since
   1914', in T. Dickson and J. Treble (eds), *People and Society in Scotland 1914–1990*
   (Edinburgh, 1992); W. H. Fraser, *Conflict and Class* (Edinburgh, 1983); A. J. McIvor,
   'Were Clydeside Employers More Autocratic ?', in W. Kenefick and A. J. McIvor
   (eds), *Roots of Red Clydeside 1910–1914?*.

Source material relating to employer collective behaviour is sparse, and especially so where small firms are concerned. Consequently, to gain an insight into the strengths and weaknesses of employer unity, a wide range of evidence has been used. Chamber of Commerce minute books offer an important insight into capitalist concord at the highest level – although their usefulness regarding labour relations is limited. Employers' organisation minute books constitute the strongest evidence. However, as these may present a biased picture of the strength of employer solidarity – and because many such records are missing or incomplete – trade journals have also been extensively trawled. Similarly, parliamentary papers and newspaper reports have also been used to gain a more objective perspective on employer action, as have Board of Trade records of industrial disputes and collective agreements. Finally, although some reference has been made to company records, the severe shortcomings of this type of source material for gaining an understanding of collective employer behaviour did not warrant its extensive use.

This book is arranged in eight chapters. Chapter 2 sets the scene by describing Clydeside's business and organisational structure. There are two main aims here: firstly, to illustrate how, despite its worldwide fame for producing capital goods, the economy of the West of Scotland was a rich mixture of varied industries. Secondly, the chapter will also show how beneath this industrial structure lay a hidden network of employer collaboration in industries as diverse as shipbuilding, building, and printing. Chapter 3 goes on to explore the degree to which various Clydeside employers regulated competition, and assesses the impact which this had on capitalist collective identity. Once again the focus is as much on small employers as larger industrialists. Chapter 4 then enters a neglected dimension of middle-class identity by illustrating how employer class consciousness was frequently sustained away from the immediate sphere of the market – in such social activities as clubs, charities, and annual excursions. Chapter 5 analyses the political activities of West of Scotland employers and suggests a reformulation of the assumption that capitalists were marginalised from political power. Chapter 6 investigates Clydeside employers and industrial relations, and considers to what extent employer organisation was successful in facing up to organised labour throughout the period. A prime concern here is to determine how the Clydesdie evidence relates to the ongoing debate regarding the centrality of employers to the development of collective bargaining. Chapter 7 then engages with the hypothesis that Clydeside employers were more authoritarian than those in other parts of the British Isles. Finally, Chapter 8 draws the threads together in a conclusion.

CHAPTER TWO

Clydeside's Business and Organisational Structure

Full details of the West of Scotland's employer community are hard to arrive at as a great many business activities went unrecorded. We can go a long way, however, by looking at census evidence and Post Office Directories. According to the 1891 census – which was the first to inquire whether individuals were employers, employed, or self-employed – just under 40% of Scotland's employers operated their businesses in the Clydeside region.[1] In Clydeside in 1891 there were 23,998 employers and 351,690 workers – which means that employers made up around 5% of the working population of the West of Scotland. But changes in census compilation make it difficult to compare population trends over time. However, in 1901 we find that the percentage of the Clydeside workforce listed as employers had dropped to 4% – while the Scottish percentage was 5%, reflecting the fact that the more industrialised areas had the lowest ratios of employers to workers, which is borne out by looking at the individual Clydeside regions. Lanarkshire, for example, the most industrialised of the Clydeside counties, had the smallest employer-to-employee ratio with 3% of its working population listed as employers, while Renfrewshire had the largest at 7%.

There is a tendency within labour history to concentrate on urban employers. However, such an emphasis ignores the fact that the Clydeside region was an important farming area too, and farmers constituted a large proportion of the region's employers. Mixed farming was predominant, but this masks important variations across the region. Dunbartonshire, for example, had a large area of mountain land and most of its inhabitants were concentrated in the arable southern part of the county. In contrast, Ayrshire in 1867 – according to one eyewitness – resembled the landscape of the English Home Counties.[2] Dunbartonshire, Renfrewshire, and Lanarkshire were Clydeside's main dairy-producing regions, and this was a principal reason for the number of small farms there.[3]

1. Census of Scotland 1891.
2. *Transactions of the Highland Society*, Volume 1, 4th series (Aberdeen, 1867), p. 231.
3. See T. M. Devine, 'The Making of a Farming Elite', in *Scottish Elites* (Edinburgh, 1994), pp. 62–76.

Consequently, Clydeside agriculture was essentially an industry dominated by small employers. Scottish Office returns for farm rentals in 1906 make this quite clear. Thirty-six percent of Clydeside farmers, according to one survey, paid annual rentals of less than £30 and Lanarkshire and Dunbartonshire were the counties with the smallest average farm size.[4] But despite the continued importance of farming to Clydeside, the region's economy was dominated throughout the period by urban industry.

Initially boosted by the manufacture of textiles in the early nineteenth century, by the 1880s the West of Scotland's economy depended upon a close integration – closer than in any other part of Britain – of the iron, steel, coalmining, and heavy engineering industries. In 1884 there were over 700 engineering companies in Glasgow alone, and the British Association's 1901 survey of Clydeside listed 120 major mechanical engineering firms.[5] Glasgow, of course, was the main centre. However, there were other significant engineering towns. Kilmarnock in Ayrshire, for example, was the home to five major engineering companies.[6] By 1900, 40 percent of Scottish male workers were employed in the heavy industries – compared to 25% in Britain as a whole. Over the 1870–1914 period heavy engineering, textiles, railways, and investment companies grew to dominate the Scottish economy.[7]

The growth of monopoly capitalism in Britain has been extensively researched, and it is not the purpose of this book to make a detailed examination of the merger movement in the West of Scotland.[8] What is significant, however, is the increasing number of cross-linkages that were formed between Clydeside capitalists. By 1905, 85% of the 108 top Scottish companies were linked through interlocking directorships – although the number dropped between then and 1920 – and this was at its densest on Clydeside.[9] These connections drew the region's main industries even closer together and connected businesses that were involved in a wide diversity of markets. Moreover, the effect of this merging tended to set off a chain reaction:

4. *Glasgow Herald*, April 29, 1907, p. 12.
5. *Industries of Glasgow and the West of Scotland* (Glasgow, 1901), pp. 37–91.
6. A. Kay, *History of Kilmarnock* (Kilmarnock, 1909).
7. J. Scott and M. Hughes, *The Anatomy of Scottish Capital* (London, 1980), p. 17.
8. See, for example, F. R. Jervis, *The Economics of Mergers* (London, 1971); L. Hannah, *The Rise of the Corporate Economy* (London, 1976); H. W. Macrosty, *The Trust Movement in British Industry* (London, 1907); H. Levy, *Monopoly and Competition* (London, 1911); P. L. Cook (ed.), *The Effects of Mergers* (London, 1958); G. C. Allen, *Monopoly and Restrictive Practices* (London, 1968).
9. L. Hannah, *Corporate Economy* (London, 976), pp. 17–28; J. Scott & M. Hughes, *Anatomy* (London, 1980), p. 20.

When companies interlock with one another they also become elements in a broader network of interlocking directorships. The creation of a direct interlock between two companies induces a set of indirect interlocks between these companies and those to which each of them is separately connected.[10]

Moreover, the trend towards interlocking directorships was accompanied by increasing vertical and horizontal integration, underpinned by a general movement towards business expansion. For example, by 1896 J. & P. Coats had bought out four of its principal rivals to become the world's leading thread manufacturer. In the textile dyeing and bleaching industry three Clydeside companies combined to form the United Turkey Red Company in 1898 – this was a response to the imposition of tariffs on cotton goods by the Indian government as well as a strategy to beat English competition. In 1899, 14 Clydeside textile printing firms joined with 32 similar English companies to form the Calico Printers' Association – which quickly commanded 85% of the British calico printing trade.[11]

It was a similar picture in engineering. The Renfrew company Babcock and Wilcox took over its main competitor – Stirlings – in 1906. Similarly, the amalgamation of the Hyde Park, Atlas, and Queen's Park railway locomotive manufacturing companies in 1903 created the North British Locomotive Company – a combine capable of turning out 600 engines a year, primarily for overseas markets.[12] The Clyde shipbuilding industry also depended to a great extent on the export market. By 1900, 38 major shipbuilding companies operated on the Clyde and the structure of the industry mirrored its national shape, with a large number of relatively small family firms predominating.[13] This small-scale structure, though, did not prevent rationalisation, and by 1918 the principal shipbuilders had taken over the Clydeside steel industry in an effort to assure themselves of future supplies of raw material.[14]

The Clydeside region was well endowed with coal deposits, and in

10. J. Scott & M. Hughes, *ibid.*, pp. 37–38.

11. H. W., Macrosty, *Trust Movement* (London, 1907), p. 10. For a detailed case study of the formation of this organisation, see P. H. Cook (ed.), *The Effects of Mergers* (London, 1958), pp. 133–208.

12. *Southern Press*, 21 April 1911, p. 1. See also G. Huchison and M. O'Neill, *The Springburn Experience* (Edinburgh, 1989), *passim.* It has been estimated that 48% of this company's locomotives went to colonial buyers.

13. *Industries of Glasgow and the West of Scotland*, p. 98. The industry had contracted from the beginning of our period, as there were 43 companies in 1870.

14. See M. S. Moss and J. R. Hume, *Workshop of the British Empire: Engineering and Shipbuilding in the West of Scotland* (London, 1977), p. 42.

1913 almost 26 million tons of coal were produced in the area.[15] In the early part of the period the ownership pattern of Scottish coal companies was characterised by a high number of large firms operating mines across several counties.[16] William Bairds, for example, owned mines in Ayrshire and Lanarkshire, and was the first British company to secure its own ore mines in Spain.[17] Throughout the period, Lanarkshire was the most important of the Clydeside coalfields. In 1868 half of Scotland's collieries were located here, and it was still the most important by 1913 – although by this time the more accessible seams were exhausted.[18] The trend towards business integration, so apparent in engineering and textile dyeing, also affected the Clydeside coal industry: in 1902, 24 companies amalgamated to form United Collieries.[19] The formation of this combine meant that by 1913 the ten largest Scottish coal companies employed 45% of the Scottish mining labour force.[20] There was, therefore, a general movement towards big business across Clydeside. However, this should be kept in perspective, given that as late as 1938 the ownership pattern of Clydeside industry was still dominated by medium-sized businesses, and that most large factories were confined to heavy industry.[21]

It has been said that British industrialists involved in the staple industries made insufficient effort to combine in the face of intensifying foreign competition.[22] This ties in with a broader argument that British industry failed to compete because of its inability to transform its industrial relations strategy, rationalise its organisation, and improve its management structures.[23] As a consequence – the argument goes – markets dwindled and industries atrophied. There certainly were such cases on Clydeside. For example, in engineering the output of boilers fell by 50% between 1913 and 1935 – precipitated by competition from the new internal combustion engine – and a similar fate met the

---

15. Report H. M. Inspector of Mines (Scotland) 1913 [Cd. 7439], p. 7.
16. R. Church, *The History of the British Coal Industry*, Volume 3, 1830–1913 (Oxford, 1986), pp. 400–402.
17. R. D. Corrins, 'William Baird and Company, Coal and Iron Masters 1830–1914', unpublished Ph.D. thesis, University of Strathclyde (1974), p. 296 and *passim*.
18. D. Bremner, *The Industries of Scotland 1868* (Edinburgh, 1969), p. 10; B. Supple, *The History of the British Coal Industry*, Volume 4, 1913–1946 (Oxford, 1987), p. 23.
19. H. W. Macrosty, *Trust Movement* (London, 1907), p. 144.
20. R. Church, *British Coal Industry* (Oxford, 1986), p. 400.
21. C. Harvie, *No Gods and Precious Few Heroes* (Edinburgh, 1981), p. 39.
22. G. C. Allen, *Monopoly and Restrictive Practices* (London, 1968), p. 52. Allen allows that there were some cartels in the staple industries.
23. B. Elbaum and W. Lazonick (eds), *The Decline of the British Economy* (Oxford, 1986).

exporters of heavy machine tools.[24] However, in general, the failure to
rationalise – which has been exaggerated to some extent – should now
be seen in the light of recent work by business historians challenging
the notion that large-scale industrial expansion is a logical strategy.
Networks of small companies can then be seen as viable alternatives to
large-scale integration, and many Clydeside industrialists who operated
small companies are exonerated.[25]

The importance of Clydeside engineering, shipbuilding, and coalmining, cannot be disputed, and it is understandable that general texts
tend to focus closely on these industries.[26] However, there was much
more to Clydeside than ships, coal, and steam engines, and recent writing
has attempted to illustrate the diversity of business enterprise in the
region. Manufacturing was undoubtedly important here – seven out of
ten Glasgow workers were employed in manufacturing in some form
or another in 1911. But only one in six workers was actually employed
in engineering and metalworking by 1914, and even in an earlier period
the success of Clydeside's basic industries has tended to obscure the
fact that most of the region's employers were not involved in this type
of enterprise.[27] The 1861 census, for example, shows that although 52%
of males were employed in manufacturing, only 14% of Glasgow's businessmen were manufacturers.[28]

The over-concentration by historians on Clydeside's basic industries
has left many other capitalist activities under-researched, and this is
certainly the case with the building trade, which was an important
employer in the Clydeside region, and in the early part of our period
two-thirds of building in Scotland was carried out by firms based in or

24. Harvie, *No Gods* (Edinburgh, 1981), p. 40.
25. See, for example, S. N. Broadberry and N. F. R. Crafts, 'Britain's Productivity Gap
    in the 1930s: Some Neglected Factors', *Journal of Economic History*, 52 (Sept. 1992),
    pp. 531–558. M. Casson and M. B. Rose, 'Institutions and the Evolution of Modern
    Business: Introduction', *Business History* 39 (Oct., 1997), pp. 1–8. Also, M. C. Casson,
    'Entrepreuneurship and Business Culture', in J. Brown and M. B. Rose (eds), *Entre-
    preneurship, Networks and Modern Business* (Manchester, 1993); G. Cookson, 'Family
    Firms and Business Networks: Textile Engineering in Yorkshire', 1780–1830',
    Business History 39, 1, 1997.
26. For example, S. and O. Checkland, *Industry and Ethos* (London, 1984); R. H. Camp-
    bell, *The Rise And Fall of Scottish Industry 1707–1939* (Edinburgh, 1980); B. Lenman,
    An Economic History of Modern Scotland (London, 1977).
27. J. Butt, 'The Industries of Glasgow', in W. H. Fraser and I. Maver (eds), *Glasgow,
    Volume II: 1830–1912* (Manchester, 1996), pp. 196–140. Also R. Rodger's chapter
    in the same volume, pp. 161–185.
28. S. Nenadic, 'Businessmen, the middle classes and the dominance of manufacturing
    in 19th-century Britain', *Economic History Review* 44 (1991), pp. 82–85.

around Glasgow.[29] Between 1870 and 1890 the trade encountered declining labour productivity – mostly due to rising labour costs – while the establishment of local authority building departments squeezed profits too.[30] The Glasgow Bank – which held the accounts of a great many Clydeside builders – failed in the autumn of 1878, and this paralysed local industry for seven years. The extent of this paralysis illustrates how most Clydeside builders operated small-scale firms – a characteristic of the trade right up until the First World War.

Although some work has been done on Scottish building-industry entrepreneurs, little attention has been paid to the numerous small firms who made up the backbone of the industry.[31] By 1911 there were 974 building trade employers in Glasgow, and on average they each employed 20 workers.[32] These figures, of course, hide large variations. McAlpine's, for example, with a workforce of around 7000 in 1904, had little in common with a small jobbing plasterer firm employing one or two men.[33] Some indication of how small-scale the trade was is the fact that at the turn of the century there were around 400 master plumbers in Glasgow and 163 master slaters.[34] Many builders depended on speculative building, and over-speculation by small firms led to market instability during the mid-Victorian period.[35]

After the First World War the building industry expanded. Glasgow's population grew by a third between 1911 and 1921 – swelled by an influx of wartime munitions workers – and in 1919 Glasgow Corporation estimated that the city needed 57,000 new houses.[36] However, although the trade expanded to meet this demand, in 1932 the Board of Trade concluded that the shape of the industry was broadly similar to its pre-1914 structure.[37] But this tends to ignore a significant amount of change which did take place. In 1884, for example, there were 219

29. R. W. Postgate, *The Builders' History* (London, 1923), p. 324.
30. J. A. McKenna and R G Rodger, 'Control by Coercion: Employers' Associations and the Establishment of Industrial Order in the Building Industry of England and Wales 1860–1914', *Business History Review* 59 (1985), p. 211.
31. See A. Slaven and S. Checkland (eds), *Dictionary of Scottish Business Biography, Volume 1, 1860–1960* (Aberdeen, 1990), pp. 125–176.
32. Census of Scotland 1911.
33. See N. J. Morgan's short description of the Scottish construction industry in A. Slaven and S. Checkland, pp. 125–132.
34. *Post Office Directory*, 1900–1901.
35. R. Rodger, 'Structural Instability in the Scottish Building Industry 1820–1880', *Construction History* (1985), pp. 48–57.
36. Board of Trade Industrial Survey of the South West of Scotland (1932), pp. 100–102.
37. Ibid., p. 97.

builders' firms in Glasgow, but this number had fallen to 109 by 1924. Similarly, the number of glazier companies fell from 87 in 1894 to 45 in 1902, and still further to only 17 by 1924. The most spectacular decline, though, was in the number of masons' firms, from 111 in 1884 to just 11 by 1924 – which reflected the growing preference for brick rather than freestone. The number of plumbing companies remained fairly stable, and painting and paper-hanging firms increased in number.[38] So there was more of a structural change in Clydeside's building trade over the period than that allowed by the Board of Trade.

Other Clydeside industries have also suffered from the long shadow cast by shipbuilding and engineering. For example, there were on average 375 printing firms in Glasgow alone between 1900 and 1920. Here, too, we find that small capitalists prevailed. Although there were several large printing and publishing companies such as MacLehose, Collins, and Aig and Coghill, most of the printing firms in the West of Scotland were small-scale outfits.[39] Also, whereas the Clydeside cotton industry went into decline from the 1870s, the textile industry – along with clothing and shoemaking – continued to be a significant employer in the area. Together these industries employed just over 22% of Glasgow workers over the 1871–1911 period. The carpet industry was also important to the region, and there were eight carpet firms in Glasgow in 1890.[40] Clydeside also had a thriving furniture industry – centred on the Ayrshire town of Beith – which catered for a growing domestic demand, as well as for the lucrative market provided by the Clyde shipbuilding industry. Clydeside's chemical industry was also a significant employer, and 50,000 tons of soda ash and caustic soda were manufactured on Clydeside in 1876.[41] Despite its gradual decline, the Scottish chemical industry still employed 3,520 people on the eve of the First World War.[42]

Clydeside was also a major region for the manufacture and distribution of asbestos – due primarily to the scale of the shipbuilding and steam locomotive industries where it was used for insulation. It was

38. *Post Office Directory*, 1884, 1896, 1902, and 1924.
39. Glasgow Typographical Society Membership Lists 1912 and 1918. Scrapbooks of J. MacLehose, Volume 5, 1913, p. 11, and Volume 54, 1919, p. 39.
40. J. Butt, *Glasgow*, Volume II, pp. 109–110. Kilmarnock was the centre of the Scottish carpet industry in the 1840s, and even by 1891 was still a force to be reckoned with – its leading firm Thomsons operated 40 looms. See F. H. Young, *A Century of Carpet Making 1839–1939* (Glasgow, 1943), p. 18. Also J. N. Bartlett, *Carpeting the Millions* (Edinburgh, 1978).
41. W. R. Scott and J. Cunnison, *The Industries of the Clyde Valley* (Oxford, 1927) p. 20.
42. Census of Production 1913 [Cd. 5162], p. 59.

Scottish industrialists who first pioneered the manufacture of asbestos products, and the first company appeared on Clydeside in 1871.[43] By 1885 there were at least 20 asbestos manufacturing and distribution companies in the Glasgow area, and by the turn of the century this number had increased to 52. At the same time there were also 26 firms that specialised in boiler and pipe insulation, and these companies had their own employers' association from 1908.[44]

The shoe and leather trade was another prominent employer in Clydeside, and Glasgow had 535 retail boot and shoe shops in 1883. At the same time there were 31 boot and shoe makers in the Ayrshire town of Kilmarnock – where Clarks, and later Saxone, gained a reputation for producing men's shoes.[45] The Ayrshire shoe industry was strengthened by an influx of Glasgow masters in the 1880s, and the town of Maybole became an important centre for boot making – several firms here were vertically integrated from the tanning process right through to retailing.[46] Boot repairing was also an important sector of the leather trade, as was fleshing and currying of the raw material. The Clydeside region also produced heavy leather for drive belts and other industrial components – and several of these companies also used asbestos as well as leather.

Clydeside's industrialisation and urbanisation spurred a rapid growth in retailing throughout the region. In 1850, most of Clydeside's shops were small in scale.[47] However, the 1870s and 1880s saw an upsurge in the number of multiple branch stores and cooperative outlets. Lipton had seven Clydeside branches by 1880, and Templeton had over 50 shops throughout the region in 1910.[48] Glasgow also led the rest of the UK in the expansion of factory bread making, and large companies such as Beattie's and Bilslands' became large employers. But despite the shift

43. A. L. Summers, *Asbestos and the Asbestos Industry* (London, 1919), p. 10.
44. *Post Office Directory of Glasgow*, 1884–85; and 1900–01. See R. Johnston and A. J. McIvor, *Lethal Work: The Asbestos Tragedy in Scotland* (East Linton, 2000); also, 'Incubating death: working with asbestos in Clydeside shipbuilding and engineering, 1945–1990', *Scottish Labour History Journal* 34 (1999).
45. *Scottish Leather Trader*, Feb. 1883, p. 57. *Kilmarnock Post Office Directory* 1883, p. 85. See B. M. White in A. Slaven and S. Checkland (eds), *Dictionary of Scottish Business Biography 1860–1960*, Volume 1 (Aberdeen, 1990), pp. 435–439.
46. A. Fox, *A History of the National Union of Boot and Shoe Operatives, 1874–1957* (Oxford, 1958), p. 99.
47. G. Shaw, 'The evolution and impact of large-scale retailing in Britain', in J. Benson and G. Shaw (eds), *The Evolution of Retail Systems c. 1800–1914* (Leicester, 1992), p. 138.
48. W. H. Fraser, *The Coming of the Mass Market 1850–1914* (London, 1981), pp. 111–112.

towards larger retailing outlets, by the end of the period most of
Clydeside's shopkeepers and bakers were still single-shop concerns.[49]

The main point of this selective snapshot of Clydeside industry has
been to put into perspective the region's textile, coalmining, engineering
and shipbuilding industries. These were undoubtedly important, and it
was upon them that the economy of the region depended, but their
success was underpinned by a tapestry of other industrial enterprises.
Next we examine how employers in many of these industries increasingly turned towards combination as a management strategy.

EMPLOYER ORGANISATION

By 1919 on Clydeside there were 180 national and local employers'
associations designed specifically for labour relations purposes.[50] Let us
examine how some of these organisations functioned in a range of
industries, from agriculture to furniture manufacture.

Agriculture

Farmers have always been noted for their individuality, and the late
establishment of a farmers' employers' association reflected this. Most
of the early moves towards collective action among farmers were for
trade regulatory reasons, and a principal reason for this was that there
was no incentive for farmers to combine against an organised labour
force. Trade unionism amongst farm employees was difficult to achieve
because of the isolation of the workers, the high number of relatively
poorly paid women employed, and a paternalistic relationship between
employer and employee. After some earlier failures an industry-wide
trade union appeared in 1912 in the shape of the Scottish Farm Servants'
Union (SFSU). The numerical strength of the union gradually increased
throughout the Clydeside region, and as the following graph illustrates,
significant inroads had been made into most farming areas by the end
of 1914.

The SFSU pursued a gradualist strategy in its early years, and it
was not until the the inter-war period that it began to adopt a more
aggressive stance.[51] It is primarily because of this that no direct link
has been made between its launch and the arrival of the first employers'
association for Scottish farmers a year later.

49. *Ibid.*, p. 115.
50. There had only been 22 in 1902. Directory of Industrial Associations in the United
    Kingdom 1902 and 1919.
51. R. Anthony, 'The Scottish Agricultural Labour Market, 1900–1939: A Case of
    Institutional Intervention', *Economic History Review*, 46, 3 (1993), p. 536.

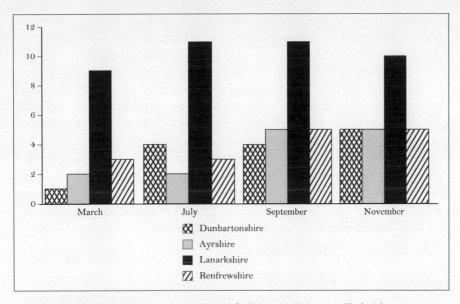

GRAPH 2.1. Growth of the Scottish National Farmers' Union in Clydeside.
Source: The Scottish Farm Servant, March, July and Sept. 1914.

The initiation of the National Farmers' Union for Scotland (NFUS) was a response to the success of the NFU in England – combined with a need to regulate the milk trade between farmers and wholesalers.[52] However, the fact that an agricultural trade union had been set up in Scotland may also have been a factor that encouraged farmers to organise. A newspaper report written during the planning stage of the NFUS, for example, cites rising agricultural wages as a principal reason for its initiation.[53] We should also note that the first branches of the NFUS were concentrated in the Clydeside area where the union was strongest – ten of the NFUS's 13-man executive in 1915 were Clydeside farmers – and there were 34 branches in the region by 1916.[54]

The timing of the NFUS's launch, then, and the similarity of growth patterns between it and the trade union, suggest that the spread of organisation among the workforce may also have acted as a stimulant to employer collectivism. Moreover, an indication of the NFUS's interest

52. R. Anthony, *Herds and Hinds* (East Linton, 1997), pp. 111–112.
53. *Glasgow Herald (GH)*, 4 July 1913, p. 12.
54. *North British Agriculturist (NBA)*, 14 Jan. 1915, p. 29. Also *NBA*, 24 Feb. 1916, p. 125. The total number of members of these branches amounted to 1,571. In 1915 the total membership of the organisation was 2000 in 46 branches. Research Note of the Records of the NFUS (Glasgow University Library History qDC 1045 NAT3), p. 1.

in labour issues before the inter-war period was its strong protest in 1919 – along with the Highland and Agricultural Society, and the Scottish Chamber of Agriculture – over proposals to grant farm workers a 48-hour week.[55]

During the war the prestige and membership of the NFUS increased dramatically when it successfully represented the interest of Scottish agriculture during a period of state control – by 1920 there were around 20,000 members throughout Scotland.[56] But it would be wrong to see the NFUS conforming to a corporatist model, as although state encouragement gave the organisation more credibility, both employers and workers were against the idea of the state coming in to regulate wage rates.[57] The notion of a growing class consciousness amongst employers and workers during this period is also questionable given that farmers worked alongside their workers in many instances.[58]

Engineering, iron, steel, and coal

It was around the Glasgow area and within Clydeside's major towns that the main upsurge in trade union membership and employer association occurred; and it was here that class consciousness was likely to be most significant.[59] The worldwide reputation of the Clyde area rested on its shipbuilding industry, and by the turn of the century there were 38 major yards along the river turning out a wide range of vessels. Most of these companies became involved in the Clyde Shipbuilders' Association (CSA).

The roots of this organisation can be traced back to 1866 when 24 shipbuilding and engineering companies decided to form an association for mutual protection against what was viewed as increasing workers' encroachment on managerial prerogative. This organisation became one of the most powerful employers' associations on Clydeside and pre-dated by ten years the formation of the national body, the Shipbuilding Employers' Federation – to which the CSA was later affiliated. In 1892 the shipbuilders and engineers parted to form two separate associations. The leading engineering firms in the Glasgow area formed the Glasgow

55. Ministry of Labour Report PRO, Lab 2/740/13.
56. However, it was in the 1930s that the association became firmly established, especially after it successfully campaigned for an extension of the 1932 Wheat Act to include crops grown in Scotland. Research Note, p. 2.
57. R., Anthony, *Herds and Hinds*, p. 127.
58. See Anthony's chapter on social relations. It should be noted that no examination of social relations in Clydeside agriculture has been carried out. R. Anthony, *Herds and Hinds*, pp. 220–253.
59. J. Foster, 'A Proletarian Nation?', p. 212.

and District Engineers' and Boilermakers' Association – which soon changed its name to the North Western Engineering Trades Employers' Association (NWETEA).[60] Despite the departure of the engineers, though, the CSA remained an influential body, and seven years after the split 17 of the region's principal shipbuilders were members.[61] At the turn of the century, then, over half of the shipbuilding companies operating on the Clyde were members of either the CSA or the NWETEA – and many firms were members of both.[62]

It has been argued that the small-scale structure of the British engineering industry made employer organisation an unattractive option, and that what organisation there was amongst the engineering employers amounted to nothing more than 'coalition building' – in the sense that it was temporary.[63] A closer look at the main engineering employers' association on the Clyde, the NWETEA, suggests otherwise.

The chief purpose of the NWETEA was to control the labour force, either through a show of strength or by initiating collective bargaining channels – suggesting that increasing employer class consciousness precipitated by the labour threat was a significant factor. Also, whereas coalitions normally disband after the termination of a crisis, membership of the NWETEA went from strength to strength throughout the period. The notion that the structure of the engineering industry was too heterogeneous to nurture collective action amongst the employers is also called into question when we examine the membership of the NWETEA. Between 1889 and 1901, 71 firms were members. Of these, 45 (63%) had wage bills of less than £15,000 a year – and 23% paid out less than £5,000 a year. Moreover, by 1914, when the number of members had increased to 85, 60% of them still had wage bills of less than £15,000 a year – indeed, 13% paid out less than £3,000 a year in wages.[64]

60. In 1901 its membership comprised some 35 companies, among which were some of the largest employers on the Clyde. Clyde Shipbuilding Association (CSA) Minute Book 1899–1903, p. 57.
61. CSA Minute Book 1899–1903, p. 31 (TD 241/1/7).
62. Fairfields joined both associations in April 1900. However, only eight years earlier the firm had flaunted its independence to the Royal Commission on Labour. Royal Commission on Labour 1892. Mining, Engineering, Hardware, Shipbuilding and Cognate Trades, p. 361. [c. 6795]. The importance of Clydeside as a centre of production is reflected in the fact that the Engineers' Employers' Federation (EEF) had its headquarters there until 1908. J. Foster and C. Woolfson, *The Politics of the UCS Work-in* (London, 1986), p. 83.
63. J. Zeitlin 'The internal politics of employer organization', *The Power to Manage?* (London, 1991), pp. 52–80.
64. NWETEA Register of Members' Voting Power, Wage Returns and Levies 1890–1929, Strathclyde Regional Archives (SRA) TD 1059/5/1&2.

Therefore, despite the presence of large enterprises like John Brown's or Beardmores, most NWETEA members were small to medium-sized businesses. Finally, the principal organiser of the NWETEA, Thomas Biggart, actively encouraged employers in industries divorced from engineering and shipbuilding to adopt a harder line with their workers. This further suggests that collectivism amongst engineers was more than a trade-wide coalition, and that a class dynamic was at play

Clydeside's ironfounders were also well organised at this time in the Scottish Ironfounders' Association (SIA). This initially came into being purely as a trade regulatory body, but a change in its constitution in 1914 enabled it to become fully involved with industrial relations. More power to the SIA's elbow was achieved in 1918 when it affiliated to the newly formed National Ironfounding Employers' Federation.[65] There was also the Scottish Iron Manufacturers' Association which comprised 17 firms in 1892, employing over 7000 workers; and the Directory of Industrial Associations indicates that a further five employers' organisations represented Clydeside's engineering and foundry employers.[66]

Employers engaged in the West of Scotland steel industry operated in export-oriented markets that were not conducive to welfarist labour control strategies. However, the levels of craft autonomy enjoyed by Clydeside steelworkers were rarely challenged by their employers. This – coupled with the acquiescence of unskilled workers in a system which offered them the eventual reward of skilled status – is said to have been a principal reason for there being stable industrial relations in steel-making throughout this period.[67] However, notwithstanding this self-regulating labour relations system, their employers were still organised against any potential labour threat.

There was a loose association of Scottish and North of England steel producers in the mid-1890s, but in 1896 steps were taken to form a permanent organisation along the lines of the Cleveland Ironmasters' Association – which regulated wages and industrial relations. In 1894 the Siemens Ingot Making Trade of the North of England and the West of Scotland came into being – later called the Steel Ingot Makers'

65. Statistical Branch of the Ministry of Labour, National Ironfounding Employers' Federation, PRO, Lab 69/34. See also Scottish Ironfounders' Federation, Minute Book 2, 3, May 1914.

66. Directory of Industrial Associations in the United Kingdom, [cd. 945XLVI 561]. See also Royal Commission on Labour 1892, Mining, Engineering, Hardware. Shipbuilding and Cognate Trades [c. 6795].

67. A. McKinlay, 'Philosophers in Overalls? Craft and Class on Clydeside c. 1900–1914', in W. Kenefick and A. J. McIvor (eds), *Roots of Red Clydeside?* (Edinburgh, 1996), pp. 86–106.

Association (SIMA). Eventually all the major Clydeside steelworks became members of an affiliated body of the SIMA: the West of Scotland Steel Makers' Association – John Colville played a leading role in the founding of this organisation, and he was elected president of the SIMA shortly before he died in 1901.[68] The SIMA kept a fairly tight rein on its membership, although there was frequent disagreement over issues such as the introduction of sliding scales. Questions of labour relations were attended to in the first instance by a network of what were termed 'urgency committees'. The composition of these committees was pre-determined, and the system was designed to enable the employers to meet at short notice to address local problems.[69] This 'buddy system' strengthened the backbone of the national association and cemented regional employer unity by creating a rapid response service capable of facing up to any labour threat.

Trade collaboration amongst West of Scotland shipbuilding and engineering companies suggests that an increasingly organised work-force was a prime cause of employer unity. However, neither the shipbuilders nor the engineering companies along the Clyde enjoyed production runs big enough – or operated in markets stable enough – to allow them to build up a long-term workforce. The delegation of industrial relations to a detached association of fellow employers, then, was a rational managerial decision. This was also the case in the Clyde-side mining industry where all the coalmasters' associations were established primarily to deal with labour relations too. Three main employers' organisations represented West of Scotland coalowners: the Airdrie and Slammanan Coalmasters' Association, the Ayrshire Coal-masters' Association, and the Lanarkshire Coalmasters' Association (LCA) – while the quarrymasters were represented by the Glasgow-based West of Scotland Whinstone Quarrymasters' Association. However, as the LCA's operational range extended over Clydeside's largest coalfield, it is best to focus on this association.

It has been argued that the effectiveness of the LCA in the early part of the period was fairly limited because of the refusal of several large employers to join – Archibald Russell, for example.[70] Also, in the Scottish

68. Steel Ingot Makers' Association, Minute Book 1, p. 268.
69. For example, James Dunlop's assigned urgency committee comprised repre-sentatives of the Steel Company of Scotland and the Glasgow Iron and Steel Company; while a representative from Dunlop's – together with one from Colville's – sat on the urgency committee of Stewart and Lloyds. Steel Ingot Makers' Association Minute Book 2, p. 221.
70. S. Renfrew, 'Militant Miners?: Strike Activity and Industrial Relations in the Lanarkshire Coalfield 1910–1914', in W. Kenefick and A. J. McIvor (eds), *Roots of Red Clydeside?*, p. 158.

coal industry employers' associations were said to be fairly weak – the LCA, for example, failed to bring about sliding-scale wage agreements.[71] This weakness, though, may have been over-stated as it ignores the influence that such organisations had beyond the confines of their own membership. The LCA was formed in 1886 and initially comprised 37 members. It is difficult to determine how representative the organisation was as its records do not list membership details. However, by 1897 it held sway over 9128 workers, and had a 'fighting fund' of £30,000 as insurance against labour trouble.[72] However, the numerical strength of the association was not the only indicator of its power and influence. For example, in 1892 its decision to reduce wage rates encouraged all the non-member Lanarkshire coal masters to do likewise. Not only that but the Ayrshire Coalmasters' Association, the Fife Coalmasters' Association, the Airdrie and Slammanan Coalmasters' Association – together with the mineral oil employers of the central belt – all agreed to follow the lead of the LCA and enforce a wage reduction.[73]

The LCA was also active in encouraging nationwide combination. Following the general strike of 1893, 86 coal masters – from all the employers' organisations in the trade – formed the Coal Masters' Association of Scotland.[74] This example of effective unity inspired the LCA to forge a Scottish-wide federation, and in 1899 the Scottish Midland Coal Owners' Association came into being – although by 1903 efforts were still being made to form a more extensive federation.[75] The strength of the LCA increased in the pre-war period. Archibald Russell was one of the largest coal owners in the region, and this firm and 13 other companies joined in 1907. By 1912 its membership had risen to 63.[76] Organisation among Clydeside coalmasters, therefore, stemmed, as with the engineers, from a need to show a united employer front to a strengthening labour movement.

71. R. Church, *British Coal Industry Volume 3*, pp. 681–689.
72. Royal Commission on Labour 1892, Evidence of Mr. Smellie on behalf of the Larkhall miners, pp. 44–55. Coal and Ironmasters of Scotland Record Book, 1894–1895, p. 11.
73. LCA Minute Book 1, 13 April 1892.
74. There were 33 companies from Lanarkshire, 18 from Slammannan, Airdrie and Bathgate, 6 from the Lothians, 10 from Fife and Clackmannan, and 19 from Ayrshire. The non-associated masters also gave their support. Scottish Coalmasters' Association, Minute Book 1, 1893, p. 2.
75. LCA, Minute Book 5, 1900–1905, 24 June 1903.
76. A. Renfrew, 'Mechanisation and the Miner: Work, Safety and Labour Relations in the Scottish Coal Industry c 1890–1939'. Unpublished Ph.D. thesis, University of Strathclyde (1997), p. 167.

Building

The biggest outlay faced by builders was their wage bills. Consequently, it was almost inevitable that – for the sake of profits – a regularisation of labour relations within the industry should be sought. The easiest way for small firms to do this was to combine, and a witness told the Royal Commission on Labour in 1894 that the establishment of strong building trade unions and employers' associations was needed to ensure peaceful labour relations in the building trade.[77] By 1905 this had largely come about, and a comprehensive system of collective bargaining in the building trade was firmly established.[78] To a great extent this system was engineered and sustained by the building trade employers' associations.

An average of 12 local and national building trade employers' organisations operated on Clydeside over the 1902–1919 period, and the Glasgow Master Masons' Association (GMMA) is a good example. Between 1875 and 1914 the average membership was only 50. However, in 1892 its members employed over 2000 operative masons, 800 labourers, and a fluctuating number of railway navvies.[79] Moreover, like the LCA in coalmining, the influence of the GMMA in the Clydeside building trade extended much further than its membership numbers would suggest. Even although there were known to be 78 employers in the region who remained outwith the GMMA, the standard wage rate for masons in the Glasgow area – of member and non-member firms – was determined by the conciliation machinery agreed between the GMMA and the operative masons' trade union.[80] This conciliation

---

77. Royal Commission on Labour 1892, Textiles, Clothing, Chemicals, Building and Miscellaneous Trades, Vol. 2. [c. 6795], Mr. D. MacGregor's evidence, pp. 305–308.

78. R. Price, *Masters, Unions and Men* (London, 1980), p. 190.

79. Royal Commission on Labour, MacGregor's evidence. This witness may have exaggerated the number of non-associated firms. The 1891 census lists only 45 master masons in the Parliamentary Burgh of Glasgow and 12 working on their own account. Furthermore, in 1902, the minutes of the Association state that 1500 operatives were pressurising its members for a pay increase. As there was a total of 1378 working at the trade in Glasgow in 1911, it would appear that most of their employers were members of the employers' organisation. Minute Book No. 4 of Glasgow and District Master Masons' Association, April 1902, p. 155; and Census of Scotland 1891 and 1911.

80. A. J. McIvor finds this to have been a characteristic of building trade employers' organisations in the North-West of England too. *Organised Capital* (London, 1996), p. 69. It is also worth noting that the GMMA stipulated tendering rates – including allowances for country work. This was also common among building trades employers' organisations in North-West England. *Ibid.*, p. 73, fn. 45.

agreement was reinforced annually at meetings with the workers'
representatives, and a clearly stated disputes procedure was generally
adhered to.

Employers' associations such as the GMMA represented all areas of
the Clydeside building industry. In 1913, for example, 98% of Glasgow's
master joiners were members of the Glasgow Master Wrights' Association.[81] This organisation came into being in 1890, but the impulse
behind its formation can be traced to frustration over workers using
their collective strength during the tight labour markets of the mid-
1870s.[82] In a similar way the Glasgow Master Slaters' Association was
formed in 1873, also to face up to growing labour unrest in the slating
trade. In 1875 a conference with the operative slaters was held and
thereafter wages and working conditions were fixed annually.[83] Forty
percent of Glasgow's master slaters were members of this employers'
association in 1887, and by 1895 this had risen to 65% – by which time
there were 30 'country members' from various parts of Clydeside.[84]

The extensive urbanisation of the Clydeside region called for a large
number of plumbers to maintain and install piping and sanitary equip-
ment – there was also a significant market in ships' plumbing in the
Clyde shipyards – and the 1911 census indicates that there were just
over 450 master plumbers in the region. The vast majority of these
were small employers, and most of them were members of the Glasgow
and West of Scotland Master Plumbers' Association (GWSMPA).[85]

Unlike most building trade employers' associations – which were
initially formed to deal with labour relations – the GWSMPA came
into being in 1856 specifically to regulate trade.[86] By 1911 the majority
of Clydeside's master plumbers were members, and six years later
practically all the plumbers in the region had joined – by which time
the membership stood at 640.[87] By now it was one of the strongest

81. This fact is referred to in Glasgow Master Slaters' Association Minute Book 4,
    27 Feb. 1913.

82. See report of operative joiners' agitation in *GH*, 17 April 1875, p. 6.

83. Glasgow Master Slaters' Association (GMSA) Minute Book 1, Sept. 24, 1875.

84. GMSA Minute Book 1, 4 Sept. 1879; Minute Book 3, Sept. 1895; and *Post Office
    Directory* 1880, and 1895.

85. Census of Scotland 1911, p. 383. Membership of the plumbers' association had
    increased over the immediate pre-war period from 173 in 1905 to 400 in 1913.
    GH, May 19, 1906; and GMMA Minute Book 1913.

86. GWSMPA Rule Book, 1912.

87. *Plumbing Trade Journal* (*PTJ*), April 1915, p. 14. Also *PTJ*, May 1917, p. 27. By
    1923 the GWSMPA was known as the Glasgow and West of Scotland Plumbers'
    and Domestic Engineers' (Employers) Association.

and richest building trades employers' organisations in the whole of Britain.[88]

Clydeside's master painters were another well-organised group of small-scale capitalists. The Glasgow Master Painters' Association was set up in 1857 following a strike; and the Association subsequently amalgamated with the Association of Master Painters in Scotland (AMPS) when it was formed in 1878.[89] At the outset all the regional master painters' associations retained their autonomy within this national organisation. However, during the war a need to check rising wage rates convinced many of the members that the loose structure of the AMPS hindered united employer action, and in 1919 all the local associations merged to form the National Federation of Master Painters in Scotland – within which local associations were represented in proportion to their membership strength.[90] Unlike the plumbers, then, the initial reason for employer collectivism in the painting trade was the need to deal with labour issues. However, the organised master painters quickly realised the trade regulatory potential of their organisation and capitalised on it by agreeing on fixed-rates for painting and decorating work – which further enhanced the Association's appeal.

There were several attempts from the 1890s to forge a Scottish employers' body for the building trade. In 1890 the Scottish Building Trades' Association (SBTA) was formed 'out of a deep and widespread conviction that the time has come when the important and ever-reaching interests of the various branches of the Building Trades rendered an organisation of this kind absolutely necessary'.[91] This strengthened employer class consciousness in the Scottish building trade, as the SBTA assumed an important co-ordinating role which kept the various

---

88. *PTJ*, May 1917, p. 27. Its secretary was also secretary of the Ironmongers and Allied Trades' Association, and this connection benefited both associations. *PTJ*, Oct. 1916, p. 18.

89. Another strike was defeated by the new association in 1860, and the following year the Glasgow masters came to the assistance of the Greenock Master Painters' Association by refusing to employ any painters involved in a dispute in the Greenock area. *Scottish Painters' Journal* – Gallagher Memorial Library, Glasgow. The *rationale* behind the formation of the national organisation was defensive: 'to promote unity of action in the settlement of all questions arising between employers and their workmen with a view to preventing lockouts or strikes against members of the Association'. The initial membership was 134. *Scottish Decorators' Quarterly Review* (1956), p. 52. See also the account of the initial Edinburgh meeting to form the national body in *GH*, 12 Jan. 1878, p. 8.

90. *Scottish Decorators' Quarterly Review* (1956), p. 54.

91. GMSA Minute Book 3, 12 Sept. 1895. See also GMMA Minute Book 3, 30 June 1895.

industry-specific employers' associations informed of any workers' agitation taking place in Scotland. In 1899, for example, there was a lock-out of joiners in Dumfries, and the SBTA circulated its member firms to advise them not to take on any men from the Dumfries area.[92] However, the organisation had only limited success in the pre-First World War period. The Glasgow master masons withdrew in 1902, and the Glasgow Master Wrights' Association (GMWA) also pulled out at this time. In 1916, though, the GMWA – which by now was committed to forging strong cross-trade links in the building industry – breathed new life into the SBTA and it was given a new constitution and a new name: the Scottish National Building Trades' Federation.[93]

The Glasgow and West of Scotland Employers' Council (GWSEC) – formed in 1902 – was another example of cross-trade employer cohesion, and stemmed from a need by employers in all branches of the Clydeside building trade to show a united front against labour. A note in the minutes of the GMWA illustrates this:

> Only by having such a council could the masters hope to hold their own with the very strong opposition presently experienced from the trades unions. The workmen have Trades Councils which help them keep in touch with each other and trade affairs generally – consequently the Masters should also combine for self-protection.[94]

The Employers' Council sent a delegate to London in 1911 to join the Employers' Parliamentary Council's deputation to protest against the National Insurance Bill.[95] The Council also tried to persuade Clydeside's building trade employers' organisations to affiliate with the Employers' Parliamentary Council – initiated in Manchester in 1894 as a counter to the parliamentary council of the TUC. However, this idea attracted little support.[96]

Like the SBTA, the GWSEC had a relatively short life, and by 1914

92. Ibid., 11 March 1899.
93. The masons initially refused to join this new body as they disagreed with the terms of its constitution and rules. However, by 1918 the GMMA had joined the association which now controlled over 3,000 operatives. GMMA, Minute Book 7, July 1916, p. 256. Also Minute Book 8, Feb. 1919, p. 27.
94. Glasgow Master Wrights' Association (GMWA) Minute Book 1, 8 Dec. 1902.
95. GMWA, Minute Book 6, p. 58, July 1911, Minute Book 6, p. 163, Sept. 1911.
96. The Employers' Council performed a useful trade regulatory role too. For example, it fought the case of the city's building trade employers against the implementation of stricter building regulations in 1908, and this forced the town council to concede considerable amendments. GMWA Minute Book 2, 6 Aug. and 4 Oct. 1909, pp. 52 and 57.

it was in decline. Its failure to usurp the trade regulatory role of the smaller employers' associations, the rise of Glasgow's Building Trades' Exchange – discussed in the next chapter – combined with the growth of state-induced arbitration channels, made it out-of-date. However, it should be seen as a further example of cross-trade collectivism in the Clydeside building industry which grew organically and independently of any government-enforced corporatism, and for a while strengthened the linkages between capitalist groups.

There was a gradual change in the structure of the Clydeside building industry over the period: more general builders came into being, and smaller units became less numerous. This altered the shape of employer collectivism too and we can see this in the metamorphosis of the GMMA. Despite the decline in the number of Clydeside stonemasons over the period, the GMMA did not go into decline, but shifted its orientation from the parochial to the national.[97] More and more big firms joined its ranks, and by 1920 the organisation – which had started off as a group of small Glasgow employers – now represented major firms such as the likes of: James Brand, William Fyfe, Melville Dundas and Whitsun, Sir Robert McAlpine, Leggat, Loudon, Sir Thomas Mason, and Sir William Arrol. Its name was changed to reflect its new orientation and it became the Scottish Building Contractors' Association, although the directors expressed their regret at the severance of the historic link with the Glasgow masons' trade. By 1919 it had outgrown the Scottish National Building Trades' Federation and had resigned from this body. McAlpine announced at this time that closer cooperation of Clydeside's building contractor and civil engineering trades was now a principal aim.[98] To this end a committee was established to bring about collaboration with the Federation of Civil Engineering Contractors, and this cohesive dynamic was sustained throughout the inter-war period – the Caledonian Portland Cement Company, for example, joined in 1928, and ten asphalt contractors became members in 1934.[99]

97. Its membership list shows that by 1919 only 34 of the 167 member firms had been members in 1900. Also, between 1910 and 1922, 17 firms which had been members in the pre-1900 period resigned or were removed from the list. GMMA Roll of Members 1919.
98. Scottish Building Contractors' Association (SBCA) Minute Book 8, April 15, 1919.
99. SBCA Membership List. This source also reveals that the Association sent information on a regular basis to the CSA, Glasgow Corporation Electricity Department, the Iron and Steel Employers' Association, and several other important employers' associations.

Textiles and clothing

In the 1820s and 1830s, strong employer organisation in the Clydeside textile industry effectively destroyed trade unionism.[100] Consequently, for most of the pre-First World War period collective bargaining was poorly developed in this industry. This, coupled with the widespread use of company paternalism, rendered employer cooperation for labour relations purposes largely superfluous – although there were still 16 national and local Scottish textiles and clothing employers' associations by 1904.[101]

From the early years of the twentieth century, however, paternalism in textiles – which was now dominated by the thread industry – began to break down under pressure from encroaching trade unionism.[102] A consequence of this – and the imposition of trades boards and industrial councils – was that employers' associations once again became important labour control agencies. The Newmilns Manufacturers' Association (NMA) initially performed a trade regulatory role. However, in 1914 the organisation became involved in labour relations too.[103] Similarly, the Scottish Lace Manufacturers' Association – which shared the same secretary as the NMA – represented eight firms from the Newmilns District by 1918.[104] The principal Kilmarnock firms involved in yarn spinning had an employers' association which also dealt with labour relations, and in 1917, 22 Clydeside companies established the West of Scotland Textile Association.[105]

The clothing industry was also dominated by small employers, and it too had its share of employers' associations. The Scottish Wholesale Clothing Association emerged in 1910 to deal with the imposition of a Trade Board on the clothing industry. By 1914, 18 companies were members, rising to 24 by the end of the war.[106] Similarly, 14 firms formed the Glasgow Shirt Manufacturers' Association in 1913, also as

100. W. H. Fraser, *Conflict and Class* (Edinburgh, 1988), pp. 114–170. There was also a flurry of organisation in the early years of the nineteenth century. See Association of Master Cotton Spinners Minute Book 1, 20 Oct. 1810. SRA, T-M J/99.

101. Abstract of Labour Statistics of the U.K., 1902–1904 [cd 2491], p. 128.

102. W. Knox and H. Corr, 'Striking women': Cotton workers and industrial unrest *c.* 1907–1914', in Kenefick and McIvor (eds) *Roots of Red Clydeside?*, pp. 107–129. See also C. M. M. MacDonald, 'Weak Roots and Branches: Class, Gender and the Geography of Industrial Protest', *Scottish Labour History* 33 (1998), pp. 6–31.

103. Collective Agreement Between the Scottish Madras Manufacturers' Association and Newmilns and District Textile Workers' Union, 1926, PRO, Lab 83/1299.

104. Ministry of Labour (ML) Report, PRO, Lab 2/274/8.

105. ML Report, PRO, Lab 2/261/12.

106. Scottish Wholesale Clothing Association, Chairman's Reports Dec. 1914 and March 1919. SRA, TD 967/5/2.

a response to the initiation of a Trade Board.[107] Employers involved in the hat trade in Glasgow were organised throughout the period in the Wholesale Cloth Hat and Cap Manufacturers' Association (Glasgow Branch).[108] By 1920 the Scottish Retail Drapers' Association was based in Glasgow. There was even a Glasgow Kilt Manufacturers' Association – comprising 21 firms – which became involved in collective bargaining with the Workers' Union in 1917.[109] And – although not technically part of the clothing industry – the Glasgow and District Umbrella Manufacturers' Association represented all the major employers in the trade by 1918, and had initiated a collective bargaining agreement with a general union in 1919.[110]

However, compared to the building trade, employer collectivism in textiles and clothing was more reactive and hesitant. Employers, long used to effective labour control, formed organisations in response to increased trade unionism and state-induced collective bargaining.

Baking

Baking was an important industry on Clydeside, and the region is credited with being the cradle of factory bread making. Twenty employers' organisations represented Clydeside's food, drink, baking and confectionery trades by 1919.[111] Seventy percent of these were in baking and confectionery where trade unionism was well established – illustrating yet again the correlation between the labour threat and employer organisation. In 1897 the Scottish Master Bakers' Association (SMBA) represented 42% of the country's master bakers, and Clydeside was its principal stronghold.[112] Glasgow had three master bakers' associations which quickly affiliated to the SMBA when it was established in 1889.[113] By 1907 the Glasgow Master Bakers' Association had 361 members,

---

107. Glasgow Shirt Manufacturers' Association Minutes, 3 April 1913. SRA, TD 967/6/1. The organisation became the Scottish District of Shirt and Collar Manufacturers – although most of its members were from Clydeside – and later The Scottish Collar and Tie Manufacturers' Federation (Scottish District), in 1920.
108. Collective Agreement between the Wholesale Cloth Hat and Cap Manufacturers' Association (Glasgow Branch), and the Undergarment workers Trade Union, 1919, PRO, Lab 83/5534.
109. PRO, Lab 83/1545.
110. ML Report, PRO, Lab 2/556/6.
111. Directory of Industrial Associations 1919.
112. By 1906 the SMBA had 2062 members and funds of over £2000, and by 1910 the membership stood at 2193 – 97% of Scottish master bakers. *British Baker*, Nov. 1897, and 30 July 1910, p. 17.
113. Cohesion amongst the city's master bakers was strengthened even further in 1919 when the three organisations merged. *The Bailie*, 24 March 1920, p. 3.

and Sir William Bilsland noted that 'however keen might be rivalry in the baking trade, the members were always friendly to each other'.[114] Glasgow was also an important centre of biscuit production, and by 1918 the Glasgow-based Association of Biscuit Manufacturers represented virtually all of Britain's biscuit makers.[115]

In contrast to the uncertain markets in which shipbuilders, engineers, and builders operated, bakers and biscuit makers produced fairly homogeneous products for a relatively stable market. Consequently some of the larger Clydeside bakeries operated successful company welfarist policies. Bilslands, for example – one of the most anti-union employers in the industry – set up its own welfare scheme in 1900. This effectively kept trade unionism at bay, and was well worth the 39/6d per employee– per year which it cost the firm.[116] Its effectiveness would suggest that the company's membership of the SMBA was largely superfluous. However, although Bilslands' – and other large welfarist-oriented bakers such as Beattie's and Montgomerie's – did not really require the labour relations' services of the SMBA, it did value the trade regulatory role which the Association provided. On the other hand, smaller firms – in which company welfarism was harder to achieve and sustain – derived positive benefit from the united employer front which the SMBA represented, as well as from market regulation.

Furniture making

The most important market for Clydeside furniture was the Clyde shipbuilding industry. This dictated that the furniture makers – like the shipbuilders – made bespoke products, which largely prevented the manufacturers from adopting factory mass-production, and compelled them to employ a highly skilled workforce. These factors, combined with the relatively small-scale nature of the firms, rendered employer cooperation a more viable labour management strategy than internal company control – which was more suited to larger, unskilled and poorly unionised workforces. The principal employers' association for the furniture trade on Clydeside – and, indeed in Scotland – was the Beith-based Scottish Furniture Manufacturers' Association (SFMA).

By 1890, the industry was under attack from two sides. Firstly, there was increased competition from other regions which produced cheaper,

114. *GH* 18 April 1907, p. 7; and *GH* 23 Nov. 1907, p. 6.
115. Statistical Branch of the Ministry of Labour, Information regarding the National Association of Biscuit Manufacturers, PRO, Lab 69/34.
116. Bilslands' Minute Book 4, 15 Jan. 1926 – the company had 440 employees at this time.

machine-made furniture.[117] The second threat was the increasing strength of organised craft labour – membership of the Scottish Union of Cabinet Makers grew by 76% between 1887 and 1891.[118] It was as a response to these threats that the SFMA came into being in 1890, and by 1898 it represented over 100 firms.[119] The organisation dealt primarily with labour relations, and its most notable success was in 1898 when it initiated and sustained a lock-out of the workers over the issue of managerial prerogative. During the labour unrest of 1912 membership of the SFMA increased by 70% – further illustrating that the organisation was primarily geared to countering the labour threat.[120] However, in the aftermath of the 1898 dispute the SFMA became much more concerned with strengthening collective bargaining channels. Initially hostile towards organised labour, the SFMA propagated and nurtured union agreements to ensure untroubled production throughout the period.[121]

The role of the state

By the end of our period many Clydeside employers had been brought into government-sponsored conciliation agreements.[122] However, despite this, many also remained apathetic. This is underlined by the lukewarm reaction which many employers gave to the idea of industrial councils in the years following the First World War. The emergence of these councils in the inter-war years has been taken to indicate an upsurge in corporatism.[123] This, though, suggests a higher degree of acceptance of the councils than was actually the case. The TUC rejected the industrial councils as 'a stratagem to circumvent collective bargaining'.

117. These manufacturers paid lower wages, and the principal trade union with which they had to deal – the Alliance Cabinet Makers' Society – represented the growing semi-skilled sector of the industry: its membership increased by 387% between 1887 and 1891. D. Blankenhorn, 'Our Class of Workmen: The Cabinet-Makers Revisited', in R. Harrison and J. Zeitlin (eds), *Divisions of Labour* (Sussex, 1985), p. 43.

118. D. Blankenhorn, p. 43.

119. SFMA Minute Book 1, 3 Nov. 1898, p. 66.

120. SFMA Minute Book 2, 25 Nov. 1913, p. 82.

121. By 1923 the Association was the linchpin of a Scottish-wide agreement which affected over 3,000 workers. Collective Agreement between the Scottish Furniture Manufacturers' Association and the Scottish Furnishing Trades Advisory Committee, 1923, PRO, Lab, 83/1872.

122. Directory of Industrial Association *1919* [cmd. 328], pp. 9–44.

123. W. Knox, 'Class, Work and Trade Unionism in Scotland', in A. Dickson and J. H. Treble (eds), *People and Society in Scotland* vol. 3, 1914–1990 (Edinburgh, 1992), p. 129.

Further – despite the fact that there were estimated to be 3.5 million workers under the schemes by the end of our period – the general reaction throughout the country was lukewarm.[124]

This was certainly the case on Clydeside. For example, the Glasgow and West of Scotland Master Plumbers' Association rejected the idea of industrial council wage bargaining primarily because the Association disliked the preponderance of English members on the council.[125] Similarly, although the SFMA initially welcomed the Furnishing Trades' Industrial Council when it was formed in 1918, it too withdrew support, complaining that the Council marginalised Scottish issues.[126] The Scottish Carpet Manufacturers' Association pulled out of the carpet trade's industrial council in 1920 in protest at a decision to standardise wages in the carpet industry throughout Britain.[127] And the SMBA resigned from the baking trade's industrial council in 1922 because its Glasgow members simply refused to have anything to do with it.[128]

Throughout the period the government shunned the idea of imposing any legally binding collective bargaining scheme and preferred voluntary agreements to a 'cast iron system imposed by law'.[129] This was very much in tune with the views of the organised employers, and in 1935 the Federation of British Industry (FBI) concluded that voluntary association was much more beneficial to industry than compulsory association.[130] A great deal of conciliation between capital and labour came into being therefore without any government prompting whatsoever. This was especially so in the Clydeside building industry. Here, although the role of the Board of Trade's representative George Askwith in forging conciliation agreements and inter-trade cohesion was important, the main impetus came from the employers' associations themselves. This is clear from the cross-trade employers' organisations, and from the fact that as early as 1910 practically all of Clydeside's

124. K. Middlemas, *Politics in an Industrial Society* (London, 1979), p. 138.
125. *GH*, 3 April 1920, p. 9.
126. SFMA, Minute Book 2, 25 Nov. 1919, p. 197.
127. Minutes of Conference between Scottish Carpet Manufacturers' Association and Scotch Carpet Union, 10 March 1921, p. 2.
128. *GH*, 7 April 1922. Such apathy was a characteristic of the system of industrial councils nationally, which was 'under pressure for most of its existence'. See C. Wrigley, *Cosy Co-operation under Strain: Industrial Relations in the Yorkshire Woollen Industry 1919–1930* (University of York Borthwick Paper No. 71 (1987), p. 2). This article gives an account of one of the more successful industrial councils.
129. Final Report of the Committee on Industry and Trade, 1929 [Cmd. 3282], p. 89.
130. James Lithgow was the chairman of this committee. Federation of British Industries, Report of the Committee on the Organisation of Industry (1935), pp. 14–15.

building employers and their workers – around 12,000 of them – were
bound by some form of conciliation machinery.[131] The notion of the
state coming in to separate two previously warring camps, therefore, is
untenable.

This also applies at the national level. The Federation of British
Industry came into being in 1916, and three years later 946 firms and
174 associations were members.[132] However, many employers remained
indifferent. The Lanarkshire Coalmasters' Association, for example,
believed that it would be impossible to find common ground with other
employers as coalmasters produced a commodity which other capitalists
consumed.[133] The Scottish Carpet Manufacturers' Association was
indifferent to the idea of membership of the FBI.[134] And the Scottish
Furniture Manufacturers' Association declined its invitation to join the
FBI in 1916 because its members could see no benefit in such an
affiliation.[135] The Engineers' Employers' Federation (EEF) consistently
distanced itself from what it saw as state-induced collectivism that
interfered with management prerogative.[136] And in 1918 it was instrumental in setting up an alternative body to the FBI in the National
Confederation of Employers' Organisations – specifically to counter the
growing influence of the Labour party and the TUC.

Limitations of employer organisation
Although employers organised more strongly and consistently on Clydeside than some writers would allow, their organisational strength should
not be overstated. Many Clydeside employers were not members of
employers' associations – although it is difficult to determine how many
as there are few membership lists available. The important factor of
trade union strength was not significant enough in some industries to
stimulate organisation as a collective defence – a prime example here
would be the textile employers throughout the earlier part of our period.
This was the case in retailing. It was not until 1967 that the Retail
Consortium came into being. The government's late involvement with
an industry which remained 'one of the last strongholds of competition',

---

131. Report on Collective Agreements Between Employers and Workpeople in the
     United Kingdom 1910 [Cd. 5366].
132. However, its immediate strength and political influence were fairly weak before
     1920. J. Turner (ed.), *Businessmen and Politics: Studies of Business Activity in British
     Politics 1900–1945* (London, 1984), pp. 33–49.
133. LCA Minute Book 10, 24 Nov. 1918, p. 198.
134. Scottish Carpet Manufacturers' Association Minutes, 10 Sept. 1918.
135. SFMA Minute Book 2, 28 Nov. 1916, p. 241.
136. E. Wigham, *The Power to Manage* (London, 1973), p. 80.

combined with the fragmented and small-scale nature of the industry, made it especially difficult for trade unionism to gain a foothold. It might be added that, like the Clydeside cotton industry of an earlier period, retailing was dominated by poorly organised women workers.[137] The labour-threat factor, then, was insignificant in this industry throughout our period.

Sometimes there was local indifference to collective organisation. In 1911, for example, the firm of George Robertson and Sons withdrew from the Scottish Coppersmiths' Employers' Association as none of the coppersmith firms in the company's home town of Paisley had bothered to join.[138] This illustrates that a critical mass had to be achieved before employer unity could be initiated and sustained. The Scottish Master Plasterers' Association (SMPA) struggled to attain this critical mass – its national membership was only 95 in 1899.[139] In 1902 – during a building boom – only half of Glasgow's master plasterers were members of the Association. Moreover, when these employers ignored a SMPA decision and conceded a wage claim, their colleagues in Hamilton and Paisley immediately left the association – those in Kilmarnock, Greenock, and Coatbridge also drifted away over the next five years.[140]

A similar fate befell the Clyde Ship Riggers' Employers' Association – initiated in 1920 to deal with industrial relations issues affecting those responsible for shifting vessels in harbour. This association began with a structural weakness in that many master riggers were employed directly by ship brokers and remained outwith the new association.[141] Also, the organisation had to deal with two trade unions – operative riggers on the lower reaches of the Clyde were members of the Sailor's and Firemen's Union, while those further upriver belonged to the Ship Riggers' Society.[142] It was primarily because of these structural weaknesses that the Association was dissolved in 1924 – by which time it had only six members.

137. W P Grant and D. Marsh, 'The Representation of Retail Interests in Britain', *Political Studies*, 22 (1974), pp. 168–177.
138. Scottish Coppersmiths' Employers' Association, Minute Book 2, 11 Feb. 1913, p. 34.
139. Scottish Master Plasterers' Association Minute Book 1, 15 Aug. 1889.
140. The situation was so bad in 1905 that the remaining members came very close to winding up the organisation. SMPA Minute Book 1, April 1905. An attempt was made in 1907 to re-affiliate the lost Clydeside masters with some success. SMPA Minute Book 1, Sept. 1907.
141. Clyde Ship Riggers' Employers' Association Minute Book 1, 17 Feb. 1920, p. 2; 4 April 1920, p. 16; and 3 June 1920, p. 26.
142. Ibid., 14 Oct. 1921, p. 49.

Sectionalism within industries could also make united action difficult to achieve. Glasgow's master tailors were split between merchant tailors – who catered mostly for the high-quality bespoke trade – and master tailors, many of whom employed semi-skilled workers under a division of labour system. An article in the *Sartorial Gazette* drew attention to this weakness in 1910:

> The first class house may condescend to recognise a 2nd class house, but will entirely ignore the 3rd class house ... Class barriers must be broken down ... there is no earthly reason why if the 3rd class workers strike the 3rd class firms, the two higher classes should not come to their assistance.[143]

A consequence of these divisions was that two employers' associations represented the Clydeside tailoring trade: the United Kingdom Association of Master Tailors and Foremen Cutters, and the National Federation of Merchant Tailors.[144] The Glasgow branch of the latter had only 70 members in 1907.[145] Moreover, of 25,000 merchant tailors in Britain in 1916, only 1,000 were members of the National Federation of Merchant Tailors.[146]

Sometimes effective employer paternalism made employer organisation unnecessary. Paternalism was used to good effect in the Paisley textile mills for much of the period. This was also the case in the Clydeside railway industry. By the 1890s most of Clydeside's railway companies were members of the Railway Companies' Association. However, this was essentially a defensive organisation aimed at opposing government interference in the railway industry.[147] Labour relations, on the other hand, tended to be dealt with at company level where a long tradition of welfarism normally soaked up any labour radicalism.[148]

The leather industry also had a history of welfarist labour control. For example, in 1884 over 600 people attended the annual festival of the Ayr Leather Trades, where one of the principal employers lectured

143. *Sartorial Gazette*, Volume 17, 1910, p. 130.
144. The correspondent in the *Sartorial Gazette* illustrated that master tailors – many of whom were employers of sweated labour – had no place in the Merchants' Association. Merchant tailors had to deal directly with the public and be employers of labour. *Ibid.*, p. 146.
145. *GH*, Report of Annual Dinner of Glasgow Branch of National Federation of Merchant Tailors. 20 Dec. 1907, p. 10.
146. *Sartorial Gazette*, Oct. 1916, p. 275.
147. See G. Alderman, *The Railway Interest* (Leicester, 1973).
148. See R. Fitzgerald, *British Labour Management and Industrial Welfare 1846–1939* (London, 1988), pp. 46–48.

the crowd on the beneficial effects of belonging to a benevolent society compared with trade union membership.[149] Similarly, at the Gryffe Tannery's annual soirée in 1889 the owner lambasted trade unionism and praised the good sense of his workforce for steering well clear of it.[150] However, the leather industry produced a diverse range of products and it was generally only the larger firms that could rely on paternalistic labour control. Once again, the most rational strategy for the smaller companies to adopt was that of collaboration. Consequently, we find that Clydeside's saddle makers were organised in the Glasgow and West of Scotland Master Saddlers' Association – although by 1928 there were just over 100 workpeople involved in this trade in the West of Scotland.[151]

The most significant sector of the leather industry was the boot and shoe trade, and company paternalism was well established here. Even as late as 1906, many of Glasgow's shoe manufacturers were successfully tempting workers away from trade unionism and into their own welfare schemes.[152] Despite this, the growing significance of trade unionism stimulated employer unity throughout the period. Workers' organisation began with the National Union of Boot and Shoe Operatives in 1874, and by 1877 the Glasgow branch had around 450 members.[153] This growth resulted in the formation of the Glasgow Master Shoemakers' Association, which by the 1880s was involved in collective bargaining with the union. Further, the growing significance of trade unionism also resulted in the formation in 1891 of the Federation of Boot and Shoe Manufacturers, to which the Glasgow Master Shoemakers affiliated.[154] Increasing trade unionism accompanied sweeping changes in methods of production, and by the end of our period only 120 workers were employed in the hand-sewn sector of the Glasgow shoe trade – although their trade union still had a collective agreement with the Glasgow Master Bootmakers' Association.[155]

149. *Scottish Trader*, March 1884, p. 329. There was a Scottish Hide and Leather Provident Society which had been established in Glasgow in 1834. *Scottish Trader*, April 1884, p. 360.
150. *Scottish Leather Trader*, 3 Jan. 1889, p. 27.
151. ML File, PRO Lab 83/1473, 'Collective Agreement Between Glasgow and West of Scotland Master Saddlers' Association, and Union of Saddlers and General Leather Workers, 1928.'
152. Glasgow Trades Council Minutes 1906, p. 3.
153. A. Fox, *A History of the National Union of Boot and Shoe Operatives 1874–1957* (Oxford, 1958), p. 30.
154. *Shoe and Leather Trader*, Jan. 1900, p. 6.
155. 'Collective Agreement Between Glasgow Master Bootmakers' Association and the City of Glasgow Operative Boot and Shoe Makers' Trade and Funeral Society, 1920', PRO Lab 83/1588. Clogs were never as popular in the West of Scotland

Changing production methods, then, combined with intensifying trade unionism, resulted in the decline of paternalism in the leather trade, and employers' associations increasingly assuming responsibility for collective bargaining. Testimony to this is the fact that by 1920 an agreement between the Federated Association of Boot and Shoe Manufacturers in Scotland and the National Union of Boot and Shoe Operatives affected over 3,000 workpeople.[156]

Even when employers were members of associations, their loyalty was not guaranteed. In 1907 several members of the Glasgow Master Horseshoers' Association insisted on paying lower wages than those agreed by the Association.[157] In 1911, the Light Castings section of the West of Scotland Iron and Steel Founders' Association (WSISFA) refused to concede an advance authorised by the parent association following a strike by moulders.[158] And during a lock-out in 1901 – to enforce a wage reduction – several members of the Glasgow Master Wrights' Association took down their reduction notices, forcing the association to impose a £50 penalty to deter future backsliders, and changing its constitution so that no lock-outs could take place until members employing at least two thirds of the operatives agreed.[159] Such 'free riderism' was a characteristic of employers' associations in other countries, and penalties such as this were often imposed to ensure membership loyalty.[160] Another good example from the end of our period is that of the Shipbuilding Employers' Federation's scheme to ensure greater unity of employer action against the trade unions. This had a clause which stated 'voluntary observance of these rules and regulations cannot be satisfactorily and solely relied upon and that a penalty for breach is in some form or another essential'.[161] It has been argued that compulsion such as this was a necessary component of group action, and that, just as the state had to frequently resort to coercion to produce patriotism, so too did employers' organisations to ensure members' loyalty.[162]

as in some parts of England. However, by 1924 the Amalgamated Society of Journeymen Cloggers had a collective agreement with several Glasgow firms. See PRO, Lab 83/1603.

156. ML File PRO, Lab 83/1586.
157. *GH*, 25 April 1907, p. 13.
158. West of Scotland Iron and Steel Founders' Association, Minute Book 3, 13 Dec. 1911.
159. Glasgow Master Wrights' Association, Minute Book 1, 30 April 1901.
160. Van Waarden, 'Organizational emergence'. p. 20.
161. Shipbuilders' Employers' Federation Scheme 1919. Mitchell Library Glasgow TD241/15/5.
162. M. Olson, *The Logic of Collective Action* (London, 1965), p. 13.

To sum up, then, operational necessity, complete indifference, determined individualism, and intense competition: all were ever-present forces acting against effective capitalist combination. The idea of a unified employer class, therefore, is difficult to sustain. However, the following chapters will show that there is more evidence of employer association holding firm on Clydeside than of its breaking apart.

CHAPTER THREE

Clydeside Employers and the Regulation of Trade

Adam Smith wrote in *The Wealth of Nations* that 'people of the same trade seldom meet together, even for merriment and diversion, but the conversation ends in a conspiracy against the public, or in some contrivance to raise prices'.[1] These famous sentiments were echoed a hundred years later by a writer in the *Glasgow Herald* who noted that: 'Our landlords have associations to keep up our rents, our grocers and provision dealers have their soirées and recreations, ostensibly for conventional sociality, but really for the purpose of making us pay more for supplies'.[2] Later still, in 1928, the Balfour Committee found that when employers organised collectively, they always resorted to trade regulation practices.[3] And in 1982 Olson concluded that the very effectiveness of trade regulation amongst British capitalists caused an 'institutional sclerosis' that stifled the country's economic competitiveness.[4] Regulation of trade, then, according to some sources, has been a fundamental characteristic of capitalist production.

This perception of employer behaviour, though, clashes with another school of thought which sees British capitalists prevented from working together effectively by the strong individualism and self-sufficiency that made them successful capitalists in the first place.[5] This chapter will take a broad view of Clydeside capitalism and highlight the dense web of trade collaboration that spread throughout the region. Adam Smith's

1. In A. Clayre (ed.), *Nature and Industrialisation* (London, 1982), p. 193.
2. *GH*, 5 Jan. 1876, p. 7.
3. I. McGrath, 'Wool Textile Employers' Organisations', unpublished Ph.D. thesis, University of Bradford (1991), p. 191.
4. M. Olson, *The Rise and Decline of Nations* (New Haven, 1982). p. 77 and *passim*. For a supporting argument, see S. N. Broadberry and N. F. R. Crafts, 'Britain's productivity gap in the 1930s: some neglected factors', *Journal of Economic History*, 52 (Sept. 1992), pp. 531–558. For a recent attack on Olson's theory, see A. Booth, J. Melling, and C. Dartmann, 'Institutions and Economic Growth: The Politics of Productivity in West Germany, Sweden, and the United Kingdom 1945–1955', *Journal of Economic History*, 57, 2 (June, 1997), pp. 416–444.
5. For example, P. L. Payne, 'The Emergence of the Large-scale company in Great Britain, 1870–1914', *Economic History Review* 2nd. series, 20 (1967), p. 523.

depiction of capitalist behaviour is the more appropriate, as in most industries capitalists increasingly turned towards non-competitive trading practices in an effort to keep their profits up. The focus will again be on capitalists large and small, as there has been a tendency among business historians to concentrate only on the restrictive practices of large employers, and to view nineteenth-century price associations as the unsuccessful forerunners of a modern multi-divisional industrial structure.[6]

COLLECTIVE POLICIES AMONGST LARGER CAPITALISTS

Iron and Steel

Chapter 2 highlighted how the iron and steel industries were central to the economic development of the West of Scotland. From the 1880s industrialists and merchants engaged in these industries were subjected to intensifying competition from within and beyond the region. As a response to this threat to profits they regulated prices.

A prime example of how easily this could be achieved was the creation of the Glasgow Iron Ring in 1881. This came about as a direct response to competition from the Cleveland industry and quickly became a barometer for the state of the whole of the United Kingdom's iron trade – it was to last until iron dealing in Glasgow was brought to an end by the Ministry of Munitions in 1916. Rings such as this were distasteful to any non-members who had to deal with them, and one Sheffield steel producer branded this particular cartel 'one of the greatest curses ever saddled upon a respectable industry'.[7]

Like the iron merchants, the Clydeside steel makers also turned to collaboration when their profits were threatened. In this case the catalyst was falling steel prices in the early 1900s caused by increasing foreign competition. Fortnightly meetings were held, penalty clauses were imposed, and a territorial agreement was struck with steel makers in the North of England. By 1904 these tactics successfully pushed steel prices

---

6. For example, L. Hannah, *The Rise of the Corporate Economy* (London, 1976); Also, F. R. Jervis, *The Economics of Mergers* (London, 1971). For a reappraisal of the importance of small family firms see *Business History*, 35, Oct. 1993, 4. See also M. C. Casson, 'Entrepreneurship and business culture' in J. Brown and M. B. Rose (eds), *Entrepreneurship, Networks and Modern Business* (Manchester, 1993); Also G. Cookson, 'Family firms and business networks: Textile engineering in Yorkshire, 1780–1830.' *Business History* 39, 1 (1997).
7. *Scottish Ironmerchant*, April 1899, p. 9. Also, *Scottish Ironmerchant*, 13 July 1900. For more information on this cartel, see J. L. Carvel, *The Coltness Iron Company* (Edinburgh, 1948), pp. 48–49.

back up.[8] Price regulation amongst Clydeside steel makers continued in the pre-war period, and this reflected a national picture in which a fifth of all British price associations by 1914 were in the iron and steel industry.[9] The extent to which the individual producers adhered to these agreements and for how long requires further research. However, by 1918 most of the major steel makers on the Clyde were involved in some form of association, as Table 3.1 shows.

TABLE 3.1

Association	Member Companies
Scottish Steelmakers' Association	Beardmore, Colville, James Dunlop, Glasgow Iron and Steel Company, Lanarkshire Steel Company, Motherwell Iron and Steel Company, Lanarkshire Steel Company, The Steel Company of Scotland, Stewart and Lloyds
Scottish Ironmasters' Association	Baird, Carron, Coltness, Colville, Dalmellington Iron Company, Dixon, James Dunlop, Glasgow Iron Company, Langloan Iron Company, Summerlee Iron Company
Scottish Bar Manufacturers' Association	Colville, Etna Iron and Steel Company, W. Martin and Company, Pather Iron and Steel Company, Scottish Iron and Steel Company, Smith and McLean, Williams and Company
Scottish Black Sheet Metal Makers' Association	Braby and Company, Carntyne Iron and Steel Company, Coatbridge Tinplate Company, Pather Iron and Steel Company, Smith and McLean, John Williams and Company, George Wolfe and Sons.

Source: National Federation of Iron and Steel Manufacturers Minutes 1918.[10]

Several of these firms were also members of the Siemens Steel Ingot Makers' Association (SIMA). The SIMA was initially concerned with the co-ordination of sliding-scale wage agreements. However, it also acted as a pressure group on behalf of its members. In 1894, for example, the Association complained to Lloyds that its standards were too

8. H. W. Macrosty, *The Trust Movement in Britain* (London, 1907), p. 66.
9. O. M. Westall, 'The Competitive Environment of British Business, 1850–1914', in W. Kirby and M. B. Rose (eds), *Business Enterprise in Modern Britain* (London, 1994), p. 224.
10. This list contains over half of the iron and steel producers listed by the British Association in their *Local Industries of Glasgow and the West of Scotland* (Glasgow, 1901).

rigorous when it came to testing and certifying certain thickness of steel plate. After sustained pressure from Scottish and North of England producers – orchestrated by the SIMA – Lloyds agreed to lower its standards.[11] In this case, therefore, determined collective employer pressure resulted in reduced safety margins. Metal refining also saw increasing organisation – although this came towards the end of our period. The Scottish Metal Refiners' Association came into being in early 1919, and grew out of an agreement among West of Scotland metal refiners the year before to regulate prices. The subsequent creation of a permanent accord meant the refiners could grant discounts to approved merchants, and regulate the percentage of copper and tin in their product.[12]

Few areas of the Clydeside metal industries, then, were untouched by trade regulation practices, and the increasing acceptance of collaboration further undermines the notion that capitalists were by nature individualistic. On the eve of the First World War the major weakness of the Scottish steel industry was its close dependence on the Clyde shipbuilders. By 1920 the bond was even stronger, as the Clyde shipbuilding companies had taken over the industry in an effort to ensure future supplies of the raw material. Consequently, the intricate web of price regulation and interlocking directorships in Clydeside's heavy industries had become even more complex.

Coal

Coalmasters experienced a similar trend towards collaboration, although they found price agreements much more difficult. The nature of Scotland's nineteenth-century coal industry matched the national picture in which wages were sporadically regulated but prices tended not to be.[13] There was a certain amount of *ad hoc* collaboration up to 1900. For example, in 1875 the principal West of Scotland ironmasters met to try and work out a collective policy to prevent men leaving the pits due to the low wages of the time.[14] Similarly, in 1900 the coalmasters held the local iron industry to ransom by withholding their stocks to force up the price of coal. Malleable iron works, foundries, and pig-iron works were all affected by the coalmasters' concerted action, and many plants were were forced to close. Testimony to the success of the ploy

11. Siemens Steel Ingot Makers' Association Minute Book 1, 5 March 1894–Oct. 1894, pp. 139–78.
12. Scottish Metal Refiners' Association Minute Book 1, 21 Jan. 1919, p. 12.
13. R. Church, *British Coal Industry* Vol. 3 (Oxford, 1986), pp. 66–68. Also, O. M. Westall, 'Business Enterprise', p. 225.
14. *GH*, 24 June 1875. p. 5.

was the fact that by August the journal reported that high Scottish coal prices had given a boost to the Irish peat industry.[15] However, there are few examples to compare with this successful exercise in coalmaster combination at this time, and the establishment of United Colliers in 1902 was really the culmination of a long period of unsuccessful price collaboration.

Twenty-four Scottish coal companies – mostly in Lanarkshire – formed this combine which eventually controlled a fifth of Scotland's coal output. Among the initial aims of the cartel was the complete elimination of competition, the regulation of wages, a reduction of carriage charges, and the opportunity to purchase materials and services at a discount.[16] The combine became an influential member of the Lanarkshire Coalmasters' Association, and nine years after its formation it followed the LCA line by agreeing to restrict output – the masters' associations in Fife, the Lothians, and Ayrshire were also involved in this strategy.[17]

The main area of trade regulation in the Scottish coal industry was amongst the exporters and merchants. The Scottish Coal Exporters' Association (SCEA) was established in 1899, and by 1901, 36 companies were members – 11 Glasgow firms joined in 1900. One of the Association's early goals was to introduce a uniform purchase note between coal exporters and collieries and a standard sales note for foreign transactions.[18] However, although primarily established to regulate the coal exporting trade, the SCEA soon became involved in more routine business. In 1908, for example, it was busy investigating complaints from its members of widespread short measure of their coal wagons – the Association found that only 7% of wagons had the correct weight; more importantly, 80% of these were to the collieries' advantage.[19] By 1919, the benefits of belonging to an organisation were so apparent to the coal merchants that plans were afoot to form a Federation of Coal Exporters' Associations with an office in London – D. M. Stevenson and Sir R. Mackie were nominated to represent the Scottish interest.[20]

Twenty-one coal distribution companies – 15 from Clydeside – formed the Scottish Coal Merchants' Association (SCMA) in 1907 to combat the monopoly position of the railway companies – of which more later.[21]

15. *Scottish Ironmerchant*, 12 Jan. 1900.
16. H. W. Macrosty, *Trust Movement*, p. 144.
17. Lanarkshire Coalmasters' Association Minute Book 8, 15 May 1911, p. 63.
18. Scottish Coal Exporters' Association (SCEO) Minute Book, 1 May 1899.
19. Ibid., 18 March 1908.
20. SCEO Minute Book 3, 26 March 1919.
21. Scottish Coal Merchants' Association (SCMA) Minute Book 1, March 1910, p. 14.

Eight hundred pounds was raised at the first meeting and this was put
in a fund to cover legal costs should any company refuse to pay de-
murrage or siding rent. By 1910 this had risen to £1,687, and this
financial muscle subsequently enabled a member firm to take on the
Glasgow and South Western Railway Company. The winning of this
test case in 1911 was hailed as a victory by the members, and vindicated
the long-term continuation of the organisation.[22] Consequently, the
Association was put on a permanent basis 'for the purpose of watching
over the interests of coal merchants in all matters affecting their trade
or business.'[23] The influence of the SCMA grew, and by 1915 there
were almost 200 members – 120 Glasgow firms joined in 1915
alone.[24] Testimony to its growing prestige was the fact that during the
war the Association worked with Glasgow Corporation to persuade
domestic consumers to buy coal direct from clearing houses rather than
the city's street hawkers, whose excessive charges were thought by the
government to be a threat to civilian morale. Subsequently, the Corporation suggested a programme of joint action between the Association
and Glasgow's retail merchants. However, the SCMA found it was
powerless to bring order to the bottom end of the trade, as most of
Glasgow's small-scale coal hawkers were beyond the organisation's control.[25] The Board of Trade faced the same problem in 1916 when it
tried to persuade coal merchants and middlemen to take only moderate
profits for the coal they sold to domestic customers. Once again, despite
the acquiescence of the SCMA – which acted as the principal negotiating
body for the Scottish trade – the sheer number of small traders beyond
the Association's control rendered a voluntary scheme impossible to
apply, and the government was forced to initiate the Price of Coal
Limitations Act.[26]

Textiles and clothing
There was a negligible amount of trade regulation in the Scottish textile
industry before 1900. The Glasgow Cotton Supply Association was
mainly concerned to regulate the quantity of raw cotton coming into
the city. Also, although a Power Loom Cloth Manufacturers' Association
was formed in the 1880s, it soon disappeared. From the 1900s, though,

22. The coal masters and coal exporters were also actively involved in this campaign
    against excessive railway demurrage charges. See Lanarkshire Coal Masters'
    Association, Minute Book, 5 Oct. 1908, and Minute Book 7, 3 Nov. 1909.
23. SCMA Minute Book 1, 20 Dec. 1911, p. 65.
24. SCMA Minute Book 2, 16 Oct. 1915, p. 164.
25. SCMA, Minute Book 1, 10 Nov. 1915, p. 171. Ibid., 7 November, 1916, p. 210.
26. Ibid., 7 Nov. 1916, p. 210.

as competition intensified, paternalism atrophied, and markets shrank, there was a growing tendency towards collaboration in the Clydeside textile and clothing trades.[27] 1904 saw the launch of the Tapestry Manufacturers' Association, and by 1919, eight Glasgow companies were listed among its 50 members.[28] The West of Scotland Retail Drapers' Association also emerged in 1904 to bring order to the local drapery trade. By 1916 this Association was powerful enough to put pressure on the government to amend an early closing order to the benefit of its Glasgow members.[29] The Scottish Wholesale Clothing Association was launched in 1910 in response to the imposition of a trade board, and this was also the reason for the initiation of the Glasgow Shirt Manufacturers' Association in 1913. The carpet trade also saw more organisation at this time and in 1917, eleven companies formed the Scottish Carpet Manufacturers' Association – this organisation was heavily involved with the Joint Industrial Council for the Carpet Trade in the immediate post-war years.[30]

The war was an important trigger of combination amongst the region's textile and clothing employers – although this did not filter down to the tailoring trade which remained wracked by sectionalist jealousy, because tailors continued to produce for different classes of customer.[31] Twenty-two clothing companies formed the West of Scotland Textile Association (WSTA) in 1917. During the war the WSTA dealt with government contracts, the allocation of scarce raw material, and the regulation of wages and prices. In the post-war period the Association expanded and nine Clydeside companies joined in 1918 alone. When a trade board was formed in the textile industry, several members of the WSTA represented the employers. Moreover, when the local trade board was extended to include Renfrewshire, Lanarkshire, and Ayrshire in 1919, the Association increased in strength when a further 15 companies from these areas joined.[32] An attempt by woollen

27. Similar concern was felt in Lancashire where employers responded to increased foreign competition by colluding on pricing and short-time working. S. Bowden and D. M. Higgins, 'Short-time working and price maintenance: Collusive tendencies in the cotton-spinning industry, 1919–1939', *Economic History Review*, 51, 2 (1998), pp. 309–343.

28. Tapestry Manufacturers' Association Minute Book 2, p. 75. UGD/265/1.

29. *Shoe and Leather Trader (SLT)*, Dec. 1916, p. 4.

30. Scottish Carpet Manufacturers' Association, 1st Annual Report, 1919, p. 2.

31. See the article in *Sartorial Gazette*, Oct. 1915, p. 308, in which the clothing association is held up as a 'power in the land' in contrast to the lack of unity in tailoring.

32. WSTA Minutes, 18 Nov. 1918. Also 28 Dec. 1917, 18 Nov. 1918, 29 March 1919, 3 June 1918, and 12 Aug. 1918.

manufacturers to impose unreasonable trading conditions on woollen merchants in 1916 resulted in the formation of the Federation of Woollen Merchants. Faced with this sudden emergence of concerted power – 200 firms were members of the Association – the manufacturers quickly moderated their terms.[33] Several important factors, then, could push capitalists into collaboration, although they were all normally linked to falling profits: increasing competition, organisation amongst the labour force, and aggressive monopoly trading by other groups of capitalists. This last factor deserves more examination as it became more prevalent as the period progressed.

The increasing regulation of trade amongst Clydeside capitalists over this period must be seen against a background of a growing number of cartels. The rise in the number of cartels in Britain from the 1880s was a response to intensifying foreign and domestic competition, combined with the absence of legislation along the lines of the Sherman Anti-Trust Act in the USA. Throughout the country trade regulation became increasingly common, and by the early twentieth century there were cartels in glass manufacture, the biscuit trade, brick production, building sand, furniture manufacture, the salt industry, the tobacco trade, and many more industries.[34] Cartels became a feature of the Clydeside economy, although many disliked the new trend. For example, the growing number of shipping rings in the 1900s was condemned by many merchants and industrialists. However, the Glasgow Chamber of Commerce defended such collaboration in the shipping industry.[35] The Glasgow company Ogston and Tennant was a member of the national soap trust headed by Lever in 1909. An intense newspaper campaign was launched against this trust which ended in some firms securing damages from several English and Scottish newspapers.[36] In 1921 the Glasgow paint manufacturer Alexander Ferguson was involved in a complex tangle of price associations, which included the Scottish Non-ferrous Association, the Scottish Paint Association, the Glasgow Lead Association, the Scottish Colour, Paint, and Varnish Association, a London-based keg syndicate, the Scottish Lead Sellers' Association, and the Scottish Lead Manufacturers' Association. The company fully realised that its

33. *Sartorial Gazette*, Aug. 1916, p. 216.
34. Standing Committee on Trusts, Interim Report [Cnd. 1066].
35. *GH*, 26 Jan. 1907, p. 7.
36. See *GH*, 10 March 1910, p. 10. Also, N. J. Reader, 'The United Kingdom Soapmakers' Association and the English Soap Trade', *Business History* 1 (1958–59), pp. 77–83. See also L. Hannan, *Corporate Economy* (London, 1976), pp. 45–46, and R. Cohan's chapter on the soap industry in P. L. Cook (ed.), *The Effects of Mergers* (London, 1958), pp. 133–208.

customers would dislike the tightly regulated trading conditions, as a note in its minutes makes clear: 'The consumer, who naturally kicked at the new conditions, is gradually settling down and becoming used to them'.[37]

Despite the spread of cartels there were some industries where the nature of production and the peculiarities of the market precluded this form of collaborative trading. The most notable on Clydeside were the shipbuilding and heavy engineering industries which produced mainly bespoke goods for volatile imperial markets. Regulation of prices amongst industrialists who built ships or steam locomotives to specification would have been difficult to attain. A fairly standardised product or service was required before comprehensive trade regulation could be achieved. Consequently, although there was a cartel in the furniture trade, this was primarily amongst those companies that made cheaper machine-made furniture, and did not affect the Clydeside manufacturers who concentrated on high-quality goods – mostly for the shipbuilding industry.

COLLECTIVE POLICIES AMONGST SMALLER CAPITALISTS

The pressures on profits that compelled larger employers to combine also affected smaller firms. When the worldwide reputation of Clydeside industry was being made by big companies such as Arrols, Lithgows, and Beardmores, a plethora of small firms formed the backbone of the region's economy. Most of these companies have disappeared, leaving us no records. However, many were compelled to collaborate in response to the growing number of cartels. The records of their organisations allow us a rare glimpse into a neglected area of capitalist production.

Plumbing

The plumbing trade is a prime example of how small firms were practically forced into trade combination by the changing nature of the market. The trade in Scotland was much more organised than it was south of the border. This remained the case until the war, and in 1914 the chairman of the National Light Castings Association urged English plumbers to follow the example of their Scottish counterparts and organise more effectively in order to get better terms from his own and similar associations.[38]

37. Private Ledger of Alexander Ferguson and Co., 1920. Also Directors' Minute Book 1, pp. 69–368. Glasgow Business Archives, UGD 258.
38. *Plumbing Trade Journal*, March 1914, p. 32.

The plumbers were perhaps more at the mercy of trade combinations than any other trades. For example, following a massive drop in the price of lead, lead producers formed themselves into the Scottish Lead Manufacturers' Association (SLMA) in May 1909. There were seven founder members – including Fergusons – and the organisation attempted, through its links with various English associations, to bring about a uniform price for lead throughout the UK.[39] The price ring secured a firm hold over the industry: members contacted the Association before agreeing discounts to customers; and there was a trading agreement between the Association and the Scottish Lead Sellers' Association.[40] In December 1912 the SLMA reached an agreement with the Glasgow and West of Scotland Master Plumbers' Association (GWSMPΛ) and the Glasgow and West of Scotland Metal Merchants' Association (GWSMMA) over discounts for master plumbers and metal merchants. Clearly, then, one immediate advantage of membership of the master plumbers' association was the ability it gave small firms to survive in an increasingly regulated market.

Another example from the plumbing trade further illustrates the growing complexity of the situations. The Glasgow and West of Scotland Metal Merchants' Association (GWSMMA) was established in 1913 specifically to arrange a trading agreement between Clydeside's metal merchants and the GWSMPA – which had almost 500 members by this time.[41] For its part, though, the Metal Merchants' Association agreed trading terms with the Scottish Lead Manufacturers' Association, the National Light Castings Association, the Cast Iron Flushing Cisterns' Association, the Sanitary Earthenware Manufacturers' Association, the Ironmongers' and Allied Trades' Association, the Enamelled Fireclay Manufacturers' Association, the Scottish Fireclay Manufacturers' Association, and, later, the National Association of Copper Cylinder and Boiler Makers.[42] Therefore – to use an example at building site level – in order to purchase cisterns from metal merchants, who were all members of the Scottish Metal Merchants' Association, master plumbers working on Port Glasgow's new housing scheme in 1917 had firstly to be members of the GWSMPA. However, the cisterns were originally sold to the metal merchants – with a 5% discount – by member firms of the Cast Iron Flushing Cisterns' Association.[43] Membership of a trade

39. *Ibid.* Also Scottish Lead Manufacturers' Association Minute Book 1, 2 May 1909.
40. Ibid., 20 Sept. 1909.
41. Glasgow and West of Scotland Metal Merchants' Association Minute Book 1, 27 May 1913, p. 11.
42. GWSMMA Minute Book 1, 8 Dec. 1915, p. 53, and 18 Feb., p. 144.
43. Ibid., 19 Sept. 1917.

association, therefore, was not just a rational choice for some small-scale capitalists, but a necessity.

The boot trade

The same process affected other industries dominated by small employers, and this was certainly the case in certain sectors of the boot and shoe industry. By 1905 Glasgow's boot industry was facing serious competition from Northampton and Leicester, where the employers had been well organised for some time.[44] As a response to this the Glasgow Boot Retailers' Association (GBRA) was formed, and it quickly affiliated to the Federated Association of Boot and Shoe Manufacturers when it came into being in 1890 as a reaction to trade union agitation. By the end of that year 70 of Glasgow's principal boot retailers were members of the GBRA, and they were determined to work in harmony to end the sectionalism that had burdened the trade for so long.[45] By 1903 the GBRA was a force to be reckoned with as it represented 450 firms.[46]

Sectionalism was rife in the boot trade, and this was apparent to the Board of Conciliation for the boot and shoe industry in 1895 which acknowledged three categories of manufacturers – and consequently three classes of wages.[47] In the mid-1890s a trade association appeared among Glasgow's shoe retailers in the high-quality bespoke sector. However, it failed to initiate a common pricing policy and quickly faded.[48] Unity was stronger outside Glasgow, though, and the Ayrshire Master Boot and Shoe Makers' Association was influential enough in 1873 to arrange a 20% wage advance affecting nine Ayrshire towns.[49]

Trade unionism amongst boot repair workers dated from 1902, and this stimulated collaboration between the masters. However, the master boot repairers also reacted to profit-killing undercutting and an unfair pricing policy pursued by the leather merchants. The repairers formed themselves into three regionally based associations in 1909 and set about establishing a minimum price for footwear repairs throughout Glasgow. The three associations amalgamated in 1913, and then affiliated to the newly formed National Federation of Scottish Master

44. The Northampton Manufacturers' Association was formed in 1879 – although re-organised in 1911 – and the Leicester Boot Manufacturers' Association appeared in 1870. *Scottish Leather Trader (SLT)*, May 1915, p. 16; also *Shoe Manufacturers' Monthly*, Mid-Aug. 1911, p. 115.
45. *SLT*, Dec. 1905, p. 15.
46. *SLT*, Feb. 1903, p. 16.
47. *SLT*, Feb. 1902, p. 13.
48. *SLT*, Dec. 1905, p. 14.
49. *GH*, 25 Feb. 1873, p. 4.

Bootmakers, Boot Retailers, and Boot Repairers in 1918.[50] Once again combination spawned further combination, networks spawned further networks.

Difficult trading conditions during the First World War quickened the pace of collaboration in the boot and shoe industry. In an effort to preserve dwindling supplies of leather the government prohibited the sale of women's high boots – despite the fact that many retailers had stockpiles of these boots ready for the winter season. As a direct response to this the Retail Section of the Shoe Distributors' Association (Scotland) was formed, and lost no time in enlisting the support of the Glasgow Chamber of Commerce to help fight the new order.[51] Finally, towards the end of the war the prioritisation of iron and steel for military use resulted in a shortage of studs, rivets, segs, etc., used in boot manufacturing and repair – known in the trade as grindery. The majority of the firms which manufactured grindery were small, and this was the main reason behind their coming together in the Scottish Leather and Grindery Federation. In 1919, this federation – along with another twelve bodies – became a founder member of the National Federation of Leather and Grindery Merchants' Associations, which eventually organised 86% of firms in this particular trade.[52] It has been said that 'tradesmen's individualism was little more than a front, capable of being discarded when circumstances dictated'.[53] Evidence from Clydeside broadly supports this contention.

Farmers

A leader in the *Scottish Farmer* illustrated that in 1896 farmers were just as likely to suffer at the hands of price associations as other business people: 'If farmers would only more freely combine', said the columnist, 'they would be less at the mercy of other combines than they are.'[54] There was some movement towards co-operation within the farming community but progress was slow, and in 1914 a commentator in the *Glasgow Herald* remarked that 'farmers are still the most wretchedly organised class on the face of the earth'.[55]

Collaboration amongst farmers had its roots in the mid-1860s when

50. The national organisation started in Dundee in 1910. See *SLT*, March 1911, p. 9. Also, Feb. 1913, p. 11. *SLT*, Sept. 1918, p. 7.
51. *SLT*, Feb. 1918, p. 2; March 1918, p. 8.
52. *SLT*, June 1919, p. 7.
53. M. J. Winstanley, *The Shopkeeper's World* (Manchester, 1983), p. 91.
54. *Scottish Farmer*, 25 Jan. 1896, p. 65.
55. Report of Glasgow and West of Scotland Discussion Society, *GH*, 22 Jan. 1914, p. 16.

the Scottish Chamber of Agriculture was formed. This organisation, though, was primarily a centralised version of the regional chambers of agriculture, and its membership never exceeded 1000 in the early twentieth century.[56] However, a more determined effort to improve farmers' trading terms was the establishment of the Farmers' Supply Association (FSA) in 1884 – which had 1,530 members by 1914.[57] This organisation began marketing its own manure and feeding stuffs, and by 1906 had secured special terms with all the leading producers of fertilisers.[58] In 1905 the Scottish Agricultural Organisation Society (SAOS) was launched.[59] The SAOS encouraged and promoted co-operation among Clydeside's dairy farmers, and one of its members commented on how this was sorely needed: 'Anyone who has seen the endless procession of separate farmers' carts pouring into Glasgow, or making for stations in Lanarkshire, Ayrshire, and Renfrewshire, must wish for a rapid extension of the co-operative system'.[60] The most significant force behind the movement towards effective trade collaboration amongst the farmers was their general disgruntlement with the milk wholesalers. This led in the 1900s to the formation of the West of Scotland Federation of Dairy Farmers, and the Federation of Dairy Farmers' Associations of Scotland.[61] The NFUS also played a much-needed trade regulatory role from its inception in 1913. In 1916, for example, its Ayr branch – which had established greater co-operation between farmers and local creamery associations – sold over 4,000 gallons of milk on behalf of its members.[62] Previously the Glasgow dealers had been guilty of playing off one creamery against the other.

Therefore, trade regulation against middle men and combines – but especially against the milk wholesalers – was a major stimulant to collaboration among this most individualistic group of Clydeside capitalists.

We now turn to two short case studies which further illustrate how trade regulation by one group of capitalists could result in a collective response from others.

56. R. Anthony, *Herds and Hinds* (East Linton, 1997), p. 111.
57. *Scottish Journal of Agriculture* (*SJA*), No. 1, 1918, p. 183.
58. *GH*, 29 March 1906, p. 12.
59. *SJA*, No. 1, 1918, p. 181.
60. *SJA*, No. 1, 1918, p. 184. See also *GH*, 4 Aug. 1906, for an account of co-operation among Ayrshire dairy farmers. There was also the North Ayrshire Co-operative Dairy Association which opened a creamery in Stewarton in 1910. See *Kilmarnock Standard*, 14 Sept. 1939, p. 10.
61. R. Anthony, *Herds and Hinds* (East Linton, 1997), p. 111.
62. *SJA*, 20 Jan. 1916, p. 45. Also AGM of Scottish Agricultural Society 1912, in *The North British Agriculturist*, 4 April 1912, p. 771.

Collective responses to the railway companies

The Scottish Coal Merchants' Association came into being as a collective defensive movement against high railway charges. The railway companies were the largest organisations in Britain throughout most of our period, and were the first enterprises to be subjected to government intervention during the era of *laissez faire*. From the 1890s the government tried to prevent railway firms charging excessive rates, but even by 1913 the companies were still allowed to increase charges if they felt it was justified.[63] As a defence against government interference the main railway firms formed the Railway Companies' Association. All the principal Scottish companies joined this organisation which persistently campaigned to keep railway carriage rates at profit-maximising levels.[64] Another example of railway capital combining for protection was the formation of the Scottish Railway Stockholders' Protection Association in 1918. This association provided insurance for those with financial interests in the railway companies, and by 1921 there were 32,000 members.[65]

At one level, then, those who controlled railway capital formed themselves into a significant power bloc to protect their interests. However, those who used the railway services to transport goods were alarmed at what they saw as a monopoly situation. Dissatisfaction reverberated through all levels of the business community. The Glasgow Chamber of Commerce asked the government in 1884 to repeal duty on railway passenger traffic.[66] Four years later several small Clydeside leather firms – denied the benefit of a trade association – complained to the Chamber about the high costs they had to bear when sending small parcels by rail.[67] The issue of railway rates was 'the one factor and one alone' which brought the Timber Trades Federation into existence in 1892.[68] In 1893 the United Kingdom Commercial Travellers' Association opened a Glasgow branch, and one of its aims was to secure cheaper rail transport for its members.[69] Ayr master bakers argued that the higher than average cost of loaves in Ayrshire was due primarily to

63. J. Walker, *British Economic and Social History* (London, 1968), pp. 146–148. See also P. J. Cain, 'The British Railway Rates Problem 1894–1913', *Business History*, Number 20 (1978), pp. 87–99.
64. See G. Alderman, *The Railway Interest* (Leicester, 1973).
65. *The Bailie*, 2 Feb. 1920. p. 3.
66. Report by the Directors of the Glasgow Chamber of Commerce, 1884, p. 20.
67. *SLT*, 4 April 1889, p. 126.
68. R. Fitzgerald and J. Greneir, *Timber, A Centenary History of the Timber Trades. Federation 1892–1992* (London, 1992), p. 33.
69. *Scottish Trader*, March 1897, p. 9.

high railway costs.[70] In 1909 several large Clydeside companies – among them the Scottish Co-operative Wholesale Society (SCWS), the Falkirk Iron Company, and Brown and Polson the mustard and starch manufacturer – formed the Scottish Railway Traders' Association, which had several aims: to secure better railway rates by combination, to pay legal costs of any disputes between members and the railway companies, and to closely monitor any new railway legislation.[71] The Scottish National Farmers' Union expressed its concern in 1915 that high railway charges were detrimental to the farming interest.[72] And the expense of sending furniture by rail compelled the Scottish Furniture Manufacturers' Association to pressurise railway companies for discounts for its members in 1914.[73]

A principal spur to collective action, then, was the comprehensive regulation of trade practised by the railway companies. This was a common problem throughout the period, and as late as 1929 the government was still receiving complaints from trading associations regarding the cost of rail transport.[74]

Collective responses to the Co-op
Major changes took place in consumer goods distribution from the middle years of the nineteenth century: the introduction of packed and branded products, the rise of large-scale retailing firms, and the expansion of the co-operative movement. These forces precipitated a collaborative response from traditional retailers who frequently pressurised manufacturers to initiate retail price maintenance.[75]

By 1899 the SCWS's trade was valued at around five million pounds a year.[76] This phenomenal success jeopardised the profits of many small individual traders and provoked a great deal of hostility throughout this level of retailing.[77] Communities were sometimes split in two. In February 1898, for example, the master bakers of Largs warned their

70. *British Baker*, 11 March 1898, p. 89.
71. Directors' Minute Book of Alexander Ferguson And Co., Feb. 1909. Glasgow Business Archives UGD 258.
72. *North British Agriculturist*, 4 March 1915, p. 32.
73. Scottish Furniture Manufacturers' Association, Minute Book 2, Oct. 1914, p. 121.
74. Final Report of the Committee on Trade and Industry 1929 [Cmd 3282], pp. 70–73.
75. B. S. Yamey (ed.), *Resale Price Maintenance* (London, 1966).
76. J. Campsie, *Glimpses of Co-operative Land* (Glasgow, 1899).
77. This was a familiar response by small traders throughout Britain. See M. Purvis, 'Co-operative retailing in Britain', in J. Benson and G. Shaw (eds), *The Evolution of Retail Systems c. 1800–1914* (Leicester, 1992), p. 119. Also, M. J. Winstanley, *The Shopkeeper's World*, pp. 83–88.

employees that if their families continued to shop in the town's new co-operative store they would all be dismissed.[78] Similarly, the Traders' Defence Association (TDA) asked the management of the North British Locomotive Company (NBLC) in Springburn to sack all employees who were members of the Cowlairs Co-operative Society – then the largest retail organisation in the north of Glasgow. The company duly obliged, and six employees were immediately given their notices. However, they were subsequently reinstated in the face of community outrage.[79] An article in the *Scottish Leather Trader* spoke of small dealers being 'squeezed to death between the two millstones of large retailers and co-operative stores'.[80] Moreover, many private traders were incensed at the exemption from income tax which the co-operative societies enjoyed – the Scottish Wholesale Clothing Manufacturers' Association, for example, expressed its concern over this issue in 1917.[81] As in the case of the railway companies, then, hostility towards a common enemy acted as a powerful unifying agent among private traders and producers. These capitalists increasingly turned to collective action and price regulation as a rational form of defence.[82]

Nationally, the British grocery trade had a significant level of trade regulation by the First World War – the National Federation of Grocers' Associations had over 1400 members by this time.[83] This level of collectivism was apparent in the West of Scotland too. In 1863, for example, the Glasgow Hamcuring and Wholesale Provision Merchants' Association was established, and this was complemented by the Glasgow Provision Trade Association in 1888.[84] However, by the end of the war, the two most vociferous enemies of the co-operative movement were the Traders' Defence Association which appeared in the 1890s, and the Scottish Grocers' Federation, established in 1918.[85]

The official journal of the TDA, the *Scottish Trader*, pushed a strong anti-Socialist message: 'This co-operative movement carries in its bosom

---

78. *British Baker*, 25 Feb. 1898, p. 1345.
79. G. Hutchison and M. O'Neill, *The Springburn Experience* (Edinburgh, 1989), pp. 17, 25.
80. *Scottish Leather Trader*, 5 May 1887.
81. Wholesale Clothing Manufacturers' Association Minute Book 3, April 11, 1918.
82. O. M. Westall, 'Business enterprise', p. 227.
83. M. J. Winstanley, *Shopkeeper's World*, p. 77.
84. For a comprehensive account of the activities of this Association see M. Moss, *One Hundred Years of Provisioning Scotland: The History of the Scottish Provision Trade Association* (Glasgow, 1989).
85. Another organisation which declared itself opposed to the principle of co-operative trading was the National Federation of Scottish Merchants' Associations which emerged in 1913. See the Report of its first AGM in *SLT*, April 1914, p. 4.

the seeds of decay and death ... Socialism is destructive to individual effort and enterprise and the sooner it is relegated to the limbo of forgotten "isms" the better for this country'.[86] The TDA fought a hard campaign and targeted the grassroots support on which the co-operative movement thrived. Its machinations with the NBLC's management have already been noted, but another example can be found in 1898 when the Association inquired of the North West Engineering Trades Employers' Association if engineering foremen used their influence to force other employees to shop in co-operative stores.[87]

Several committees were set up by the TDA to represent small businesses battling against co-operative competition. As we have seen, Clydeside's shoe and leather traders were already encountering intense competition from England. Consequently, they fully supported the work of the TDA's Boot and Shoe Committee – which in 1898 received pledges from over a thousand Scottish firms not to sell co-op manufactured goods.[88] Also in the leather industry, agitation against co-operative trading led the TDA's Fleshers' Protection Committee to instigate a boycott of Glasgow's meat auctioneers and butchers – in an attempt to force them to stop trading with co-operative societies.[89] Moreover, in the grocery trade, the TDA claimed that 90% of Clydeside's grocers sympathised with its cause.[90]

British retail trade associations sometimes organised their own bulk buying schemes, and this form of defence against intensifying competition was practised on Clydeside too.[91] The Glasgow Grocers' and Provision Merchants' Association was established in 1893, and soon after its launch it introduced a scheme to buy margarine in bulk and pass on the saving to its members. The TDA applauded this plan and recommended that it should be extended to encompass all areas of private trading. Under such a scheme, said the TDA, all Glasgow's shopkeepers would form 'one large trading concern with millions of pounds of capital'.[92] In effect, individual private capitalists were being pressed into co-operative trading.

The Scottish Grocers' Federation (SGF) was also anti-co-operative.

86. *Scottish Trader*, Oct. 1897, p. 30 and July 1897, p. 6.
87. NWETEA Minute Book 2, 18 May 1898, p. 50.
88. *Scottish Trader*, 1 Jan. 1898, p. 238.
89. For a full account of the 'beef boycott', see J. Kinloch and J. Butt, *History of the Scottish Co-operative Wholesale Society Limited* (Glasgow, 1981), pp. 255–263.
90. *Scottish Trader*, 1 Jan. 1898, p. 239. The TDA also claimed to have a list of over 600 manufacturers who supported its principles.
91. M. J. Winstanley, *Shopkeeper's World*, p. 78.
92. *Scottish Trader*, 5 April, 1910, p. 17.

The SGF was formed during the war and soon became a champion of the small trader. The editorial in its journal *Fingerpost* in 1918 trumpeted a similar message to that of the TDA: 'Grocer shops conducted as self-contained units will before many years be displaced by the co-op store and the multiple shop, just as surely as the hand loom was replaced by the power loom'.[93] The SGF also offered potential members the chance to socialise: 'The Federation makes mutual help possible; troubles are lessened when they are shared. It offers opportunities of meeting together, pleasant intercourse, human fellowship, which in the days of every man for himself were impossible'.[94] The SGF's appeal was so successful that by October 1918 it had 13 branches throughout Clydeside alone.[95] Moreover, by 1924 the organisation claimed to represent 75% of Scottish grocers.[96]

Clearly, therefore, the co-operative movement both divided and unified capitalists. However, co-operation itself was a form of employers' organisation; and this brings us to an examination of a neglected aspect of the co-operative movement: the extent to which alliances were formed between co-operators and private capitalists in order to trade successfully within a capitalist trading system.

Historians of the Scottish co-operative movement have emphasised its socialist orientation, and have examined its structure as though it somehow stood outwith the capitalist system.[97] Labour historians, for their part, have largely overlooked the fact that the co-operative movement was one of the largest employers in the West of Scotland, and there is an ongoing debate over the extent to which the movement abandoned its Utopian principles.[98] Evidence from Clydeside suggests that the co-operative movement accepted the finality of capitalist trading before the First World War.

In 1893, for example, the chairman of the SCWS told the Royal Commission on Labour: 'The fact that we will not unite with other employers in Association in any industry has not been taken advantage

93. *Fingerpost*, Dec. 1919, p. 1.
94. *Ibid.*, May 1918, p. 1.
95. *Ibid.*, Oct. 1918, p. 7.
96. By this time the Association had a Parliamentary Committee, and an Emergency Committee, ran its own insurance scheme, and was planning to establish a benevolent fund. *The Bailie*, 9 April 1924
97. See, for example, J. Kinloch and J. Butt, *History of the Scottish Wholesale Society* (Glasgow 1981), J. A. Flannagan, *Wholesale Co-operation in Scotland* (Glasgow 1919), W. Reid, *History of the United Co-operative Baking Society, 1869–1919* (Glasgow, 1920), and J. Birchall, *Co-op: The People's Business* (Manchester, 1994).
98. See P. Gurney, *Co-operative culture and the politics of consumption in England 1870–1930* (Manchester, 1996), pp. 22–23, p. 167, pp. 143–168, and *passim*.

of by the men to use as a lever to raise wages'. Further, when describing the nature of the United Co-operative Baking Society (UCBS), he declared: 'the Society is not in union with other master bakers'.[99] However, this was not the case, for only a year earlier the *British Baker* noted that the Ayrshire Master Bakers' Association had the support of all the co-operative societies in the county.[100] More importantly, in mid-1896 a representative of the UCBS attended meetings of the Scottish Master Bakers' Association, and the thorny question of UCBS involvement with the SMBA was raised at the Society's quarterly meeting that year. There was some discomfort at the UCBS's presence in this bastion of capitalism, and the Chairman lamely explained to the directors that the SMBA was not a properly constituted employers' organisation but only 'an informal gathering of people engaged in the same business' – a clear distortion of the truth.[101] In any event a motion that the Society should have no further dealings with the SMBA was defeated, and although the question frequently cropped up at general meetings, the connection between the UCBS and the SMBA was allowed to remain.[102]

The UCBS operated one of the largest bakeries on Clydeside. In 1894 it produced around 1500 bags of flour a week, employed over 200 people, used only trade union labour, and traded solely with members of its own federation.[103] However, the dilemma it and other co-operative societies faced was expressed by an historian of the movement in 1919 when describing the SCWS's wages strategy: 'The SCWS does aim at keeping a little ahead of the capitalist employers, but in a world of competition it cannot go very far ahead of its competitors without jeopardising its trade'.[104] The need to regulate competition, therefore, and determine to what extent it was ahead of the capitalists, led the UCBS into an unholy alliance with some of its most anti-trade union competitors. Bilslands', for example – a member of the Glasgow Master Bakers' Association – maintained a stifling paternalist labour management policy throughout the period, and remained extremely hostile to the very concept of trade unionism. Bilslands' minute books show that this company sometimes colluded with the UCBS and several other Glasgow bakers on a private level. In March 1922, for example,

99. Royal Commission on Labour 1893 [c. 7063–1], Evidence of William Maxwell, pp. 33–38.
100. *British Baker*, May 1892, p. 613.
101. W. Reid, *History of the UCBS* (Glasgow, 1920), p. 136.
102. *Ibid.*, p. 136.
103. Royal Commission on Labour 1893, William Maxwell's evidence [c. 7063–1], p. 39.
104. J. A. Flannagan, *Wholesale Co-operation in Scotland* (Glasgow 1919), p. 267.

Bilslands', Beattie's, MacFarlane's, Stevenson's, and the UCBS, agreed the price of discounted bread they sold to large Clydeside institutions.[105] And in September of that year they resolved to link the price of their bread to the cost of London flour.[106] Wages too were sometimes co-ordinated. In July 1926 Bilslands' was informed by a UCBS representative that the Society was cutting its bakers' wages. Consequently, a meeting of the other firms involved in the pact was quickly called to discuss the feasibility of a similar reduction.[107]

However, it was not just in the baking trade that co-operators found themselves rubbing shoulders with capitalists. The SCWS was a founder member of the Scottish Railway Traders' Association in 1909.[108] The Co-operative Society was trading rubber for profit on the international market in 1921.[109] In 1908 the UCBS joined the Glasgow Chamber of Commerce.[110] In January 1918 the SCWS became a full member of the Scottish Furniture Manufacturers' Association – notorious for its brutal ten-month lock-out in Beith and Kilwinning twenty years earlier.[111] The Glasgow Master Masons' Association regularly sent wage rates and price lists to the SCWS's building department.[112] The SCWS tried to join the Glasgow Master Slaters' Association in 1918 but its application was turned down.[113] The Scottish Coal Merchants' Association had eleven co-operative societies as members in 1909.[114] The Paisley Co-operative Manufacturing Society was a founder member of the West of Scotland Textile Association in 1917.[115] The SCWS was a member of the Tapestry Manufacturers' Association.[116] And its printing department was a member of the Glasgow Master Printers' Association – and later the Scottish Alliance of Master Printers. The SCWS sent a secret letter to a leading Glasgow printing firm asking for information regarding

105. Bilslands' Minute Book 2, March 1922.
106. Ibid., Sept. 1926.
107. Ibid., 23 July 1926. Similar concerted action occurred in April 1927. Ibid., 29 April 1927.
108. Directors' Minute Book of Alexander Ferguson And Co., Feb. 1909. Glasgow Business Archives UGD 258.
109. *The Fingerpost*, Oct. 1921, pp. 59–67.
110. W. W. Reid, *History of the United Co-operative Baking Society 1869–1919* (Glasgow, 1920), p. 207.
111. SFMA Minute Book 2, 1917–1919, 21 Jan. 1918, p. 44.
112. GMMA Minute Book 8, membership role 1919.
113. GMSA Minute Book 5, 10 Sept. 1918.
114. SCMA Minute Book 1, 24 Nov. 1909.
115. West of Scotland Textile Association Minutes 28 Aug. 1917.
116. Scottish Tapestry Manufacturers' Association, Minute Book 2, 1919 membership list.

foremen's holiday entitlement – in which it was requested that the reply should be in the strictest confidence.[117] And this report of a SCWS meeting, published in the *British Baker*, further illustrates how the union between co-operators and employers' associations – in this case the Master Printers' Association – was something of a shotgun marriage:

> One point of special interests was pressed to a division, viz., the proposal of the directors to affiliate with an association of master printers. A number of the trade unionists present declared that the affiliation of the wholesale with such an association would simply mean that the hands of the directors would be tied, and that it would be no good to the movement, and do harm to the workers. The Chairman's explanation was that information was required that could best be got through membership of the association; and he quelled the fears of the trade unionists by pointing out that the wholesale could withdraw from the association if its presence there was found to involve them in anything.[118]

What these examples illustrate is that the compulsion upon traders and manufacturers to nullify market forces through combination was so overwhelming that even the Co-op, the enemy of the individual capitalist trader, was forced to seriously – and somewhat furtively – compromise its principles.

Bakers

When examining master bakers' associations in 1906, Macrosty stated that 'price fixing is unquestionably the one which most attracts the members'.[119] An examination of the Scottish Master Bakers' Association confirms this. In 1898 – only seven years after its formation – this association represented virtually all of the Scottish baking trade, and by 1905 the bakers were reckoned to be the most organised of Scotland's shopkeepers.[120] Clydeside's bakers sold both a service and a product, but unlike the engineering companies their product was fairly standardised. Consequently, trade regulation between bakers involved regularisation of prices as well as services. Glasgow, from the 1880s,

---

117. Letter from D. Campbell, Manager of SCWS Printing Department, to J. Mac-Lehose, dated 13 June 1913. MacLehose Scrapbooks, Volume 5, 1913, p. 10.
118. *British Baker*, 28 April 1916, p. 9.
119. H. W. Macrosty, *Trust Movement*, p. 266.
120. *British Baker, Confectioner and Purveyor*, Vol. 13, 4 March, 1898. Also, *SLT*, Nov. 1905, p. 10. Winstanley refers to the 'bakers' comparative failure to organise effectively on a national basis by 1914 ...' This was clearly not the case in Scotland. Winstanley, *Shopkeeper's World*, p. 76.

led the rest of the United Kingdom in the adoption of factory bread making – indeed, the process was initially known in the trade as the 'Scotch factory bread system'.[121] With the increasing dominance of large factory bakeries in Glasgow – such as Montgomerie's, Beattie's, Bilsland's, and the UCBS – Clydeside consumers came to expect a high-quality cheap supply of bread and confectionery. The intense competition among factory bakers, therefore, ultimately led to price regulation and a certain standardisation of service.[122]

A good example of the latter was the successful campaign at the turn of the century to abolish the practice of giving Christmas and New Year presents to customers. The *British Baker* had strong views on the subject: 'The indiscriminate giving of Christmas presents cannot be too seriously condemned'.[123] It was impossible for individual bakers to opt out of this tradition without incurring severe loss of trade, and the only solution was to take concerted action through the employers' associations. Glasgow bakers once again led the field and stopped giving Christmas boxes in the late 1890s. Other Clydeside regions then followed suit. In October 1900, for example, the Lanarkshire master bakers circulated all their customers intimating that no presents would be given during the festive season.[124]

Other employers' associations followed the bakers' example, but with less success. The West of Scotland Confectioners' Association (WSCA) began a campaign to stop the giving of trade favours in 1907. However, solidarity was harder to achieve, and by 1913 the WSCA was still complaining that some of its members persisted with the practice.[125] In 1910 the Glasgow Master Boot Repairers' Association (GMBRA) also condemned the habit of giving New Year gifts to customers. However, the Association fully realised the difficulty of a complete cessation, and recommended that its members begin giving small calendars as a way of easing themselves out of the custom.[126]

The building trade
The predominately small-scale structure of Clydeside's building industry

---

121. *The Northern Miller and Baker*, 1 Oct. 1885, p. 14.
122. Mechanisation and centralisation of production within bread making spread quickly throughout the UK, and by 1914 most of the present-day characteristics of the industry were developed. See J. Burnett, 'The Baking Industry in the 19th Century', *Business History* 5 (1962–63), pp. 98–108.
123. *British Baker*, 19 Oct. 1900, p. 388.
124. *British Baker*, 16 Nov. 1900, p. 602, and 7 Dec. 1900, p. 309.
125. *Confectioners' Union*, 15 April 1910, p. 497, and 18 Oct. 1913, p. 1295.
126. *SLT*, Feb. 1911, p. 7.

meant membership of an employers' organisation was the most rational way for many employers to bring order to the trade. In Chapter 1 we saw how the Glasgow Master Painters' Association emerged out of a need to come to terms with worker radicalism. The Association, however, also played a valuable role in standardising prices, and this was a characteristic of many associations connected with the building trade.

The Glasgow Master Painters' Association 1892 rule book gave clear guidelines on prices members should charge for their work. The difficulty, though, was getting the members to comply, and this was especially difficult in times of slack trade – during the war the secretary of the Scottish Master Painters' Association branded the amount of undercutting going on as 'conflict within our own gates', and spoke of painters keeping down costs by using poor-quality materials and employing unscrupulous workmen and young boys.[127] Renegade behaviour by members was a problem faced by many associations, and was especially common amongst smaller organisations. To combat this, many associations used an element of compulsion. This was evident in the 1924 version of the Glasgow Master Painters' Association rule book which had a separate price list marked 'Strictly Private and Confidential':

> Members are requested to rigidly adhere to the undernoted prices as the absolute lowest to be charged. Discounts should only be allowed to house factors ... members who know of any master painter in Glasgow or district, whether a member or non-member of any association, charging less than the minimum rate for any item ... are specially requested to report same, without delay, to the Secretary.[128]

Although the main reason for forming building trade employers' associations was the need to regulate labour relations, in most cases once the initial unity had been established, trade regulation followed too. This was the case with the Glasgow Master Masons' Association which introduced a price list in 1896, which determined rates for journeymen, foremen, apprentices, labourers, and for the hire of horses and carts.[129] Similarly, the Scottish Electrical Contractors' Association had a comprehensive price list which stipulated uniform job rates, the regulation of wages, hours, and overtime, the payment of travelling expenses, a covenant to confine competition to quality rather than cheapness, and a stipulation dictating conditions of employment for

127. Report of AGM of Scottish Master Painters' Association, *GH*, 23 Jan. 1915, p. 9.
128. Minimum Price List for Jobbing Work 10 March 1924. Glasgow District Master Painters' Association. SRA.
129. GMMA Minute Book 3, July 1896.

apprentices.[130] Also, only two weeks after its formation, the Glasgow Master Wrights' Association in 1891 brought out a jobbing price list which remained in force – with frequent amendments – until the Restrictive Practices Act of 1964 rendered it illegal.[131]

Price regulation was as important an inducement to membership of building trade employers' associations as labour control. This is borne out by the fact that many organisations campaigned for new members solely by advertising the benefits of co-ordinated pricing. For example, between December 1911 and January 1912, the GMWA embarked on a frenzied recruiting drive on this issue alone. The result was a doubling of the Association's membership – which meant that by 1913, 95% of the Glasgow joinery trade adhered to the GMWA price list.[132] This performance was replicated by the Glasgow and West of Scotland Master Plumbers' Association which also embarked on a recruitment campaign at this time. What is interesting, however, is that these membership increases occurred against a general upsurge in employer association membership in response to the labour threat – for example, membership of the Scottish Furniture Manufacturers' Association (SFMA) rose by 70% during this period.[133] However, although a defensive reaction to organised labour was the main reason for the SFMA's rise in members, the principal attraction of the plumbers' and wrights' associations was their trade regulatory role.[134]

The Glasgow Master Slaters' Association scored a major victory for its members in 1895 when it took on a major slate syndicate. A consortium called Highland Slate Quarries – whose principal member-firm was Ballachulish Slate Quarries Ltd. – was the main supplier of roofing slates to the Clydeside area. However, a persistent difficulty faced by slating firms was the irregularity of slate sizes. A standard slate was supposed to measure 15″ × 8″, but the slaters had to contend with a great many under-sized slates. This caused problems on site, and the extra cost of the useless slates had to be borne by the master slaters themselves. The widespread annoyance at this state of affairs led the GMSA to organise a meeting between representatives of all Clydeside's

130. This Association also kept a register of unemployed electricians and a note of their qualifications. *Scottish Electrician*, Feb. 1901, p. 21.
131. GMWA, Minute Book 1, 26 Jan. 1885.
132. Ibid., 14 Jan. 1913.
133. One hundred and fifty new members joined the Association at this time. GMWA, Minute Book 3, 9 Jan. 1912. GMMA, Minute Book 6, 4 Feb. 1913. SFMAScottish Furniture Manufacturers' Association, Minute Book 2, 25 Nov. 1913, p. 82.
134. The SFMA did not really become involved with concerted pricing policies, although in 1914, eight of its firms colluded to regulate the price of suites. SFMA Minute Book 1, 16 June 1914, p. 102.

master slaters' organisations and an official from the slate consortium. The result of what the pitiable official called 'the most formidable deputation he had ever seen' was a promise from Highland Slate Quarries to improve its quality control.[135]

Membership of the GMSA shrank following a successful seven-month lock-out in 1908, and one of the reasons for this was dissatisfaction among the members at the organisation's inability to curb the extent of undercutting in the trade.[136] The membership situation was so grim by 1913 that a deputation from the Glasgow Master Wrights' Association was invited to advise the slaters on how to organise an effective recruitment drive. The determined shake-up which this pep talk engendered involved the implementation of a binding price list, and a new rule which rendered members' books liable to investigation by a third party if undercutting was suspected by other member.[137] The immediate result was that 50 new members joined the Association in 1913.[138]

Once again, therefore, trade regulation, and not labour regulation, was the main appeal of an employer association. Consequently, although the increase in the number of British employer associations during the pre-war period was due largely to labour militancy and government intervention in capitalist production, these examples from the Clydeside building trade show that the factors underlying the rise in membership of established associations during this period were much more complex.

In some English districts building trade employers' associations also attracted members through their ability to standardise prices and services, as well as being agencies for regulating labour relations. However, whereas the main impetus for the growth of these associations was the enforcement of a strict inter-trading rule – which compelled members to deal only with fellow members – this does not seem to have been a major factor among the Clydeside associations.[139] The practice was

---

135. Glasgow Master Slaters' Association, Minute Book 2, 8 Feb. 1895, and 12 Dec. 1895. The number of undersized slates was reduced. However, as late as 1905 the association was still pushing for better quality slates. Minute Book 3, 27, January 1905.

136. GMSA, Minute Book 4, 11 Feb. 1923.

137. GMWA Minute Book 4, 14 March 1913.

138. Ibid.

139. J A McKenna and R. G. Rodger, 'Control by Coercion: Employers and the Establishment of Industrial Order in the Building Industry of England and Wales 1860–1914', *Business History Review*, 59, 1985, pp. 223–331. McIvor also finds this practice was common in the construction industry of the North West of England, but questions whether it was as significant as McKenna and Rodger suggest. A. J. McIvor, *Organised Capital* (London, 1996), p. 83.

certainly not unknown amongst West of Scotland trade associations. For example, Clause 21 of the Clyde Master Sailmakers' Association's Rule Book stated that 'no Member or Subscriber shall do work for, lend men to, or give work to, any sailmaker in the Clyde district who is not a Member or Subscriber to the Association'.[140] The relative lack of general builders on Clydeside, though, coupled with the absence of an overall regional employers' organisation for most of the period – comparable to the Manchester, Salford, and District Building Trades Employers' Association, or the Liverpool Master Builders' Association – rendered inter-trading stipulations unworkable. Moreover, at the local level the Scottish Building Trades' Federation (SBTF) was not strong enough in the pre-war years to implement an inter-trading policy. It was not until the federation grew in the post war years that the potential for comprehensive inter-trading was achieved – by which time the Glasgow Master Masons' Association had evolved into the much wider Scottish Building Contractors' Association.

Although limited in scope, the Glasgow Building Trades' Exchange, established in 1894, was an important exercise in collaboration in the building trade which pre-dated state-induced collectivism during the war. Among the objects of the Exchange were the promotion and protection of the building trade, the initiation of uniformity of contract, the dissemination of business information among members, and the settlement of disputes by arbitration. The Exchange did not become involved in labour relations issues at building-site level – although it petitioned against the proposed Trades Disputes Bill in 1902 which was eventually passed in 1906 – and in 1903 its members were drawn from the whole range of Clydeside's building industry.[141] However, a major weakness of the Exchange was that it tended to duplicate some of the trade regulatory functions that the building trade employers' associations already provided. Consequently, these associations gave the exchange little support.[142]

Before leaving the building trade, the issue of state-induced price regularisation deserves one final examination. The government's chief industrial troubleshooter throughout this period was G. R. Askwith.

140. Membership Book of Clyde Master Sailmakers' Association, 1906, p. 8. SRA TD241/10/2.

141. The Building Trades' Exchange of the City and District of Glasgow Ltd., Fifth Annual Issue, p. 14.

142. See account of a letter from the Secretary of the Glasgow Building Trades' Exchange to the GMWA, complaining about the indifference shown to the Exchange by the employers' associations. GMWA Minute Book 4, 8 Feb. 1917, p. 64.

With the passing of the 1896 Conciliation Act, Askwith was assigned the responsibility of persuading employers and employed to embrace the terms of this voluntary legislative measure. This task was so large that a labour relations' department was set up within the Board of Trade in 1911, which Askwith headed as Chief Industrial Commissioner.[143]

However, Askwith was not just concerned with labour relations but with the regularisation of industry in general. In 1915, for example, he became involved in a dispute between Clydeside's architects and surveyors over the correct mode of measurement to be adopted for joiners' work. The resultant Glasgow Mode of Measurement was adopted by the whole of the Scottish building trade and became 'the first National Building Code produced by any country'.[144] But although Askwith in his autobiography claimed the lion's share of credit for this innovation, it was principally the Glasgow Master Wrights' Association that was responsible for ensuring the acceptance of this code of practice by all the parties concerned.[145] It may also be added at this point that although Askwith played a valuable refereeing role regarding inter-trade collaboration in the post-war Clydeside building industry, it was once again the GMWA that successfully drummed up co-ordination between the different building trades employers.[146]

Several local employers' associations also played a valuable trade regulatory role without any prompting or guidance from government departments. For example, In 1915 the Paisley Master Plumbers' Association successfully persuaded the town council to issue plumbing contracts on a rotational basis to the various local firms. Similarly, in August of that year the Kilmarnock Master Plumbers' Association forged a deal with the town council regarding gas-cooking, and heating work – despite protestations from some quarters that such work could have been undertaken by corporation direct labour.[147] Also, when wartime labour shortages hit the Clydeside ironmongery trade in 1916, it was the Glasgow Ironmongers' Association which orchestrated a rational closure of premises at midday.[148] The idea of a government-induced

143. See R. Davidson's comments in *Industrial Problems and Disputes* (Brighton, 1974), pp. vii–xiv.

144. G. R. Askwith, *Industrial Problems*, pp. 411–412.

145. GMWA Minute Book 3, 8 July 1915, p. 413.

146. GMWA Minute Book 3, Dec. 1913, p. 265; Minute Book 4, Sept. 1916, p. 75; Minute Book 6, Feb. 1923, p. 85.

147. *Plumbing Trade Journal*, July and Aug. 1915, p. 40 and p. 42. A. J. McIvor notes that building trade employers' organisations in Lancashire played a similar watch-dog role over direct labour issues. A. J. McIvor, *Organised Capital*, p. 74.

148. *Plumbing Trade Journal*, Jan. 1916, p. 38.

collectivist ideology amongst building trade capitalists, therefore, should be treated with suspicion.

Shipbuilding and repairing

Despite the high level of organisation among Clydeside shipbuilding and engineering companies there seems to have been a negligible amount of trade regulation. This was in contrast to the situation in the North-West of England where some local associations of the Engineering Employers' Federation (EEF) were engaged in price fixing.[149] The main difference, however, was that whilst English companies tended to produce standardised products, the majority of the companies involved with the North West Engineering Trades Employers' Association (NWE-TEA) made bespoke goods. On the other hand, Clydeside ship boiler repair companies sold services rather than products, and this facilitated trade regulation. The Glasgow and District Engine Boiler and Ship Repairers' Association was formed in 1891 'to arrange a uniform rate of prices for labour and material in repair work'.[150] The constitution of the Association incorporated a rule which bound members to report to the Secretary the names of any employers on the river charging less than Association rates. Two years after its launch the Association persuaded a similar organisation in Greenock to bring its rates into line with its own, and in 1894 it amalgamated with the Ship Repairers of the United Kingdom – a body based in Newcastle. This larger body had recently reached an agreement with the Boilermakers' Society regarding wages for ship repair work. In engineering, therefore, when trading conditions were conducive, price regulation could take place.

Collective responses to risk

The need for mutual insurance was an ever-present stimulant to employer organisation. This could manifest itself as a defence against organised labour, the state, or a monopoly. Here, we specifically examine how capitalists insured themselves against financial loss.

The need for mutual insurance was the main reason that Clydeside's shipowners first formed an association. Lloyds' Insurance did not cover all the risks which shippers frequently faced. Consequently, several associations came into being throughout the UK to fill this gap. The first such organisation was the North of England Insurance Association, formed in 1856, and by 1889 there were 40 similar organisations

---

149. A. J. McIvor, *Organised Capital* (London, 1996), p. 74.
150. Glasgow District Engine Boiler and Ship Repairers' Association, Minute Book 1, 12 Aug. 1891; 11 Oct. 1893; 28 Feb. 1894.

throughout the UK. These were all affiliated to a central body called the Chamber of Shipping for the United Kingdom, which was based in London.[151] On Clydeside the two affiliated organisations were the Clyde Sailing Ship Owners' Association (CSSOA) – formed in 1883 – and the Clyde Steamship Owners' Association (CSOA) – formed in 1884.

The CSSOA was established to insure sailing ship owners against costs incurred through lengthy loading and unloading times at docks – a risk not covered by Lloyds. The effectiveness of the organisation was put to the test only three years after its launch when a vessel called the *Loch Torridon* berthed at Hull. The owners were informed that it would be discharged at the rate of 130 tons per day, which was judged by the CSSOA to be too slow. The case was taken to court and the result was a complete victory for the Association in the form of full reimbursement for the owners and a new discharge agreement at Hull docks policed by the Hull Chamber of Commerce.[152] By 1891 the CSSOA was responsible for over 300 sailing ships. However, technology was changing, and the Association was eventually wound up in 1924, by which time there were no sailing ships operating on permanent trade from the Clyde.[153]

Like the CSSOA, the CSOA was oriented towards insuring its members against any eventualities not covered by Lloyds – interestingly it was instrumental in persuading Lloyds to open a Glasgow office in 1900.[154] However, at its outset the CSOA was also concerned to ensure that its members were properly represented on the forthcoming Royal Commission on Shipping.[155] The CSOA represented the bulk of the Clyde steamship trade, and by 1910 had over 500 vessels on its list – which amounted to over a million tons of shipping.[156]

Both these organisations, then, were primarily established to provide insurance cover. However, over and above this role, they also monitored the activities of the Clyde Trust, and kept a watchful eye over any potentially damaging government legislation.

With the introduction of workmen's compensation legislation from

151. 'The History of Steamship Protection Societies', Unidentified newspaper clipping, 1889. The Glasgow Chamber of Commerce became involved with this issue, and in 1886 helped establish a sliding scale of loading and unloading charges at the port of Glasgow.

152. Clyde Sailing Ship Owners' Association (CSSOA), Minute Book 1, 4th Annual Report.

153. CSSOA Directors' Report, 1891, p. 2. CSOA Report 1924.

154. CSOA Directors' Report, 1900, p. 3.

155. Ibid., 1900, p. 3.

156. Ibid., 1910, p. 2.

the 1890s, employers frequently resorted to collective insurance against claims by their workers. This was especially the case after the 1897 Act rendered employers liable for compensation claims regardless of fault. The shortcomings of this act included delay in settling claims, the difficulty faced by workers in pressing claims in the first place, and certain stipulations from which employers could legally extricate themselves.[157] An act of 1906 removed some of these anomalies, but the scope of workmen's compensation was still limited by 1945. Moreover, it was not until after the Second World War that the notion of compensation was replaced by a new ideology in which benefits were provided irrespective of the causes of particular accidents.

With the passage of the 1897 Act it was assumed that employers would cover themselves against claims, although there was no legal stipulation compelling them to do so. This sharpened employer class consciousness on Clydeside, and several mutual insurance schemes were established. For example, the *Scottish Farmer* branded the extension of workmen's compensation to cover farm hands in 1900 'the worst framed and most iniquitous act ever passed', and suggested: 'the best plan is to shunt responsibility at the earliest possible opportunity on to the Insurance Companies'.[158] But it was not until 1923 that the National Farmers' Union Mutual Insurance Society – founded in 1919 – had any Scottish representation.

This was in contrast to urban employers who had a longer history of dealing with workmen's compensation. Under the supervision of the legal firm Biggart and Lumsden the Repairers' Liability Insurance Committee was formed to cover those involved in ship repairs throughout the UK. By the end of our period all the major Clyde ship repair companies – employing around 7000 workers – subscribed to this association. These included the likes of the Ardrossan Dockyard Company, Barclay Curle's, Scotts, and D. & W. Henderson. However, the Association also covered most of the British ship repairers in the United Kingdom. Consequently, the potential claims of around 60,000 workers were monitored by Biggart and Lumsden.[159]

Biggart and Lumsden were also in charge of the affairs of the Mutual Insurance Company of the Federated Engineering and Shipbuilding Employers. In 1898 Dr Arthur Mechan was taken on by the company

---

157. See P. W. J. Bartrip and S. B. Burman, *The Wounded Soldiers of Industry* (Oxford, 1983).
158. *Scottish Farmer*, 7 March 1903, p. 185.
159. Repairers' Liability Insurance Committee, Wages, Returns and Premium Register 1921–1922 (UGD 339/265).

to serve as one of two visiting medical officers for the Glasgow district – by 1906 he had investigated over 5,000 cases. The senior partner, Thomas Biggart – whose activities are illustrated in Chapter seven – made it quite clear that Mechan's medical knowledge would only be required for investigative purposes:

> His duties are not to act as Medical Attendant to the injured workmen, but to examine in the interest of the Employers ... He has afterwards to watch, and report frequently on progress made. In particular, he has to see that all reasonable means are taken to promote recovery, and that a return to work is not unduly delayed.[160]

Those engaged in the Clydeside building industry also became concerned at having to pay compensation to their workers, and once again this concern was addressed by successful employer action. For example, the Glasgow Master Masons' Association secured favourable terms with the Ocean Accident Guarantee Corporation.[161] This insurance company was commissioned by the Glasgow Master Wrights' Association too, and a letter to the Association's secretary illustrates how the removal of any vestige of humanity from claim transactions was all part of the company's service: 'Employers may feel that in certain cases a liberal payment should be made, but this is usually a matter of sentiment ... with the insurance company it is entirely a matter of business ...' Consequently, the Association was told to 'act entirely under the Company's directions and take no action without its instructions'.[162]

In coalmining, the Ayrshire Employers' Mutual Insurance Association (AEMIA) was initiated in June 1898 by seven large employers – among them James Baird and W. Houldsworth. As with the engineering employers, the main motivation behind the formation of this association was a fear that the workers would abuse the compensation system. One of its prime roles, then, was to 'investigate the circumstances of any accident or alleged accident ... and to obtain any information or evidence which may seem to have any bearing upon any claims or demands made.' An example of the AEMIA in action was its refusal to compensate a worker called John Little in 1898 as it decided that his recent mining accident was caused by his own misconduct.[163] The Scottish Mine Owners' Mutual Insurance Association also acted as a detective agency to determine the authenticity of claims. In 1925, for example, a

160. Ibid., letter regarding Dr. Arthur Mechan dated 3 July 1906.
161. GMMA Minute Book 3, Dec. 1898.
162. GMWA Minute Book 1, 12, Sept. 1901.
163. Articles of Association of Ayrshire Employers' Mutual Insurance Association Ltd. Also Directors' minutes of same, 5 Oct. 1898 (UGD 162–1/1 and 2/1).

letter to the railway wagon builders Rye Pickering & Co. informed them that one of their workers was being paid compensation for a mining accident in which a serious eye injury had been sustained. Pickering's was asked to kindly verify to the insurance company that the claimant did indeed have a bad eye.[164]

Despite the fact that coalowners found mutual insurance to be more expensive than they had anticipated, such schemes frequently worked out cheaper than employing the services of a professional insurance company.[165] For example, in 1920 it was found that 53 members of the Scottish Coal Merchants' Association (SCMA) had paid out over £2,500 in premiums to insurance companies. However, there had been only one fatal accident, necessitating a £327 payment by an insurance company. As a consequence of this alarming revelation the SCMA quickly formed its own mutual insurance company.[166]

The Scottish Master Bakers' Association (SMBA) also established its own mutual insurance scheme. This was launched in 1898 as the Scottish Employers' Mutual Insurance Society, with the owner of Kingston Bakery in Glasgow as its first Director.[167] The scheme was so successful that it was quickly taken up by all the main Scottish employers' associations involved in flour milling, confectionery, biscuit making, and preserve manufacture.[168] Moreover, pressure from the SMBA successfully removed a clause – operated by the Register of Public Companies – which necessitated the deposit of £20,000 before a mutual insurance company could be registered. The removal of this financial obstacle paved the way for other employers' associations to embark on mutual insurance.[169]

Noting the sheer number of price associations in Britain in 1911, Levy stated: 'the English man of business is a much greater lover of cartels than he should be, if his adhesion to the principle of individualism were as firm as is generally supposed.'[170] Our evidence broadly supports this, and further calls into question the notion that capitalists were characterised by a reluctance to combine.

164. Minute Book of Rye Pickering, 1925. UGD 12/29/25.
165. *GH*, 4 July 1908, p. 6.
166. SCMA, Minute Book 2, 3 Nov. 1920.
167. *British Baker*, Dec. 1898, p. 826. For an account of similar responses to the Workmen's Compensation Act by employers' organisations in the North-West of England, see A. J. McIvor, *Organised Capital*, pp. 79–81.
168. H. J. Dandie, *The Story of the 'Baxters'* (Aberdeen, 1990), p. 124.
169. *Ibid.*, p. 125.
170. H., Levy, *Monopoly and Competition* (London, 1911), p. 177.

CHAPTER FOUR

The Social Activities
of Clydeside Capital

We have seen so far that although it is wrong to speak of a unified Clydeside employer class, the number of labour relations-oriented employer organisations, and the high degree of trade collaboration that went on in the region, suggest that class-based models of collective action should not be entirely discarded. Clydeside capitalists large and small were not as reluctant to combine – to face up to the labour threat or protect their profits by regulating the market – as some commentators have suggested. However, so far the focus has been on market-centred combination, and it is the aim of this chapter to illustrate that a shared capitalist consciousness was in many ways perpetuated within the social sphere too. This is a neglected dimension to which labour, business, and social historians have devoted little attention.

Chambers of Commerce
When the Glasgow Chamber of Commerce (GCC) was established in 1783, it was the first such institution on the British mainland – Jersey had a chamber 15 years earlier. The chamber came into being due to the alarm felt by many Clydeside merchants over the loss of the American colonies, and by 1884 its membership stood at over a thousand. It is difficult to determine how many of these members were actually employers as only 5% of them gave their business addresses. However, this 5% represented a wide spread of industries across the Clydeside region, such as oil cloth manufacturing, starch works, thread manufacturing, flour milling, shipbuilding, iron manufacture and locomotive building. There was a bias in the GCC during the 1880s and 1890s towards large businesses and merchants, and this was reflected in the composition of the directorship too. In 1894, twenty directors were merchants – seven of whom were iron merchants – two were engineers, three were chemical manufacturers and thread manufacturers. However, there were also two warehousemen, three shipowners, two calico printers, a turkey red dyer, a wood broker, a cotton broker, and an underwriter.[1]

1. Report of the Directors of the Glasgow Chamber of Commerce, 1894, p. 43.

The main orientation of the Chamber was to monitor commercial and industrial legislation in parliament – which is dealt with in some detail in the next chapter – and to ensure the smooth running of the region's commerce and industry within an international trading network. In 1884, for example, a memorial was sent to India – always an important area of interest for the Chamber – urging the Viceroy to put pressure on the Indian government to extend its rail system – one of the main reasons being that there was a surplus of British capital looking for investment abroad.[2] The question of free trade was also an important one, and in 1903 the GCC circulated its members to guage the extent of their concern over increasingly protected foreign markets.[3] By 1914 the membership stood at 1220, and the Chamber's first *Commercial Year Book* was published in 1915, with a trading index in four languages.[4] The GCC's growing concern over German competition is reflected in the unqualified support it gave to the establishment of the Board of Trade's Commercial Intelligence Agency in 1918: 'The unscrupulous trade organisation of Germany has made it impossible for this country to continue to rely upon the haphazard methods of past years'.[5] Further, in 1919 the President went so far as to compare 'the spontaneous and intelligent industriousness of the German prisoners, with the listless and vacant idleness of so many of our own working people'.[6] In the post-war period membership of the Chamber increased considerably – to 2,844 by 1924 – and the balance swung more towards smaller companies.[7]

Many Chamber members belonged to the top circle of Glasgow's business elite. Alexander Cross MP was a director of the Chamber, senior partner in Cross and Sons Chemical Manufacturers and Seedsmen, and Liberal MP for Camlachie division. John Wilson owned of one of the most successful mining concerns in the United Kingdom, employing over 3000 people – as Liberal Unionist MP for Falkirk and district he played an active part in framing the 1897 Workmen's Compensation Act.[8] John Stephen was Chairman of Alexander Stephens of Linthouse, and Chairman of the African Lakes Corporation of Glasgow. Sir James King Bart. was President of the Chamber between 1874 and 1876 and Lord Provost of Glasgow from 1886 to 1899. Archibald Campbell was

2. Minutes of GCC, 1884, p. 48.
3. Report of the Directors of the GCC, 1903, pp. 8–19.
4. *Glasgow Chamber of Commerce Commercial Year Book* (Glasgow, 1915), p. 101.
5. Report of the Directors of GCC, 1918, p. 10.
6. Report of the Directors of the GCC, Dec. 1919, p. 12.
7. Report of the Directors of the GCC, 1924, p. 9.
8. *Glasgow Contemporaries at the Dawn of the Twentieth Century* (Glasgow, 1900), *passim.*

FIGURE 1. Sir James King.

a shipbuilder who represented the Gorbals ward on the Town Council from 1900. However, the Chamber was not just an institution for the big industrialists, as many smaller capitalists – such as bottle manufacturers, small merchants, and traders – swelled its ranks. This organisation, then, embraced a broad spectrum of West of Scotland capitalists. Many of its members shared the same class situation in Weberian terms – in that they were dominant entrepreneurial or petit bourgeoisie – while, at the same time, they shared in the status of belonging to a prestigious civic institution.[9] Many of them also operated premises within the commercial centre of the city and came from the same social background.[10] In this case, therefore, class and status were mutually reinforcing.

A change in the GCC's constitution in 1906 gave more power to its co-opted organisations, and by 1918 several of Clydeside's most powerful employers' associations were affiliated to the chamber.[11] By the end of our period there were 25 co-opted organisations electing representatives to the Chamber on an annual basis. Among these were the City Business Club, the Federation of Calico Printers – represented by the United Turkey Red Company – the Horse and Motor Contractors' Association, the United Fleshers' Society, the West of Scotland Guardian Society, the Scottish Master Bakers' Association, and the Scottish Coal Exporters' Association. The significant influence which the GCC had in Westminster was utilised, and at the same time strengthened, by the strong industrial muscle of these employers' and trade organisations. Consequently, the Chamber of Commerce functioned as a central link

9. For a recent appraisal of the importance of the Glasgow Chamber of Commerce see E. Gordon and R. Trainor, 'Employers and Policymaking: Scotland and Ireland, *c.* 1880–1939', in S. J. Connely *et al.* (eds), *Conflict, Identity, and Economic Development: Ireland and Scotland 1600–1939* (Preston, 1995), pp. 254–267. Also, see R. Trainor's chapter, 'The Elite', in W. H. Fraser and I. Maver (eds), *Glasgow Volume II: 1830–1912* (Manchester, 1996), pp. 227–264.

10. J. McCaffrey, 'Liberal Unionism in the West of Scotland', *Scottish Historical Review*, 149, April 1971, p. 58.

11. The co-opted associations were: Clyde Shipbuilders' Association; Clyde Steamship Owners' Association; Lanarkshire Coalmasters' Association; North West Engineering Trades Employers' Association; Scottish Coal Exporters' Association; Scottish Iron Manufacturers' Association; West of Scotland Iron and Steel Trades' Association; Glasgow Corn Trade Association; West of Scotland Iron and Steel Founders' Association. These were joined in 1919 by the National Light Castings Association. The following organisations also had nominees within the chamber: Underwriters and Insurance Brokers' Association in Glasgow; Scottish Section of the Society of Chemical Industry; Glasgow Stock Exchange; Institute of Accountants and Actuaries in Glasgow; the Trades House; and the Merchant House. *Glasgow Chamber of Commerce Monthly Journal* (1918), p. 32.

in a network of capitalist influence which transcended the industrial, the commercial, the social and the political spheres.

The Greenock Chamber of Commerce was also an important institution. Initially, the membership of the Glasgow chamber included representatives of the business interest of Greenock and Port Glasgow. However, in 1813 a chamber was established in Greenock, and by 1898 it had 221 members.[12] Unlike its Glasgow equivalent, the Greenock chamber sometimes had to resort to recruiting campaigns to attract new members.[13] However, in 1903 membership stood at 237, and the occupations of 88% of these can be determined. The largest group (21%) were involved in shipping, and there was a persistent bias towards shipping, sugar refining, and shipbuilding/engineering. Like the Glasgow chamber, though, the rest of the members represented the whole gamut of the region's industrial and commercial business community.[14] Moreover, 70% of the members can definitely be identified as employers – not including those classed as merchants.[15] The Greenock chamber was never as powerful as the Glasgow body – owing to the greater numerical strength of the latter. However, its affiliation to the Association of British Chambers of Commerce (ABCC) – which the Glasgow chamber refused to join until 1910 – enhanced its influence.

Melling believes that chambers of commerce should be seen as 'voices of a civil community' that helped establish and legitimise the hegemony of the capitalist class.[16] This is appropriate when applied to Clydeside as many members of both chambers were influential in the community. However, it was not just the capitalist elite that was represented by these institutions, but a cross-section of the business community from large industrialists to small-scale merchants.

The orientation of the chambers does not fall neatly into a corporatist model, as the chamber of commerce movement grew independently of state inducement – indeed for some time the ABCC was dissatisfied with the activities of the Foreign Office and the Board of Trade. Moreover, a deep distrust of state intervention in free market capitalism was apparent in the attitude of chamber members to post-war government control of industry. In 1918 representatives from the two Clydeside

12. Report by the Directors of Greenock Chamber of Commerce, Jan. 1898, p. 10.
13. Ibid., p. 10.
14. This was broadly similar to the make up of the Greenock town council on which 13 of the members served. *Greenock Post Office Directory*, 1898.
15. Report by the Directors of Greenock Chamber of Commerce 1903, Membership List.
16. J. Melling, 'British Employers and the Development of Industrial Welfare c. 1880–1920', unpublished Ph.D. thesis, Glasgow (1980).

chambers took part in a delegation to the President of the Board of Trade to voice their concerns over the Imports and Exports Temporary Control Bill – which was to give the Board of Trade authority to control this area of production for three years after the war. The two main fears of the delegation were that the legislation would lead to even more intrusive government intervention, and that it was a stepping stone towards state socialism.[17]

Membership of the chambers brought no direct tangible benefit to individuals, companies, or organisations – in the same way as membership of an employers' association or trade association. Consequently, prestige, status, and the opportunity to enjoy a sense of belonging to the business community remained their principal attractions throughout the period. This was a much more face-to-face form of solidarity than that provided by employers' associations oriented towards labour relations. In 1884, for example, the GCC held seven general meetings, while the Directors held 36 meetings throughout the year.[18] It should also be noted that these institutions offered no special benefits to their members, as any successes which their lobbying activities brought tended to be shared by the whole Clydeside business community. Consequently, Olson's theory of collective action fails to explain their appeal, and a class or status model has much more relevance. Chambers of commerce, then, should be seen as perpetuating a common identity within and between capitalist groups, while, at the same time, functioning as central cogs in a capitalist network of influence.

The Guildry

Capitalist class identity was further bolstered by two of the GCC's most important co-opted associations: the Merchants' House and the Trades House – collectively known as Glasgow's Guildry. These institutions evolved in the seventeenth century from the medieval trade guilds. At the head of the Merchants' House the Dean of Guild presided over the city's Dean of Guild Court. This body was an important charitable institution which provided educational bursaries for merchants' children and issued pensions to 'decayed members'. Prior to 1832 the House provided all of Glasgow's town councillors, but even when stripped of this function its prestige remained undiminished. In 1879, for example, it was remarked that 'though now greatly shorn of its political privileges, the Incorporation is still regarded by the best class of citizen, as one

---

17. *Monthly Journal of the Glasgow Chamber of Commerce* (1919), 1, pp. 7–9.
18. Minutes of GCC, 1884, p. 63.

in which it is an honourable duty to enrol themselves'.[19] The House had a long association with the GCC – it shared the same premises, and many individuals served in both institutions.

Like the Chamber, the Merchants' House acted as a pressure group for the interests of the area's trade and industry – as well as serving as a valuable status institution. It petitioned for a system of decimal coinage in 1855, fought for a better postal service for Glasgow, campaigned for improvements to the Clyde's harbour facilities, and advocated proportional representation for Scotland in 1867.[20] In 1909 the institution successfully defended its privileges by defeating a clause in the Housing and Town Planning Act, which would have deprived the Dean of Guild Court of its powers. That same year the Merchants' House received its own legislation – the Buchanan and Ewing Bequest Act – which allowed it to assist in the education of merchants' sons at Glasgow University and Anderson's College. Prominent members of the House included Sir James King, John Ure, and Campbell Bannerman. However, its prestige is best exemplified by the extent of the bequests which it received from deceased members. One of the most spectacular was the posthumous donation of Lord Inverclyde – Chairman of Cunard – in 1905: 'I leave everything to the Merchants' House of Glasgow ... The Income of this Fund is to be allocated annually by the Directors of the Merchants' House to Charities or Institutions connected with Seamen or for the benefit of aged or infirm Seamen or their families'. This amounted to £185,000, and there were other examples of such benevolence towards the institution throughout the period.[21]

The second component of Glasgow's Guildry was the Trades House. Here, the Deacon Convenor presided over the affairs of Glasgow's 14 incorporated trades: the Hammermen, Tailors, Cordiners, Maltmen, Weavers, Bakers, Skinners, Wrights, Coopers, Fleshers, Masons, Gardeners, Barbers, and Dyers. In the seventeenth century these incorporations regulated entry into Glasgow's crafts, provided funds for the education of craftsmen's children, and distributed charity to old and infirm members. An Act of 1846 abolished such exclusive privileges, and the incorporations therefore concentrated on providing charity. However, in contrast to trades guilds in other Scottish cities, the Glasgow incorporations continued to attract members throughout the nineteenth and twentieth centuries, and by 1923 the total funds of the Trades House amounted to just over one million pounds.[22] A principal

19. J. Cruishank, *Sketch of the Incorporation of Masons* (Glasgow, 1879) p. 198.
20. J. M. Reid, *A History of the Merchants' House* (Glasgow, 1938), p. 57.
21. *Ibid.*, pp. 68–69.
22. *The Bailie*, 24 Oct. 1923, p. 4.

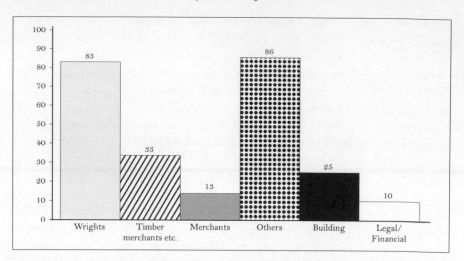

GRAPH 4.1. Occupations of those who joined the Incorporation of Wrights 1870–1889. *Source*: J. M. Reid, *The Incorporation of Wrights in Glasgow* (Glasgow, 1928).

reason for this was that, compared to the situation in Dundee, the Glasgow trades opened their membership to individuals not directly associated with the respective crafts.[23] The result of this change of policy was that although the guilds retained some connection with their historic crafts, they attracted a mixture of individuals from across the professional spectrum. This can be clearly seen in the occupations of those who joined the Incorporation of Wrights over a 19-year period from 1870.

The Incorporation was strongly linked to the Glasgow joinery trade, and many of its Presidents were also Presidents of the Glasgow Master Wrights' Association. The trade connection is fairly obvious from the number of professional wrights who were members of the Incorporation. Moreover, the category 'building' in the graph included masons, brickbuilders, measurers, architects, and lathsplitters, and this – together with the large representation of timber merchants – meant the connection between the Incorporation of Wrights and the building trade was fairly strong. However, the graph also shows that the largest group of members – the 86 designated as 'others' – was made up of a scattering of occupations including schoolmasters, clothiers, warehousemen, jewellers, etc. Moreover, there were also 23 members who were either merchants, lawyers, or accountants. Consequently, this organisation appealed both

23. See A. M. Smith, *The Nine Trades of Dundee* (Dundee, 1995). Also her *The Three United Trades of Dundee* (Dundee, 1987), for an account of trade guild activity in an earlier period in this city.

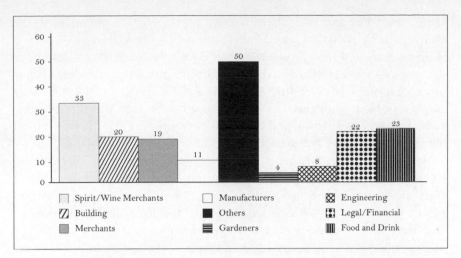

GRAPH 4.2. Occupations of those who joined the Incorporation of Gardeners 1870–1889. *Source: History of the Incorporation of Gardeners* (Glasgow, 1903).

as a trade representational body, and as a status identification body at the same time.

Not all the trades retained a historic craft link. The membership role of the Incorporation of Gardeners shows that, once again, the largest group fell into the multifarious 'others' category. However, in contrast to the four gardeners who joined over this period, the second largest group was composed of wine and spirit merchants, followed by those involved in the food and drinks industry such as grocers and bakers.[24]

Consequently, most new members of the Incorporation of Gardeners over this period were either spirit merchants or were involved in the food and drink industry. It should also be noted that 22 members were engaged in the legal or financial professions. Of most significance, though, was the wide catchment of commercial and industrial enterprises from which the Incorporation drew its members – from the building trade, to commerce, to engineering, etc. Moreover, this broad occupational sweep reflected an equally wide social sweep, as we find large-scale capitalists such as William Bilsland on the membership list together with a brush manufacturer, pawnbrokers, and a collector of canal dues.[25]

The principal appeal of this institution, therefore, was that it provided members with an important badge of status, and this was the case with the trades guilds in general. This is borne out by the fact that a large number of individuals were members of several incorporations at the

24. *History of the Incorporation of Gardeners* (Glasgow, 1903), pp. 19–119.
25. *Ibid.*, p. 22.

same time. For example, Lauchan A. McGeoch – a founder of the Glasgow and West of Scotland Ironmongers' Federation – was a Hammerman, a Wright, and a Mason.[26] Similarly, W. F. Russell – senior partner in a successful coal exporting company – was a member of four incorporations: the Wrights, Hammermen, Coopers, and Gardeners.[27] Sam Stevenson, the President of the Glasgow Master Wrights' Association in 1905 – instrumental in the formation of a conciliation board for disputes in the Clydeside joinery trade – was a Hammerman, and a Mason.[28] And John Grimond, the Chairman of the West of Scotland Hosiery Manufacturers' Association from 1921, was a Baker and a Gardener, as well as being a member of the Merchants' House.[29] Further, by the end of our period a commentator in the *Bailie* could still remark that the 'Incorporations maintain their prestige in attracting the flower of the business and industrial life of Glasgow'.[30]

There was a significant overlap between the Guildry and the GCC – indeed, the Merchants' House and the Chamber still share the same George Square premises. Both McGeoch and Russell were members of the Chamber – indeed, Russell was a President. J. T. Tullis was a member of the GCC while serving on the board of the Merchants' House. Tullis was also a Deacon of the Incorporation of Bakers, and Deacon Convenor of the Trades House.[31] Similarly, James Gilchrist was both a member of the Merchants' House and the Trades House as well as Deacon Convenor of the Hammermen.[32] J. Inglis was both a Director of the Merchants' House and the GCC.[33]

All of the individuals shared the same economic class. Tullis was a leather belt manufacturer, director of a Lanarkshire-based coal mining consortium, and was involved in several other Clydeside enterprises. Gilchrist was Chairman both of Barclay Curle and of the locomotive company Sharp and Stewart. Inglis was a wealthy shipbuilder; while Gilchrist served on the board of the North British Railway Company and was President of the Institute of Engineers and Shipbuilders. They were, therefore, part of Clydeside's industrial elite, and although it would

26. *The Bailie*, 20 Oct. 1920, p. 3.
27. *The Bailie*, 8 Feb. 1922, p. 3.
28. *The Bailie*, 26 Sept. 1923, p. 2.
29. *The Bailie*, 25 July, 1923, p. 2.
30. *The Bailie*, 10 Oct. 1923, p. 2.
31. *Glasgow Contemporaries*, p. 206. See also S. Slaven and S. Checkland, *Directory of Business Biography 1860–1960* (Aberdeen, 1990), pp. 469–471.
32. *Ibid*. Gilchrist was also Vice-President of the Institute of Engineers and Shipbuilders.
33. *Glasgow Contemporaries*, p. 184.

FIGURE 2. Sir Frederick C. Gardiner.

be difficult to argue that they came from the same class as the small business people and merchants with whom they shared membership of the Guildry and the Chamber, they were, nevertheless, part of the same network. A good example to illustrate this point is that of Sir F. C. Gardiner. Gardiner was a member of the GCC from 1899, its Director in 1909, and its President ten years later. He was also involved with several trade incorporations, several charities, was President of the Clyde Steamship Owners' Association, was a member of the Shipping Federation, and was a member of the Old Glasgow Club.[34] Consequently, the connections through which Gardiner could exert his influence – and through which he could draw upon the influence of others – extended from the economic to the social sphere. The same could be said of James MacFarlane, biscuit manufacturer, leading member of the Glasgow Master Bakers' Association – which had two representatives on the GCC – initiator of the Glasgow Pastry and Family Bakers' Association in 1917, and one-time Deacon Convenor of the Trades House.[35] Also, the tailor S. B. Slater was a member of the Federation of Master Tailors as well as being a Deacon of the Incorporation of Tailors.[36] To a significant extent, then, collective identity amongst capitalists large and small was perpetuated by a criss-crossing of connections both in the social sphere – through institutions, incorporations, involvement in charities and shared life styles – and in the economic sphere – through such agencies as employers' associations and interlocking directorships.

With this in mind we take a look at another trade incorporation: the Hammermen. The Incorporation of Hammermen had a strong connection with Clydeside's engineering, shipbuilding, and metal-working industries. Indeed, in 1910 Lord Rosebery commented that 'the Hammermen craft represents perhaps the most powerful of all the manufacturing interests, because it represents so many'.[37] This is borne out by the percentage of engineers, shipbuilders, ironfounders, ironmasters, and ironmongers, who joined between 1870 and the end of 1889.[38]

However, despite this, and notwithstanding the presence of Clydeside's leading engineers and shipbuilders on the membership roll – such as J. B. Neilson, and W. Denny – the Incorporation of Hammermen, like the other Trades Guilds, took in a wide occupational sweep that encompassed the likes of coalmasters, biscuit manufacturers, bakers, and

34. *The Bailie*, 29 June 1921, p. 2.
35. *British Baker*, 5 June 1917. Also, *British Baker*, 23 Nov. 1917, p. 18.
36. *The Bailie*, 21 Sept. 1921, p. 2.
37. H. Lumsden and P. H. Aitken, *History of the Hammermen of Glasgow* (Glasgow, 1912), title page.
38. H. Lumsden and P. H. Aitken, *Hammermen of Glasgow*, Membership list.

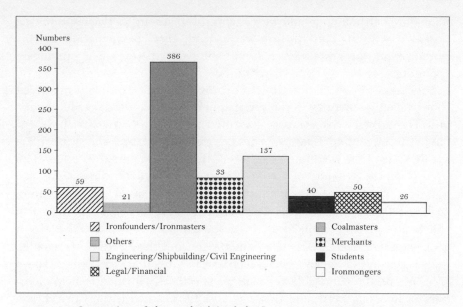

GRAPH 4.3. Occupation of those who joined the Incorporation of Hammermen 1870–
1889. *Source*: H. Lumsden and P. H. Aitken, *History of the Incorporation of
Hammermen in Glasgow* (Glasgow, 1911).

carting contractors. Like the incorporations of Wrights and Gardeners,
most of those who joined the Hammermen over this period came from
occupations too diverse to represent on a graph – among them ship-
brokers, cashiers, architects, doctors, hotel keepers, tailors, etc.[39] And
once again we find that a not insignificant number of lawyers, bankers
and accountants were members too.

As well as the Guildry, there were other more parochial incorporations and industry-specific benevolent institutions which played
important status reinforcing roles too. For example, in Paisley – which
had its own incorporations of Hammermen, Maltmen, and Grocers –
there was the Corporation of Merchants which dated from 1725, and
continued to attract members throughout our period. Here we find the
same wide spread of capitalists represented – among the 1870 Directors
were T. Coats the textile manufacturer, A. Craig, who owned an engineering firm, J. Clark, a master baker, W. Polson, of Brown and Polson's
mustard and starch manufacturers, and J. Caldwell, a wine and spirit
merchant.[40] Another important Paisley institution was the Old Paisley
Weavers' Society (1702). Several of the region's textile masters were
involved in the hierarchy of this association in the 1870s and 1880s.

39. *Ibid.*, Membership List, Appendix 2, *passim*.
40. *Paisley and District Directory, 1870–1*, p. 56.

Therefore, although employer organisation amongst Paisley's textile bosses was limited in the pre-war period, their participation in this organisation suggests closer bonds between them than previously thought.[41]

Several more associations illustrate how Clydeside capitalists bolstered their collective identity in the social sphere. The Clydesdale Merchants' and Tradesmen's Society was instituted in 1890 to cater for those excluded from joining Glasgow's trades guilds. By 1923 this was still a viable institution with 931 members – Bonar Law joined in 1905. The occupations of over 400 of these individuals can be determined, and once again we find a broad sweep of capitalist enterprise involved, from slaters to house factors, from spirit merchants to plumbers.[42] There was also the Southern Merchants' and Tradesmen's Society which dated from 1895, and had over 700 members in 1903;[43] and the Eastern Merchants' and Tradesmen's Society which boasted 300 members in 1908.[44] These were essentially charitable associations specifically formed to help members in financial need, and this was also the case with the Corn Trade Benevolent Society, initiated in 1880, the membership of which comprised corn merchants and their chief clerks.[45] The Govan Weavers' Society was established in 1756 and attracted 178 new members between 1920 and 1923.[46] In 1888 the Slate Trade Benevolent Society was established. The Anderston Weavers' Society dated from 1738, and by the end of our period – when its funds amounted to £32,500 – it still held annual dinners and social events.[47] In 1890, 140 guests attended the annual dinner of the Grocers' Company of Glasgow, formed in 1790.[48] In 1914 its President was Duncan McIntyre, President of the Glasgow Grocers' and Provision Merchants' Association, and founder member of the Glasgow Grocers' Club.[49] The Master Bakers' Friendly Society of Glasgow was formed in 1795 by bakers in the outskirts of the city determined to protect themselves against the organised bakers within, and continued

41. In 1870–71, five of the 12 Managers of the Paisley Old Weavers were involved with the textile industry. By 1890, however – after the decline of the Paisley shawl industry – there was more of a mix of trades represented. *Paisley and District Directory, 1870–71*, and *1890–91*. Paisley Central Library.
42. Membership Role of the Clydesdale Merchants' and Tradesmen's Society, 1923, SRA TD402/49.
43. *Shoe and Leather Trader*, Feb. 1903, p. 9.
44. *GH*, 21 Feb. 1908.
45. *Glasgow Post Office Directory*, 1886, p. 231.
46. *The Bailie*, 24 March 1926, p. 4.
47. *The Bailie*, 21 Aug. 1923, p. 2.
48. *GH*, 14 March 1890, p. 9.
49. *The Bailie*, 17 March 1926, p. 3.

to act as a charitable and social institution throughout the period.[50] The Glasgow-based Scottish Wine and Spirit Merchants' Benevolent Institution was set up in 1871, the Paisley and Renfrew Wine, Spirit and Beer Trade Association was initiated the same year, and a similar Greenock and Gourock-based Association came into being in 1878.[51] By 1880, the funds of the Glasgow body were almost £5,000, and its membership stood at 350 – by 1899 this had risen to over 500.[52] Finally, there was the Merchants' Club of Glasgow which dated from 1872, although this had only 22 members in 1916.[53]

The deep involvement of the legal and financial professions in the trades guilds should remind us of the difficulty of separating the industrial sphere from the financial and legal. Wiener argues for a definite compartmentalisation here:

> An important distinction must be borne in mind at the outset. Nineteenth-century economic development threw up not one but two groups of new businessmen, with differing characteristics and different fates: one based on commerce and finance and centred in London, the other based on manufacturing and centred in the North.[54]

However, regional evidence suggests that such social separation between finance and industry is too extreme. Trainor has shown that such a separation was rather blurred in the English Midlands, and Gordon and Trainor's recent work in Scotland also highlights the fallacy of making clear distinctions between industry and finance – while McCrone has illustrated the strong links which existed between the industrial and landed classes through intermarriage.[55]

Both the Glasgow and Greenock Chambers of Commerce included industrialists and bankers on their membership lists. However, the membership roles of the incorporations provide the most compelling evidence that commerce and industry did not constitute two separate camps. Here, industrialists, accountants, lawyers and bankers shared the same status. Consequently, the capitalist web stretched smoothly from the

---

50. *Ibid.*, p. 3.
51. *Paisley and District Directory, 1900–1*; *Greenock Post Office Directory, 1880–81*.
52. Minute Book of Scottish Wine and Spirit Merchants' Benevolent Institution (UGD 119 5/1).
53. *Shoe and Leather Trader*, July 1916, p. 4.
54. M. J. Wiener, *English Culture and the Decline of the Industrial Spirit 1850 1918* (London, 1992), pp. 128–129.
55. R. Trainor, *Black Country Elites* (Oxford, 1993), *passim*. E. Gordon and R. Trainor, 'Employers and Policymaking', p. 238. D. McCrone, 'Towards a Principled Society', in T. M. Devine (ed.), *Scottish Elites* (Edinburgh, 1994), p. 181.

commercial through the industrial to the legal spheres. A prime example of this was Thomas Biggart, who, although a lawyer by profession, identified wholeheartedly with Clydeside engineering and shipbuilding employers – his role in cultivating employer organisation is examined in Chapter 7. Biggart's status as a capitalist was bolstered by his membership of the Incorporation of Hammermen, which he joined in 1892.[56] The very act of membership of these associations announced a definite position in society, and this was continually defined through social mixing at their annual dinners and other such events.[57] The connections between lawyers and capitalists, therefore, deserve further investigation, and the significant involvement of solicitors in Clydeside's First World War Munitions Tribunals provides a further reason for more research into this neglected area.[58]

The Glasgow City Business Club
Another example of an institution which helped reinforce social status – especially amongst the lower echelons of the commercial and industrial class – was the Glasgow City Business Club. This organisation was formed in 1912, and by 1920 – by which time it had joined the Glasgow Chamber of Commerce – had a membership of 330. The membership of the Business Club was very wide, as the following table shows.[59]

TABLE 4.1. *Membership of Glasgow City Business Club, 1913*

Soap Manufacturer, House Factor, Bookseller, Shipping Agent Farrier, Surveyor

Shipowner, Draper, Engraver, Glass Stainer

Gunpowder Manufacturer, Fireplace Maker, Bedding Manufacturer

Tea Merchant, Artist, Brassfounder, Advertising Contractor

Optician, Tobacconist, Fruit Merchant, Auctioneer

Removals Contractor, Chemist, Outfitter, Hotel Manager

Boys' Clothier, Glass Merchant, Engineer

Motor Car Dealer, Investment Broker, Commission Merchant

Timber Importer, Billiard Table Maker, Paper Merchant

Umbrella Manufacturer, Dancing Master, Wholesale Scrap Dealer

Structural Engineer, Aerated Water Manufacturer

56. H. Lumsden and P. H. Aitken, *History of the Hammermen of Glasgow*. Membership list, p. 349.
57. See, for example, the Incorporation of Hammermen's annual dinner toast list. MU22-C. 19.
58. G. R. Rubin, *War, Law, and Labour* (Oxford, 1987), p. 41.
59. Minute Book of Glasgow City Business Club.

This broad spread of business interests was expanded still further when a one-member-one-trade rule was rescinded in 1920, and further still in 1922 when those who lived outside the city were allowed to join the Club. By 1923, then, the 625 members included master plasterers, plumbers, printers, engineers, and painters. The Club held weekly dinners throughout the period – which an average of 50 members attended during 1916. There was also an active social calendar with well attended events such as golf competitions, day trips down the Clyde, and regular talks in the Gordon Street club room on commercial, political, and industrial topics, such as 'British Industry After the War', 'The Co-operative Trading Movement and its Effects on Industrial Enterprise', and 'Politics and Business'. The Club was a bastion of free enterprise and it petitioned to have co-operative societies liable to payment of income tax.[60] Only the financially solvent were allowed to join, and from the Club's inception all prospective members were strictly vetted. This factor assisted inter-trading amongst the club's members, but also ensured that they were drawn from a particular economic class.

Other Institutions
On a broader front, the Glasgow and West of Scotland Guardian Society also ensured that class and status overlapped. This inquiry agency was formed in the 1850s to safeguard Clydeside businesses against losses incurred through bad debts. Its importance, though, is illustrated by the fact that in 1906 alone it vetted over 16,000 individual cases.[61] Moreover, like the GCC, the Guardian Society increasingly became concerned with the promotion of Clydeside capital overseas; and – like the Chamber's trade journal – its *Scottish Trade Courier* was published in four languages. The Society was affiliated to 90 kindred bodies throughout the United Kingdom – through the Association of Protection Societies – had its office in the Merchants' House, and ten Lord Provosts of Glasgow were listed among its presidents. Its Manager from 1909 was J. R. Rutherford, a member of the GCC.[62] This organisation, therefore, was an important element of the Clydeside capitalist system.

The Clyde Trust was responsible for ensuring the maintenance of the navigable river, the construction of docks, cranes, warehouses, etc., the levying of dues on vessels and goods, and the borrowing of money for capital purposes.[63] However, a position on the Clyde Trust was one of

---

60. Minute Book of Glasgow City Business Club, 23 Sept. 1915.
61. *GH*, 27 Feb. 1906, p. 8.
62. *The Bailie*, 13 April 1921.
63. *Industries of Glasgow and The West of Scotland* (Glasgow, 1901), pp. 283–288.

FIGURE 3. D. M. Stevenson.

FIGURE 4. James Brand.

considerable prestige and there was intense competition for the yearly vacancies. From 1858 Clyde Trustees were chosen from the Merchants' House, the Trades House, and the Chamber of Commerce – who each provided two members. In 1889 a movement to extend the number of trustees was set in motion, but this did not bear fruit until 1905. Thereafter 42 individuals were entitled to become trustees: 18 directly elected by the ratepayers and shipowners; 16 nominated by Glasgow Corporation and the institutions; and eight from Glasgow's adjacent burghs.[64]

The employer class's enthusiasm for the pursuit of knowledge also produced status-conscious organisations. In Paisley, for example, several of the town's leading capitalists were involved with the Philosophical Institution and the Paisley Observatory.[65] However, Glasgow once again provides an example *par excellence* of a city thirsting for learning. Glasgow had 25 literary and scientific institutions in 1886, and many dated from an earlier period. The Glasgow Athenaeum came into being in 1847 'to place within the reach of the public the fullest and most recent information on all subjects of general interest, whether Commercial, Literary, or Scientific', but also to 'provide an agreeable place of resort in the intervals of Business'. The Athenaeum had its own amusement rooms, and its reading room in 1886 had 11,000 books. Among its vice-presidents were substantial employers such as Collins, Tennant, and Orr Ewing – while J. Stirling Maxwell, Paul Rottenburg, and Andrew Bonar Law made regular donations to its upkeep. By 1918 there were over 1,600 members – 521 of whom were women.[66]

The Adam Smith Club was another important discussion society and social club, as was the Civic Society of Glasgow which combined charitable functions with regular social events. Rottenburg was involved here also, along with William Bilsland, D. M. Stevenson, James Brand, and Sir William Arrol.[67] The Scottish Christian Social Union was founded in 1901 and was also Glasgow-based. Several prominent Clydeside capitalists were represented here too, such as Beardmore, Primrose, and Templeton.[68] The Philosophical Society of Glasgow met fortnightly to 'promote diffusion of scientific knowledge', and had 850 members in 1886.[69] And the Old Glasgow Club was established

64. J. F. Riddell, *Clyde Navigation* (Edinburgh, 1979), pp. 147–148.
65. See *Paisley and District Directory, 1880–1920*, which lists the council members of both institutions.
66. Seventy-First Annual Report of The Glasgow Athenaeum. MU22-F-15. Also, *Glasgow Post Office Directory 1886–87*, p. 114.
67. Membership List of the Civic Society of Glasgow, 1899–1900.
68. Fourth Annual Report of the Scottish Christian Social Union, 1905.
69. *Glasgow Post Office Directory 1886–87*, p. 115.

in 1900 'for the discussion of matters relating to the history of the city'. This organisation met once a month, and by 1908 there were 468 members – an average of 100 new members joined every year between 1905 and 1908. Once again we find the names of Clydeside's top industrialists on the membership role – such as Bilsland, Glen-Coats, Tullis, and D. M. Stevenson. However, although the members do not give their occupations, their addresses in solid middle-class areas suggest that once again a broad sweep of business enterprises was represented.[70]

Neighbourhood identity

Although it is true that working-class consciousness depended more on neighbourhood than that of the middle class – which was manifested more through a network of connections – the effect of living near other capitalists should not be ruled out as a vital component of middle-class consciousness too.

Clearly, the idea of a unified capitalist class is contradicted by the separation of the various strata of the middle classes throughout the Clydeside region. For example, many of Clydeside's industrial and commercial elite lived in towns such as Helensburgh, Largs, Kilmacolm, Langbank, and Bridge of Weir. Amongst this high stratum of the middle class, therefore, the effect of neighbourhood was least relevant, and network factors as props of class solidarity were more important. However, further down the social scale, both neighbourhood and network factors played a part, and especially so from the 1880s when the lower middle classes began moving out of Glasgow's city centre and into newly constructed suburbs like Pollokshields, Hyndland, and Bearsden. Consequently, in 1899, we find that among those who owned houses in Barrinton Drive – in Glasgow's West End – were 'a builder, a writer, a factor, a commission merchant, four wine and spirit merchants, a grocer, [and] a female relative of the builder'.[71] The petite bourgeoisie, therefore, from the 1880s and 1890s tended to live in particular locations and this helped strengthen their class identity. Many of the members of the Old Glasgow Club, for example, lived in the Hillhead, Downhill, and Pollokshields areas – 30 from Pollokshields alone.[72] And this is repeated when we examine the residential addresses of the members of the Incorporation of Wrights – the most extensive of the incorporations'

70. Old Glasgow Club, Volume 1, Session 1906–08, p. 242.
71. C. M. Atherton, 'The Development of the Middle Class Suburb: The West End of Glasgow', *Scottish Economic and Social History*, 11 (1991), pp. 19–35.
72. Old Glasgow Club Membership List, Volume 1, 1906–08, p. 248.

membership lists – between 1870 and 1928. This reveals that of the 2,108 members who joined over this period, around 40% lived in Kelvinside, Hillhead, Partick and Newlands, while five percent were residents of the Pollokshields/ Pollokshaws area,[73] which does suggest that lower middle-class identity was increasingly bolstered by spatial as well as network factors.

Many of the large Scottish employers had little control at the civic level – due to the dominance of the propertied influence in the City Chambers – and this compelled them to provide their own company housing.[74] However, although this may have been the case for the large industrialists, by the turn of the century Scotland's small employers dominated the towns and cities, and it was they who controlled most urban property.[75] This was certainly the case on Clydeside where there was 'a close connection between ownership of a few tenements and the petite bourgeoisie'.[76] The majority of houses in Glasgow at the beginning of the twentieth century were owned or rented by private individuals; next in importance came trusts, followed by house factors. Of the private individuals, those who were involved in the building trade, provision merchants, and licensed grocers, were strongly represented amongst owners, and the income from these investments was normally destined to provide for widows or unmarried daughters.[77] A good example is the Glasgow baker and grain merchant T. M. Stevenson who died in 1906. Stevenson owned ten tenements around Kidston Street and Florence Street in Glasgow, as well as other property in Govan. The gross rental from this property amounted to almost £14,000 a year. This, combined with his numerous shares, meant his total personal estate was valued at almost £70,000.[78]

Charity, religion, and freemasonry
Social standing was further ensured by involvement in civic institutions and charitable causes. Membership of Glasgow's Guildry was an

73. Membership List of the Incorporation of Wrights. J. M. Reid, *The Incorporation of Wrights in Glasgow* (Glasgow, 1928), pp. li–ccii.
74. J. Melling, 'Scottish Industrialists and the Changing Character of Class Relations in the Clyde Region c. 1880–1918'. In T. Dickson (ed.), *Capital and Class in Scotland* (Edinburgh, 1982), p. 111.
75. D. McCrone, 'Towards a Principled Society: Scottish Elites in the 20th Century'. In A. Dickson and J. H. Treble (eds), *People and Society in Scotland Vol. 3, 1914–1990* (Edinburgh, 1992), p. 184.
76. N. J. Morgan and M. J. Daunton, 'Landlords in Glasgow: A Study of 1900', *Business History* 25 (1983), Number 3. p. 267–268.
77. *Ibid.*, pp. 268–269.
78. Trust of T. M. Stevenson. TD 974/196/1.

important stepping stone to prestigious civic positions. The Trades Guilds annually nominated 36 appointees to public institutions – two Clyde Trustees, four patrons of Hutcheson's Hospital, two Directors of the Western Infirmary, one Director of the Convalescent Homes, etc.[79] However, middle-class domination of civic institutions was the norm throughout Clydeside. In Greenock, for example, Shaw Stewart, the MP for Renfrewshire East, was President of the Greenock Infirmary in 1900, while his Vice-President was Sir Thomas Sutherland, MP for Greenock – and member of Greenock Chamber of Commerce. Moreover, among the directors of the Infirmary were Greenock's shipowning Lord Provost, A. O. Leitch; the engineer and shipbuilder Andrew Rodger; the sugar refiner Robert Kerr; the engineer J. M. Kincaid; and James MacOnie who owned a substantial engineering and foundry business.[80]

Specific charitable causes also depended on middle-class benevolence. In Greenock in 1870, for example, the MP and merchant J. J. Grieve was Patron of the Greenock Charitable Society which had a committee of 20 – most of whom were local employers. Glasgow, though, offers the prime example of middle-class charitable involvement. In 1897 there were almost 200 separate charities in the city – generating over one million pounds a year.[81] Moreover, despite a reduction in the number of religious and moral institutions over the period – discussed below – the number of charitable and friendly societies listed in the *Glasgow Post Office Directory* between 1886 and 1920 increased – 95 in 1886, 138 in 1909, and 134 in 1920.[82]

Many of these charitable organisations were of vital importance to the Clydeside area. For example, the Glasgow Home For Deserted Mothers in the city's Renfrew Street was established in 1873, and leading members of Clydeside's commercial and industrial elite were involved in its upkeep – such as Robert Gourlay of the Bank of Scotland, and Sir J. King, Bart.[83] Thomas Biggart and his family established the Biggart Memorial Home for Crippled and Infirm Children at Prestwick.[84] Other

79. W. Campbell, *The Cordiners of Glasgow* (Glasgow, 1883), p. 207.
80. *Greenock Post Office Directory*, 1900.
81. *Organised Help: Organ of the Charity Organisation Society*, Number 2, 15 Jan. 1897, p. 26.
82. *Glasgow Post Office Directories*, 1886–7, 1909–10, 1919–20. There was a similar pattern in Greenock where there were four charities listed in 1870, eight in 1880, 14 in 1900, and 12 in 1923. *Greenock Post Office Directory*, 1870–1, 1880–1, 1900–1, 1922–23. Watt Library, Greenock.
83. *Glasgow Post Office Directory*, 1891, p. 117.
84. *The Bailie*, July, 1925, p. 2.

institutions which depended upon such private philanthropy were the Glasgow Institution for Orphan and Destitute Girls – which prepared orphans for careers as domestic servants – the West of Scotland Convalescent Seaside Homes, the Mission to the Outdoor Blind, and many more.[85] Also, although individual endeavour played a significant role in the running of these charities, their main income came from a wide cross-section of industrial donations. For example, the donation list of the Glasgow Houses of Shelter for Females shows that companies such as Templeton's, N. B. Loco, Brownlee, Stewart and Lloyd, and Bilslands were regular donors.[86] Charitable involvement was not just confined to Glasgow. The Greenock Seamen's Friends' Society depended upon the generosity of a wide range of Clydeside businesses – for example Gourock Ropework, Clydeside Shipbuilders and Engineers, Scotts, and the Aluminium Casting Company.[87] Charitable involvement, therefore, was another important factor in strengthening capitalist class consciousness throughout the region. Moreover, such philanthropy cannot be dissociated from the economic and commercial spheres. Seven of the four-man directorship of the Glasgow Houses of Shelter for Females, for example, were members of the Glasgow Chamber of Commerce.[88]

A prime example of how important charitable commitment was to the network of capitalist influence – and *vice versa* – is that of the Scottish Labour Colony Association. The idea of creating a labour colony in which Clydeside's able-bodied unemployed – and its vagrants – could be placed stemmed from the general popularity of the labour colony solution at the time. However, the idea was given a significant boost when General Booth of the Salvation Army gave a speech on labour colonies at St Andrew's Halls in December 1890. After this the Adam Smith Club discussed the idea, the Glasgow Social Union gave its support, and a conference comprising all the philosophical and charitable agencies in the Glasgow area was held a year later.[89] This was followed by a public meeting in St Andrew's Halls in 1892 called specifically to discuss the problem of unemployment and vagrancy. The top circle of Clydeside's industrial and commercial elite were there, such as J. A. Cuthbertson the chemical producer; J. C. Burns who was three times President of the Clyde Steamship Owners' Association; J. G. A. Baird

85. *Glasgow Post Office Directory*, 1891.
86. Report of the Glasgow Houses of Shelter for Females 1906–1907, p. 3. MU22-e8.
87. Greenock Seamen's Friends' Society, Annual Report 1908, pp. 12–15. Watt Memorial Library, Greenock, R/668.
88. Ibid.
89. Adam Smith Club of Glasgow, Membership Book 1868–1897, p. 29. Scottish Labour Colony Association Annual Report 1900, GUA MU22-E-8.

the iron and coal master; W. Collins who owned one of the largest printing and publishing companies in Britain and was an active member of the Glasgow Master Printers' Association; T. Tullis the leather belting manufacturer; W. Bilsland the baker, and J. Brand the builder.[90] The eventual result was the founding of the Scottish Labour Colony Association, and the establishment of a labour colony near Dumfries – which, although not expanding to the initial expectations of its founders, operated for 18 years.[91]

What is significant is the complexity and strength of the web of connections. Many of the philanthophists were Chamber of Commerce members, several knew each other through involvement in company boardrooms, many were also involved with the trade incorporations, and most of them were members of employers' associations. Moreover, like most private charities, the Scottish Labour Colony Association depended on the input of the business community at large. Consequently, we find a broad range of businesses giving donations to the cause – such as the Firhill Iron Works, Ferguslie Thread Company, and Britannia Pottery.[92]

The solidarity which this type of activity engendered was also bolstered by shared religious affiliation. Religion added another important dimension to the shared identity and status consciousness of the employing classes. In an earlier period evangelicalism had been the most distinguishing characteristic of Scotland's new middle classes. This social elite embraced evangelicalism in the 1830s and 1840s, and especially so in Glasgow which became known as the 'Gospel City'.[93] A great many religions voluntary organisations were established, and these complemented the strong middle-class input into charitable associations. The deep involvement of the employer classes in crusading evangelicalism continued until the First World War – bolstered by the Moody and Sankey revival in 1873–75. And a study of the social composition of the congregations of nine Glasgow Presbyterian churches in the 1900s indicates that the higher social groups dominated the eldership.[94] Moreover, middle-class identity was further strengthened in 1900 when inter-denominational rivalry between the United Presbyterian Church and the Free Church ended with the merging of both organisations.

90. *GH*, 13 May 1892, p. 5.
91. See R. Johnston, '"Charity that Heals": The Scottish Labour Colony Association and Attitudes to the Able-bodied Unemployed in Glasgow 1890–1914', *Scottish Historical Review*, April 1998, pp. 61–79.
92. Scottish Labour Colony Association Annual Report 1900, p. 5.
93. C. G. Brown, *Religion and Society in Scotland Since 1707* (Edinburgh, 1997), p. 195.
94. *Ibid.*, p. 110.

From the 1890s, however, the middle classes withdrew from 'hands on' evangelicalism in working-class areas. This was part of the gradual exodus of the middle class from the city centres and into select residential areas such as Hyndland, Jordanhill, Bearsden, and Pollokshields.[95] This is apparent from the diminishing number of religious and moral institutions listed in the *Glasgow Post Office Directory* – from 95 in 1886, to 41 in 1901, and rising slightly to 46 in 1920.[96] There was a similar story in Greenock where there were 12 religious societies in 1870, eight in 1880, five in 1900, and only two by the end of our period.[97] However, this exodus was matched by a spate of church building within the new suburbs. Consequently, although middle-class involvement in religious charity faded as a demonstration of class consciousness, shared religious practice – now bolstered by neighbourhood identity – continued throughout our period.

Many Clydeside capitalists were also Freemasons, and membership of the Craft extended from artisanal level right up to the top flight of the region's middle classes. The Trades House had its own Masonic Lodge (No. 1241), while the Provincial Grand Lodge of Glasgow was the premier Scottish lodge and had the largest membership – and the healthiest bank balance – of all the Scottish Masonic lodges.[98] Several prominent employers were leading members of Lodge 12, Greenock Kilwinning. Among its hierarchy in 1871 we find the likes of Thomas Ballantine the distiller, Edward Blackmore the engineer, and J. B. Crawhall the sugar refiner. Similarly, Shaw Stewart the dyer and bleacher, Scott the shipbuilder, J. Niven the sailmaker, and D. J. Dunlop the engineer and shipbuilder were office bearers of the Grand Lodge Renfrewshire West between 1900 and 1916.[99] It was a similar picture in Paisley where a dyer, a grocer, a mill furnisher, and a master slater were officials of the town's St Mirren Lodge No. 129.[100] Freemasonry permeated much of Clydeside's skilled engineering and shipbuilding trades, and many companies – such as John Brown's and Scotts – had their own Masonic Social Clubs.[101] In Greenock, Kincaid's Masonic Club

95. *Ibid.*, p. 128.
96. This drop in numbers was partly due to the Unification of 1900. *Glasgow Post Office Directories*, 1886–87, 1901–2, 1919–20.
97. *Greenock Post Office Directory*, 1870–71, 1880–81, 1900–01, 1922–23.
98. *The Bailie*, 8 Feb., 1922, p. 3.
99. *Greenock Post Office Directory*, 1900–01, and 1915–16.
100. *Paisley and District Directory*, 1890–91, p. 67.
101. Kincaid and Company Works' Masonic Club Minutes 1918–1925. TD. 131/9/1. See also Register of Members, TD 131/9/2. This shows that in 1919 there were 118 members, most of whom were skilled workers such as plumbers and boilermakers.

was formed in 1917 and the staff were normally well represented at its monthly social meetings.[102] The *Greenock Telegraph* reported how at its Burns Supper of 1920,

> One of the speakers made reference to the wide representation of the gathering, and the belief was expressed that such gatherings, where employers, staff, and men, were represented in social harmony, would have an influence in allaying industrial unrest.[103]

Orangeism remained primarily a proletarian movement throughout our period. There is, though, some circumstantial evidence that some Clydeside employers gave the Orange Order their tacit support. For example, William Baird and Company were notorious for their dislike of Catholicism and for their encouragement of the Lanarkshire Orange movement from the mid-nineteenth century.[104] By 1914 many skilled shipyard workers were Orangemen – a trait which had spread from the Belfast yards in the 1850s – and this perpetuated an already strong discrimination against Roman Catholics in the region. Marshall has argued that Clydeside employers did not have to resort to utilising Orangeism as a labour control tool, as they were not faced with a homogeneous proletariat. However, the overlap between this extreme form of Protestantism and Freemasonry – one of Glasgow's Lord Provosts, James Bain, was a member of both orders – makes it likely that many employers accepted it as a necessary part of the social hierarchy. Also, in 1880 Lodge 690 was established in Glasgow, specifically to form 'an informal bridge between the Order and the Conservative party'.[105] This would have led many employers into – at the very least – an identification with the movement. Finally, Marshall argues that Orangeism was generally too proletarian to attract employers. However, whereas this may have been the case with the industrial elite, it should be remembered that many Clydeside employers were only one step removed from being working class themselves. Consequently, the extent of Orangeism within the wider employer community of the West of Scotland may have been under-estimated.

Annual dinners and day trips

Finally, we turn to a neglected dimension at which Clydeside employer

102. Ibid., Report of Meeting at Masonic Temple in Sterwart Street Greenock 21 Nov. 1918.
103. *Greenock Telegraph*, 2 Feb. 1920, p. 3.
104. See W. S. Marshall, *'The Billy Boys'. A Concise History of Orangeism in Scotland* (Edinburgh, 1996), pp. 42–44.
105. *Ibid.*, p. 84.

class consciousness was created and sustained: the social activities which many employers' associations provided.

Glasgow's master shoemakers believed socialising to be of the utmost importance, and organised regular social events and smoking concerts.[106] Members of the Glasgow Paper and Stationery Trades' Association had an annual golf tournament, while the Scottish Paper Makers' Association held annual dinners.[107] The Glasgow Grocers' Associations had a thriving bowling club throughout the period.[108] The Greenock Master Wrights' Association held annual soirées and dinner dances, and most of its members participated as guests in the Glasgow Master Wrights' Association's annual day trips.[109] The Scottish Furniture Manufacturers' Association held its first dinner in 1898 to celebrate the success of the recent lock-out, and this was so successful that it became a yearly event which helped bolster solidarity. For example, at the 1914 dinner the Chairman urged those assembled for the meal to 'take a leaf out of the workers' book and combine, combine, combine … not to find the differences that existed among them, but rather to find a common platform from which they could act hand in hand and together'.[110] The engineering industry also had social events: the Brassfounders' Association, for example, held annual dinners from 1920.[111]

There were other examples. Over 200 people attended the Glasgow Ironmongers' and Iron Merchants' Friendly Society annual dinner in the Trades Hall in 1897.[112] The Grocer Company of Glasgow held regular, well-attended functions, and this body – unlike its more ritualistic London equivalent – had strong links with the local retail trade.[113] The Glasgow Dairymen's Association – which represented many of the region's small dairy farmers – held annual soirées which complemented the organisation's important trade regulatory role.[114] Four different societies represented Glasgow's commercial travellers in 1897 and they all held frequent balls and dinners.[115] The annual dinner of the Glasgow and West of Scotland Master Plumbers' Association

106. *Shoe and Leather Trader*, Oct. 1911, p. 21.
107. The Scottish Paper Makers' Association joined its English equivalent in 1912 to form the Paper Makers' Association of Great Britain and Ireland (1912) (Incorporated). *The Paper-Maker and British Paper Trade Journal*, 1 July 1912, p. 57.
108. *The Bailie*, 17 March 1926, p. 3.
109. Greenock Master Wrights' Association, Minute Book 1, 7 May 1875.
110. *The Furniture Record*, 20 Feb. 1914, p. 198.
111. Scottish Metal Refiners' Association, Minute Book 2, Jan. 24 1924.
112. *Scottish Trader*, 4 Dec. 1897, p. 26.
113. *Ibid.*, 12 March 1910, p. 34.
114. *The Scottish Farmer*, 1 Feb. 1896, p. 95.
115. *Scottish Trader*, March 1897, p. 9.

was presided over by the city's Lord Provost and was reputed to be 'one of the biggest social events of the season'.[116] The Scottish Coal Exporters' Association had annual dinners to which representatives of Scotland's four other coal masters' associations were routinely invited – Sir Adam Nimmo attended the 1918 dinner.[117] And Clydeside's master tailors regularly attended the annual dinners of the Federation of Merchant Tailors.[118]

All the major employers' associations representing the Clydeside building trade held such events, and a notable characteristic was the participation of representatives from kindred associations. For example, at the Glasgow Master Painters' Association's annual dinner in 1909 there were guests from the Edinburgh, Leith and District Building Trades Association, the Glasgow Master Plumbers' Association, the Glasgow Master Masons' Association, and the Glasgow Master Plasterers' Association.[119] There is some evidence too that Scottish leather employers were more liable to meet together on a social basis than those in England.[120]

Some employers' associations also organised excursions to help sustain a collective identity amongst the members. The annual excursion of the Slate Trade Benevolent Association in 1908, for example, took place during a lock-out of Clydeside slaters – the event no doubt strengthened the employers' resolve to resist the workers' demands.[121] The Scottish Chamber of Agriculture's annual conferences – held in a different part of Scotland every year – involved the delegates in visiting farms and embarking on excursions throughout the locality of the guest association.[122] The Greenock Master Hairdressers' Association held annual picnics to Dunoon.[123] The furniture manufacturers spoke of the need for an excursion in 1902 to help 'cement the friendship of the members, and thus indirectly strengthen the cause for which the association exists'.[124] In 1894 the Glasgow Master Bakers' outing to Dumfries included masters from Baillieston, Coatbridge, and Hamilton.[125] The West of Scotland Wholesale Confectioners' Association held annual trips

116. *Plumbing Trade Journal*, Oct. 1919, p. 32.
117. Scottish Coal Exporters' Association, Minute Book 3, 19 Dec. 1918.
118. *Master Tailors' and Cutters' Gazette*, 1901, p. 4.
119. Glasgow Master Masons' Association, Minute Book 6, Aug. 1909, p. 10.
120. See letter from an English reader in *Scottish Leather Trader*, Jan. 1884, p. 248.
121. Glasgow Master Slaters' Association, Minute Book 4, 12 June 1908.
122. *North British Agriculturist*, July 1918, p. 574.
123. Minute Book of Greenock Master Hairdressers' Association, 3 June 1909.
124. In this case, however, it is not clear if an annual trip materialised. SFMA Minute Book 1, May 14 1902.
125. *British Baker*, Oct. 1894, p. 146.

from 1897 – which included football matches, races, and games for the members and their families.[126] Glasgow Federated Boot and Shoe Manufacturers held similar excursions – in 1900, for example, they visited Aberfoyle and the Lake of Mentieth.[127] The master bakers of Paisley held yearly excursions from 1883, and their 1898 trip is typical of the breathtaking determination of business people to cram as much as possible into a rare day away from the workplace. The company travelled from Queen Street Station to Edinburgh where they changed trains for Dunbar. At Dunbar they climbed Castle Hill and had lunch at the Marine Hotel, after which four carriages took them to North Berwick. Here, they spent an hour touring a country estate before returning to North Berwick where they took dinner before the long journey home.[128] And the same frenzied determination was evident in the Glasgow and West of Scotland Master Plumbers' Association's 1914 excursion – which the President of the Glasgow Master Wrights' Association attended. This involved a train journey from Glasgow to Larbert; a motor vehicle ride to Stirling for lunch at the town's Golden Lion; then an extensive motor vehicle tour of the Ochill Hills. Next came tea back at the Golden Lion, before returning to Glasgow in the evening.[129]

Excursions such as these were made to different parts of the country every year, and the building trade associations always tried to avoid a clash of dates – as this enabled representatives from each trade to attend. In 1886, for example, the Glasgow Master Masons' Association chartered the *Columba* from the Broomielaw to Ardrishaig; in 1889 the members went to Melrose; and in 1890 the *Duchess of Hamilton* took them to Arran.[130] The Glasgow Master Wrights' Association routinely invited as many representatives from the building trade as possible to their excursions as 'their meeting together in a social capacity would be beneficial to the trade generally'. In 1913, therefore, complimentary tickets were issued to guests from employers' associations representing Glasgow's master plumbers, masons, plasterers, painters, slaters, as well as to the Faculty of Surveyors, the Scottish National Building Trades' Federation, the Edinburgh and Leith District Building Trades' Association, and the Glasgow Institute of Architects.[131]

These activities, then, were valuable opportunities for small employers to form or reinforce acquaintance with counterparts from within and

126. *Confectioners' Union*, 15 July 1913, p. 885.
127. *Master Tailors' and Cutter's Gazette*, 5 July 1900, p. 898.
128. *British Baker*, 17 June 1898, p. 792.
129. *Plumbing Trade Journal*, July 1914, p. 41.
130. Glasgow Master Masons' Association, Minute Book 1.
131. Glasgow Master Wrights' Association Minute Book 3, July 1913, p. 295.

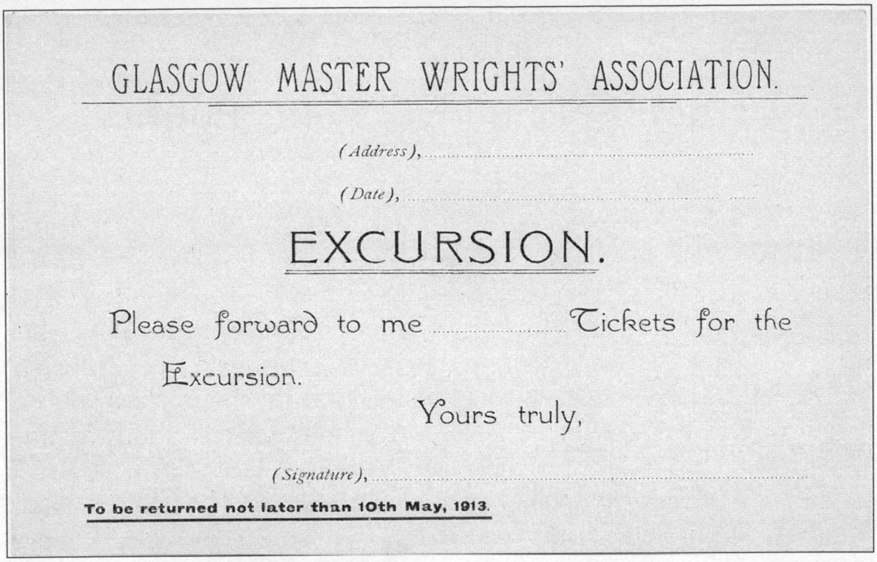

GLASGOW MASTER WRIGHTS' ASSOCIATION.

(Address),..

(Date),..

EXCURSION.

Please forward to me .... Tickets for the Excursion.

Yours truly,

(Signature),...

To be returned not later than 10th May, 1913.

FIGURE 5. Invitation card for the Glasgow Master Wrights' Association Excursion, 1913.

without their own trades. Many of the members of these associations were only one short step from being operatives themselves. However, in such company their class consciousness as employers of labour was assured and strengthened.

CHAPTER FIVE

Clydeside Employers and Politics

It has been suggested that the role industrialists played in British economic growth has been exaggerated and that their input into politics was minimal.[1] This point of view has been attacked, of course, and some historians have cautioned that we can only really gauge the influence of the industrial elite by looking beyond the economic and political spheres, and take account of capitalists' involvement in public institutions, their civic role, involvement in charities, etc.[2] There is also a leftist point of view that points to the fact that a third of British cabinet ministers between 1886 and 1950 were businessmen, and that although capitalists may not have run the country, their presence within key parts of the state system always ensured that the business interest held at least one of the reins.[3] In this chapter we examine to what degree Clydeside capital played a political role over the 1870–1920 period.

Chambers of commerce as political pressure groups
Let us begin by turning once again to Clydeside's chambers of commerce.

1. W. D. Rubinstein, 'Wealth, Elites and the Class Structure of Modern Britain', *Past and Present* 76 (1977); 'The Victorian Middle Classes: Wealth Occupation and Geography', *Economic History Review*, 2nd Series, 30 (1977); *Elites and the Wealthy in Modern British History: Essays in Social and Economic History* (Brighton, 1987); M. J. Wiener, *English Culture and the Decline of the Industrial Spirit* (Cambridge, 1981). For a more recent argument, see S. Nenadic, 'Businessmen, the urban middle classes and the "dominance" of manufacturers in 19th century Britain', *Economic History Review* 44 (1991). J. Turner also argues that the business interest was 'defensive and divided' before the First World War. J. Turner (ed.), *Businessmen and Politics* (London, 1984), p. 7. See also K. Middlemas, *Politics In Industrial Society* (London, 1979), p. 64.

2. R. Trainor, 'Urban Elites in Victorian Britain', *Urban History Yearbook* (1985); R. Trainor, *Black Country Elites* (Oxford, 1993); M. Morgan and R. Trainor, 'The Dominant Classes', in *People and Society in Scotland*, Vol. 2, 1830–1914 (Edinburgh, 1989), p. 127; E. Gordon and R. Trainor, 'Employers and Policymaking: Scotland and Northern Ireland 1880–1939', in *Conflict Identity and Economic Development, Ireland and Scotland 1600–1939* (Preston, 1995).

3. R. Miliband, *The State in Capitalist Society* (London, 1979), pp. 52–53; Melling adopts a similar line. See J. Melling, 'Scottish Industrialists and the Changing Character of Class Relations in the Clyde Region *c.* 1880–1918', in T. Dickson (ed.), *Capital and Class in Scotland* (Edinburgh, 1982).

The chambers were vital links in the chain of capitalist connections that stretched across the Clydeside region and far beyond, and their principal attraction was the prestige and sense of belonging to the business community which membership offered. However, the chambers were also important lobbying institutions that enabled Clydeside capitalists to influence central government.[4]

From its inception in 1783 the Glasgow Chamber of Commerce (GCC) acted as watchdog over the interests of Clydeside capital. The Chamber quickly established a Scotch Commercial Agency in London to promote Scottish goods and monitor parliamentary legislation deemed potentially harmful to West of Scotland commerce. It maintained this watchful attitude throughout the period. For example, in 1874 a petition was lodged against the Factory Amendments Bill – framed to reduce the hours worked in factories from 60 to 56 hours a week. Similarly, the members were horrified that the 1892 amendment to the Factory and Workshops Act had no clause that allowed employers to contract out of compensation agreements and arrange their own settlements. Subsequently, when the bill was eventually passed by the Lords, most of the clauses which the Glasgow Chamber of Commerce had complained of were removed. Also, in 1885 the Chamber petitioned against the proposed Merchant Shipping Bill – intended to ensure greater safety for seamen. The bill was withdrawn in July 1884.[5]

Many Glasgow industrialists remained dedicated to free trade and the unity of the Empire throughout this period. In 1886 the GCC petitioned against the Government of Ireland Bill, saying 'it was prejudicial to those commercial interests which it is the province of chambers of commerce to safeguard'.[6] Therefore, although at the national level business politics may have been weakened by conflicts between free traders and protectionists before 1914, on Clydeside there was much more unity on this issue among the industrialists represented by the Chamber of Commerce.[7]

Clydeside was well endowed with political clubs, and especially so after the Liberal Party split over Home Rule. In 1887, 112 (11%) of GCC members were involved with the Conservative Club of Glasgow. Further, 14 of these members were also on the Conservative Club's Political Committee. This was the fighting wing of the Club which produced political pamphlets, organised lectures, contributed towards

---

4. E. Gordon and R. Trainor, 'Employers and Policymaking', p. 262.
5. Report of the Directors of the Glasgow Chamber of Commerce, Jan. 1885, p. 3.
6. Report of Directors of the GCC, 1894, p. 163.
7. J. Turner, *Businessmen and Politics*, p. 6.

the expenses of political demonstrations, encouraged local artisanal Conservative associations, and ensured that the Club kept in touch with similar organisations all over the country. Glasgow also had its Imperial Union Club formed 'to promote the social intercourse of Unionists of all political parties ... who engage to maintain to the best of their ability integrity of the British Empire; the Union of the three Kingdoms of England, Scotland, and Ireland, and the complete supremacy of the Imperial Parliament'. Eighty members of the GCC can be identified on the Club's 1899 membership list.[8] This ties in with work on Liberal Unionism in the West of Scotland where it was found that the nucleus of the Liberal Unionist movement there was formed by a core of businessmen who depended upon world markets. The speed with which these individuals formed themselves into a political party was due largely to the fact that all knew each other through membership of the Chamber, and through involvement in public bodies.[9]

Paisley, too, had its political clubs, and their organising committees illustrate how employers were attracted by ideologies conducive to their own particular markets. The Paisley Liberal Association in 1900 had Thomas Glen Coats and James Coats among its Vice-Presidents. Its Committee of Management, however, was made up of a diverse clutch of capitalists including several solicitors, a confectioner, a furniture dealer, and a master bootmaker – in general, employers not wholly committed to empire markets. In contrast, the Paisley Liberal Unionist Club had large-scale capitalists among its hierarchy, such as A. Coats, W. A. Coats, and G. H. Coats – which illustrates how political allegiances cut through families – J. Polson of Brown and Polson, H. Smiley a thread manufacturer, G. Dobie the tobacco manufacturer, R. Barclay who owned a local engineering company, and A. Fullerton, another engineering capitalist. Moreover, the closeness in the orientation of Conservatism and Liberal Unionism is illustrated by the fact that both Dobie and Fullerton were also Vice-Presidents of the Paisley Conservative Association. The level of political enthusiasm in Paisley had not diminished by the end of our period, and by 1924 there were three Liberal associations, three Unionist clubs, and a Women's Guild of Empire Association all active in the region.[10]

The Greenock Chamber of Commerce, like its Glasgow equivalent, was frequently used to convey the grievances of the local business

---

8. Constitution and Rules of the Conservative Club of Glasgow, 1899; Constitution and Rules of the Imperial Union Club of Glasgow, 1899.
9. J. F. McCaffrey, 'Liberal Unionism in the West of Scotland', *Scottish Historical Review* 149, April (1971), p. 59.
10. *Paisley and District Directory, 1900–01*, and *1923–24*.

community to parliament. For example, along with the Glasgow chamber it petitioned against the Irish Home Rule Bill in 1886 – a principal concern of the Chamber being that a third of Greenock sugar was shipped to Ireland.[11] Also, in 1883 a memorial was sent to the Treasury asking the government to pressurise Spain into removing sugar tariffs.[12] Memorials and petitions such as these were normally first passed to the local MP, and particular care was taken to ensure politicians were amenable to the business interest. In 1885, for example, the merchant and shipowner J. Stewart resigned as Greenock's constituency MP. The Greenock Chamber of Commerce recorded its appreciation for his past efforts. However, the chamber lost no time in arranging a special meeting to interview the new MP, the shipowner T. Sutherland – who was already one of its members. At this meeting Sutherland was given 'full information respecting several matters in which his assistance as Parliamentary representative would be valuable'.[13] The issue of sugar bounties was a significant one for the Greenock area, and a constant bone of contention for the Chamber to chew on. Sutherland was back at the Chamber in January 1898, this time along with the Greenock Sugar Refiners' Association, the Town Council, and the Greenock Harbour Trust, to be briefed on the damaging effect which foreign sugar bounties were having on some of the members; however, as a shipowner himself, Sutherland would probably be well aware of the seriousness of the issue.[14] Moreover, in March of that year the Greenock chamber memorialised Lord Salisbury on this very issue.[15] Eventually pressure such as this – from Greenock and other chambers of commerce – succeeded in bringing about an abolition of sugar bounties in 1902.[16]

It has been said that in the mid-Victorian period chambers of commerce were fairly ineffective lobbying bodies.[17] Evidence from Clydeside suggests otherwise. The links between the GCC and the political arena were replicated in the orientation of its counterpart down-river at Greenock. Clydeside's two chambers of commerce, therefore, were important and effective pressure groups which carried the region's commercial and industrial concerns right to the heart of Westminster politics.

11. J. F. McCaffrey, 'Liberal Unionism', p. 67.
12. Minutes of Greenock Chamber of Commerce, Jan. 1883, p. 42.
13. Ibid., Jan. 1885.
14. Ibid., Jan. 1898.
15. Ibid., March 1898.
16. Report by the Directors of the Greenock Chamber of Commerce, 1902, p. 8.

Capitalists as constituency MPs

The idea that employers were poorly represented within the corridors of power has recently been challenged, and it has been found that at the turn of the century 18 of the 25 West of Scotland MPs were businessmen.[18] If we take a closer look at the occupations of all Clydeside's 126 MPs over the 1870 to 1920 period – 70% of whom were Liberals or Liberal Unionists – we find that 18% of these politicians were employers of labour – not including those who classed themselves as merchants. The following table shows their distribution throughout the region.[19]

TABLE 5.1. *Number and percentage of MPs identified as employers on Clydeside, 1870–1920*

District	Employer MPs	Total number of district MPs and employer %	
Paisley	3	6	(50%)
Kilmarnock	1	7	(14%)
Lanarkshire	8	31	(25%)
Dunbartonshire	2	8	(25%)
Ayrshire	3	57	(5%)
Greenock	2	6	(33%)
Glasgow	8	33	(24%)
Renfrewshire	2	10	(20%)
Total	29	158	(18%)

Many of the MPs were large-scale employers. For example, John Colville the iron and steel manufacturer held North-East Lanarkshire for the Liberals between 1895 and 1901. In Ayrshire Sir William Arrol represented Ayrshire South from 1895 to 1906; William Birkmyre, the jute and linen manufacturer, sat for Ayr Burghs between 1892 and 1895; and George Younger, the brewing magnate, represented the same constituency for 16 years after his election in 1906. Dunbartonshire was a safe Conservative seat for the earlier part of the period – due to the dominance of the agricultural interest there. However, the Conservative

17. A. H. Yarmie, 'Employers' Organisations in Mid Victorian Britain', *International Review of Social History*, 25 (1980), p. 221.

18. E. Gordon and R Trainor, 'Employers and Policymaking: Scotland and Northern Ireland 1880–1939', in *Conflict, Identity and Economic Development, Ireland and Scotland 1600–1939* (Preston, 1995), p. 262.

19. The information on Clydeside MPs is obtained from *Dod's Parliamentary Companion 1870–1924*; and M. Stenton and S. Lees, *Who's Who of British Members of Parliament*, Vols 2, 3, and 4.

FIGURE 6. Sir Godfrey Collins.

Sir Archibald Orr-Ewing – who held the seat from 1868 until his retirement in 1892 – was a merchant and an important local employer. The Liberals finally won the seat when Captain J. Sinclair was elected in 1892. However, the years 1895–1906 saw it once again in the hands of a Conservative, the large employer A. Wylie Ross – a turkey-red dyer and calico printer.[20]

Three of Paisley's MPs were powerful local businessmen. W. Holms, who held the seat for the Liberals for nine years from 1874, was a partner in a large spinning and manufacturing company with branches in Glasgow and London.[21] He was succeeded in 1884 by S. Clark of the thread manufacturing family. In 1906 the constituency fell to J. M. McCallum, a large soap manufacturer, and he retained the seat until 1920. Greenock also had its share of industrial MPs. The Liberal Unionist T. Sutherland – who held the constituency between 1884 and 1900 – was a shipowner and member of the Greenock Chamber of Commerce. His successor was the high-ranking Freemason and JP for Greenock, James Reid – Reid owned a spinning and hosiery manufacturing company. He was followed in 1906 by the even more influential employer, Sir Godfrey P. Collins. Collins was the managing director of the large Glasgow-based publishing company. During the war he became the private secretary to the Secretary for War, and by 1919 was Junior Lord of the Treasury. Collins held Greenock until 1936 and was Secretary of State for Scotland for the last three years of this term.

The Conservative Andrew Bonar Law represented Glasgow Blackfriars from 1900 until 1906. Bonar Law was initially an iron merchant, and was still a member of the GCC whilst serving as deputy Prime Minister.[22] There were other important employers among Glasgow's MPs. From 1892 until 1910 Glasgow Camlachie was represented by the Liberal Alexander Cross, a seed merchant and chemical manufacturer. A staunch free trader, Cross was also a director of GCC, chairman of the Iron Trade Association, and a founder of the Liberal Unionist party.[23] The calico printer R. Dalgleish held the Glasgow City constituency for the Liberals for 20 years from 1857. And the ironmaster A. Whitelaw represented Glasgow for the Tories from 1874 until 1879.

Important constituency changes between 1885 and 1918 mean that the above table tends to distort the picture slightly. Govan, for example, was listed under Lanarkshire until 1918, then became a Glasgow

20. See C. Wilson's Chapter in J. Hood (ed.), *The History of Clydebank* (Carnforth, 1988), pp. 23–31.
21. The following information is from *Paisley Post Office Directory* 1870–1916.
22. E. Gordon and R. Trainor, 'Employers and Policymaking', p. 262.
23. J. F. McCaffrey, 'Liberal Unionism', p. 59.

FIGURE 7. Alexander Cross.

constituency – held by Labour's Neil McLean until 1950. Consequently, the fact that five of the six Govan MPs over the 1870–1920 period were employers tends to be lost within the overall average for Lanarkshire. Several of these members had extensive business interests. Sir William Pearce was a partner in John Elder the shipbuilders; John Wilson owned tube works in Glasgow and Govan; and R. Duncan was senior partner in a large marine engineering firm. *Forward* made much of the support which Govan's working class gave to the capitalists: 'During the general election the workers of Govan were implored to vote for the employer of labour and keep the hammers going'.[24] It is also interesting that the Deputy Grand Master of the Orange Lodge of Scotland addressed Govan voters urging them to support Pearce.[25]

The table also excludes any MPs who classed themselves as merchants. So, if we put the merchants back into the picture – allowing that several would have been employers of labour too – we find an even higher level of capitalist political activity on Clydeside. Therefore, over a quarter of Clydeside's MPs over the 1870–1920 period had business interests – and almost half of those in Paisley, Lanarkshire, Glasgow, and Greenock. This must be kept in perspective as only a few managed to attain Cabinet posts. However, although not constituting a cohesive employer lobby, these capitalist MPs were nevertheless in positions to block, hinder, or, at the very least, monitor, any legislation detrimental to the commercial interest of their constituencies.

TABLE 5.2. *Number and percentage of Clydeside MPs identified as capitalists, 1870–1920*

District	Employer MPs (including Merchants)	Total number of district MPs and employer %
Paisley	6	6 (100%)
Kilmarnock	2	7 (29%)
Lanarkshire	10	31 (31%)
Dunbartonshire	3	8 (38%)
Ayrshire	4	57 (7%)
Greenock	6	6 (100%)
Glasgow	10	33 (30%)
Renfrewshire	4	10 (40%)
Total	45	158 (28%)

24. *Forward*, 20 Oct. 1906, p. 7.
25. W. S. Marshall, *'The Billy Boys': A Concise History of Orangeism in Scotland* (Edinburgh, 1960), pp. 64–65.

During the war the government-sponsored industrial truce – and the later introduction of Whitley Councils – lent impetus to the concept of national collective bargaining, and this stimulated organisation amongst capital and labour. Many leading employers had secured key roles in the prosecution of the war effort. For example, when the coal industry was taken over by the government in 1916, Andrew Duncan was given the position of Coal Controller.[26] Also, the engineering employer William Weir was made Director of Munitions, and his heavy-handed approach to the dilution of labour issue may have been a factor in the wartime labour unrest on the Clyde. By 1919 two important employers' organisations – the FBI and the NCEO – represented capital in Westminster.

With the expansion of the franchise in 1918 the political climate changed, and the expanded electorate's concern with issues such as class inequality and industrial relations made Liberalism out of date.[27] Partly as a consequence of this, the years following the end of the war saw the rise of the Labour Party on Clydeside, and by 1924, twenty-one Clydeside constituencies were held by Labour or ILP members. There was still, though, a significant employer presence among Clydeside's politicians. Indeed, two of the Labour MPs were employers. Thomas Henderson, the MP for Glasgow Tradeston, was a high-ranking manager with the Cooperative Society; and the MP for Renfrew West, Robert Murray, was a Director of the SCWS. Sir W. Alexander, the Conservative member for Glasgow Central, was the Director of several companies, and a prime example of an industrialist who gained power and prestige during wartime. He had been Minister of Munitions for three years, Controller of Aircraft Supply and Production, Director General of Purchases, and a member of the Air Council. Glasgow Cathcart had another Conservative member in Robert MacDougall, who was a piano manufacturer and member of the GCC. Moreover, several significant employers managed to retain their seats despite the Labour challenge. Sir G. P. Collins the publisher, kept his Greenock seat until 1936, Sir George Younger held Ayr Burghs, and Glasgow Maryhill was taken by the Conservative shipowner – and member of Greenock Chamber of Commerce – H. Brown in 1924. Clearly, though, Labour's rise brought a break in trend, and the broader social pool of potential MPs meant that the employer interest was not quite as prominent.

Capitalist involvement in civic government
There was little connection between parliamentary politics and civic

---

26. *The Bailie*, 5 Nov. 1919, p. 3; also, E. Wigham, *The Power to Manage*, p. 47.
27. M. Bentley, in K. Brown (ed.), *Essays in Anti-labour History* (London, 1974), p. 42.

politics up until 1914. The *Airdrie and Coatbridge Advertiser* made this
point quite clear in 1892:

> The best representatives on any Council Board are those who will
> act jointly, and independently of petty party spites, jealousies, and
> victories. The true object of all legislation is the carrying out of
> really useful social and sanitary measures which will prove beneficial
> to the community at large.[28]

Local politics, therefore, was seen to be important. Daunton has stated
that 'the industrial bourgeoisie, even if it did not seek representation
in parliament, was actively involved in the difficult task of ensuring
political and social mobility within the major urban cities'.[29] How true
is this of Clydeside?

Research on the administration of the city of Glasgow during the
1830–1912 period shows that of Glasgow's 577 councillors during this
time, 211 (37%) were manufacturers, and 208 (36%) were dealers of
some kind or another. So 73% of Glasgow's town councillors were
involved in some kind of business.[30] Taking the period 1870–1912, we
find a slightly higher percentage of capitalists involved in local politics.
Of the 312 Glasgow councillors during this period, 152 (49%) can be
identified as employers of labour, while 87 (28%) were merchants or
shipowners.[31] If we continue up until to 1920, we find that 35% of
Glasgow's 93 town councillors over this period were employers, and
15% were merchants.[32] Therefore, 50% of Glasgow councillors during
the 1912–1920 period had business interests. The fall in the number of
capitalists involved in municipal politics – from 73% to 50% of total –
may have been a reflection of the tendency for more artisans to become
involved in civic politics. However, despite this decline, the figures show
that throughout the 1870–1920 period municipal politics in Glasgow
was dominated by the employer interest.

Information on the occupations of Lanarkshire's MPs is at best patchy
over our period. However, the evidence does suggest a similar high
involvement by local businessmen in the running of civic affairs. John

28. *Airdrie and Coatbridge Advertiser*, 9 Nov. 1872.
29. M. J. Daunton, '"Gentlemanly Capitalism" and British Industry, 1820–1914', *Past
    and Present* 122 (1989), p. 157.
30. I. Sweeney, 'The Municipal Administration of Glasgow, 1833–1912: Public Service
    and the Scottish Civic Identity', unpublished Ph.D. thesis, University of Strathclyde
    (1990), Volume 2, p. 694.
31. From a list of Glasgow town councilors, 1833–1912, by I. Sweeney. Research note
    by I. Sweeney, Mitchell Library Glasgow, ref. AGN 994.
32. Compiled from *Glasgow Post Office Directory*, 1912–1920.

FIGURE 8. John Colville.

Colville was Commissioner of Supply for the county, a Justice of the Peace, a member of Lanarkshire County Council, and Lord Provost of Motherwell for seven years. Airdrie's town councillors between 1870 and 1890 included J. Brown, house painter and decorator, W. Brown, an ironstone contractor, G. Finlay, a grocer, and D. Martin, a draper.[33] Also, of the seven candidates for the 1873 Airdrie Burgh election, four can be positively identified as employers.[34] Details for Clydebank are also quite sparse. Clydebank was created as a Police Burgh in 1886 under the 1862 Lindsay Act – which allowed for the creation of police burghs in any areas with a population of more than 700. The main impetus behind the formation of the burgh was the parish's inability to deal adequately with the area's rapid population growth due to the rise of shipbuilding in the area and Singer's arrival in 1884.[35] The list of candidates for the first Burgh Commission was dominated by large local employers and small businessmen. For example, the shipbuilders R. T. Napier and J. R. Thomson – from whose shipyard Clydebank subsequently got its name – were candidates, as was the chemical manufacturer E. C. C. Stanford. However, among the other 15 candidates were four grocers, a Clyde Trust manager, and a superintendent at Singer's.[36] Nine years later there were no large employers on the Commission, which was then made up of three grocers, one provision merchant, and a plumber – along with a foreman joiner, a lock keeper, a shipwright, a clerk of works, and a house factor.[37]

It has been said that the thread manufacturers of the Paisley area ensured a high degree of control over their employees through paternalistic policies, such as the provision of company housing and acts of public benevolence.[38] It has also been suggested that Paisley's working class accepted Liberalism until 1924 because they followed the dominant political ideology of their employers: Robert Balderstone, the manager of Clarks, for example, served on Paisley's town council in the 1880s, while Sir Thomas Glen-Coats was MP for West Renfrewshire.[39] However, it would be wrong to imagine that the 'threadocracy' of Paisley also held sway at the civic level. In 1897, for example, Thomas Glen

33. J. MacCarthur, *New Monklands Parish* (Glasgow, no date), pp. 374–381.

34. Minutes of Airdrie Town Council, 1873.

35. J. Hood (ed.), *The History of Clydebank*, pp. 23–31.

36. *Ibid.*, p. 25.

37. *Clydebank Trade Directory* 1893. p. 22.

38. W. Knox, *Hanging By a Thread* (Preston, 1995), pp.122–140. For a re-appraisal of this agreement, see C. M. M. MacDonald, 'Weak Roots and Branches: Class, Gender and the Geography of Industrial Protest', *Scottish Labour History* 33 (1998), pp. 6–31.

39. W. Knox, *Hanging*, p. 128.

Coats was said to be 'sulking in his tent' after the town council had given its support to a rail extension to Barrhead against his wishes.[40]

It is reasonable to assume that a principal reason for Coats not getting his own way over the Barrhead railway was that the make-up of the council favoured smaller capitalists. The occupations of 84 of Paisley's 112 councillors between 1872 and 1915 can be ascertained. Of these, 63 (75%) can be identified as employers – again excluding merchants. There were a few thread manufacturers among these – such as James Clark, and W. H. Coats – however, the overall picture is one of large, medium, and small employers. There were 19 shopkeepers; nine were involved in the building trade; and thirteen (16%) classed themselves as manufacturers. The rest were drawn from across a wide spectrum. James Weir was an upholsterer, Robert Fulton was a packing case maker, W. Leitch was a flesher, Samuel Dougal was a coal merchant, James Barr had an engineering business, and Alex Hair was a soap manufacturer – another soap manufacturer J M MacCallum also served as a town councillor before going on to represent the constituency at parliamentary level. Clearly, therefore, although representatives of Paisley's leading industry were involved in local politics, they by no means dominated its civic administration. What is clear is that the broad range of industrial and commercial employers represented on Paisley Town Council illustrates once again that capital – large-scale and small – had a rigid hold on local politics. This was also the case on the Paisley Parish Council, which was elected every three years. Of the 19 parish councillors who served on the 1907 council – and whose occupations can be determined – 13 (68%) were employers – six of whom also served on the Paisley Town Council.[41]

Down the Clyde at Greenock there was a similar story. The occupations of 75% of the 115 town councillors between 1870 and 1916 can be determined. Of these, 60 (69%) were employers of labour – once again excluding merchants. As the orientation of its chamber of commerce indicates, Greenock was dominated by three principal business interests: sugar refining and brokering, shipbuilding and engineering, and shipping. Like Paisley, representatives from the leading industries of the town were to be found among the town councillors. Eleven (13%) were shipowners or represented shipping companies, ten (11%) were engineers and/or shipbuilders, and six (7%) were engaged in the sugar industry. However, in general – also like Paisley and Glasgow – Greenock's town councillors represented a wide range of business interests,

40. *GH*, 10 April 1897, p. 10.
41. *Paisley Directory*, 1872–1924.

such as sack manufacturers, rope manufacturers, provision merchants, drysalters, tanners, timber merchants, and spirit merchants.

Finally, at Kilmarnock, we find the same picture. In 1879 the list of magistrates on the town council lists a tweed manufacturer, the owner of a cabinet-making business, an engineering company owner, a grocer, and a master builder; the only magistrate who was not a capitalist was a station master. At the same time the Lord Provost of Kilmarnock was the local mine owner, Peter Sturrock.[42] This was the general make-up of the town council of Kilmarnock throughout the period.

The evidence from Glasgow, Greenock, Paisley and Kilmarnock town councils shows quite clearly that businessmen dominated Clydeside's local politics. Those from commercial and legal backgrounds were poorly represented – of Glasgow's councillors between 1870 and 1912 only 73 (23%) had no connections whatsoever with industry or commerce.[43] Many businessmen-councillors also attained posts in civic government. For example, ten of Glasgow's Lord Provosts and 79 of the city's magistrates between 1870 and 1912 were employers.[44] A good example of how this could be used to further business interests is that of R. G. Renfrew. Renfrew was a Glasgow councillor with a successful plumbing business. Moreover, in 1914 he was also President of the Glasgow and West of Scotland Master Plumbers' Association. As a way of stopping the rising tide of direct labour by Glasgow Corporation, Renfrew seconded a motion that the Corporation should only be allowed to employ trade union labour.[45] Not all employer/councillors used their civic positions to further their business interests. However, many were in a position to do this.

Capitalist organisations to combat Socialism
Over the 1867–1914 period, increased state welfarism, the spectre of continental socialism, and the rise of the trade union movement, provoked some of the old 'ruling oligarchy' into forming the Liberty and Property Defence League (LPDL) in 1882. This pressure group set out to 'uphold

42. *Kilmarnock Post Office Directory* 1879, p. 142.
43. Extrapolated from I. Sweeney's list of Glasgow councillors 1833–1912, Mitchell Library AGN 1994.
44. Ibid. B. Aspinwall contrasts the relative apathy towards municipal politics of American businessmen with their Glasgow counterparts, who 'were anxious to serve the city and considered their election a great personal honour'. B. Aspinwall, 'Glasgow Trams and American Politics, 1894–1914', *Scottish Historical Review*, Volume 56 (1977), p. 75.
45. *Plumbing Trade Journal*, Volume 7, Dec. 1914, p. 34. and Volume 8, Oct. 1915, p. 42.

the principle of liberty and guard the rights of labour and property of all kind against undue interference by the state, and to encourage self-help *vs.* state-help'.[46] Although initially representing the propertied interest, the LPDL had a significant input from private capital – possibly because it acted as a counterweight to the TUC – and by 1893, 150 trade associations gave it their support.[47] The main aim of the league was to oppose social legislation in parliament, and it successfully delayed the introduction of comprehensive workmen's compensation legislation until 1897. Moreover, a widespread fear of increasing 'grandmotherly legislation', combined with a strengthening labour movement, resulted in the emergence of similar organisations in the pre-war period: the Free Labour Protection Association – formed after the engineering strike of 1897 – the Employers' Parliamentary Council, formed in 1898, and the Glasgow Citizens' Union (GCU), also formed in 1898.

The principal aim of the GCU was to oppose socialist candidates in municipal and parish elections. This was done through public propaganda work, and by selecting, funding, and supporting non-socialist candidates. The GCU – which by 1906 claimed to have over 3,000 members – was fairly successful in its efforts: in 1908, 12 of its 13 recommended candidates were returned to civic government positions.[48] Lack of records means that the social composition of its membership is impossible to determine with accuracy. However, among its leading members were R. Bird, Secretary of the Liberal Unionist Association, A. Kay, who owned a large retail warehouse in the city, and H. G. Cree, a Glasgow stockbroker who later became Glasgow's Lord Provost. Several of the members achieved high positions in the Guildry, while Cree was a member of the Merchants' House and later President of the GCC.[49] It is highly likely that the membership of the GCU – although mainly property owners – would have included a significant number of employers. Firstly, one of the Union's aims was determined opposition to any form of municipal enterprise of a competitive nature – such as direct labour or municipal trading. Secondly, in 1911 many firms took advantage of the Companies Act and became limited companies. However, because only ratepayers – and not companies – were allowed to vote in municipal elections, many large Glasgow firms became disenfranchised. Alarmed at this reduction in capital's voting power against encroaching socialism, the GCU memorialised Glasgow Corporation,

46. N. Soldon, 'Laissez-Faire as Dogma: The LPDL', in K. D. Brown (ed.), *Essays in Anti-Labour History* (London, 1974), p. 208.
47. *Ibid.*, p. 213.
48. *GH*, 14 Dec., 1908, p. 5.
49. *The Bailie*, 17 Sept. 1920, p. 12. See also *GH*, 14 Dec. 1908, p. 5.

asking for a re-establishment of the franchise to companies; the Corporation, however, decided that this could only be done on a national basis and refused.[50] And thirdly, in July 1919 when the GCU re-appeared wearing the new clothes of the Good Government Committee, its inaugural meeting in the Merchants' Hall was reported to be composed of business people and professionals.[51]

The rise of the Labour Party lent further impetus to middle-class organisation, and the Middle Class Defence League came into being in 1906. This organisation really only existed on paper prior to 1914 – despite an attempt to amalgamate all British anti-socialist organisations into a citizens' union in 1911. In the post-war period, though, increased threats to property gave the movement further stimulus, and especially so on Clydeside.

For many in Britain, the 1918–1920 period was one in which revolution became a realistic scenario. Several right-wing organisations emerged as counter-measures to the socialist/Bolshevik threat – such as the National Alliance of Employers and Employed, which was supported by the Association of British Chambers of Commerce, the Anti-Socialist Union, which had evolved out of the Reconstruction Society formed in 1908, a national propaganda organisation called the Economic League the British Empire Union, and the Liberty League.[52] This was indicative of a rising capitalist class consciousness throughout Britain, which was especially apparent on Clydeside where between 1918 and 1920 almost a quarter of British Anti-Socialist Union meetings took place.[53]

The post-war Middle Class Union – or league – (MCU) was launched with great acclaim in London in March 1919, and a leaflet testified to its position:

> At last the Middle Classes are aroused! They have found their voice … Plainly the middle classes are 'up': apathy is forgotten.

The MCU purported to represent a section of the population which was being increasingly squeezed between organised capital on the one hand, and organised labour on the other:

50. *GH,* 10 Feb. 1911, p. 5; and 17 March 1911, p. 12.
51. *GH,* 22 Oct. 1920, p. 11.
52. On the Economic League, see A. McIvor and H. Paterson 'Combating the Left', in *Militant Workers.* See also S. White, 'Ideology, Hegemony and Political Control: The Sociology of Anti-Bolshevism in Britain, 1918–1920', *Scottish Labour History Society Journal,* Number 9, June 1975.
53. A. Nasibian, Attitudes on Clydeside towards the Russian Revolution, 1917–1924, unpublished M. Litt. thesis, University of Strathclyde, p. 177. See also K. D. Brown, 'The Anti-Socialist Union', in K. D. Brown (ed.), *Essays,* pp. 234–262.

Capital is organised and defends itself. It is also mobile. When menaced it can be easily and quickly transferred to other countries. Organised labour is aggressive and insistent. It demands shorter hours and higher wages – it negotiates with capital (with the approval of the Government – witness the proceedings of the Coal Commission on which non-trading consumers are unrepresented) and obtains great concessions of which the Middle Classes must be the victims.[54]

Ostensibly, therefore, this was a section of the middle class dissociating itself from the 'capitalist class' above it – indeed, one of the league's members defined the 'middle class' as 'everybody who is not a big capitalist or a manual labourer'.[55] Moreover, the first issue of the MCU's journal, *M.C.*, spoke of the need for a secret combination against capital and labour.[56] The Rent Restriction Act of 1915 fell most heavily upon the lower middle class, causing it to distance itself from the higher echelons of the bourgeoisie.[57] The MCU, therefore, may have been a manifestation of this dissatisfaction. However, the degree to which this organisation was motivated against large-scale capital is questionable, as the defence of property remained one of its guiding principles. The Left of the period certainly doubted that this was the case. The *Labour Leader*, for example, exposed many members of the MCU's Grand Council as notorious anti-labour capitalists, and questioned how 'a Union which claims to cater for the shopkeepers, clerks and lower middle classes, should be possessed of sufficient funds to pay for a full page advertisement in *The Times*'.[58]

On Clydeside – where a MCU branch opened only six weeks after the league's first London meeting – the directors of Beardmores and the Bank of Scotland were involved – which, to an extent, supports the *Labour Leader*'s claim.[59] Moreover, the league became quickly and firmly involved in Clydeside's capitalist network. The Glasgow City Business Club immediately joined.[60] Also, Rutherford, the manager of the West of Scotland Guardian Society, became a member. The MCU encouraged the formation of a 'triple alliance' comprising the Clerical Shipping Staffs'

54. MCU leaflet, c. 1919.
55. *The Bystander*, 23 April 1919.
56. This is mentioned in *Christian World*, 1 May 1919.
57. D. McCrone, 'Towards a Principled Society', in T. Dickson and J. Treble (eds), *People and Society in Scotland, Vol. 3, 1914–1990* (Edinburgh, 1992), p. 185.
58. *Labour Leader*, 16 May 1919.
59. A. Nasibian, Attitudes on Clydeside towards the Russian Revolution, 1917–1924, p. 82.
60. *The Bailie*, 25 Feb. 1920.

Guild, the Banking Clerks' Guild, and the Insurance Clerks' Guild.[61] However, not many of Clydeside's industrial elite featured on the branch's governing body – although they may well have been active behind the scenes. The first President was the Glasgow surgeon Professor Sir W. Macewen; and he was followed by J. A. Rudd who owned a successful marine engineering firm. The Honorary Secretary A. Aitken was a solicitor – emphasising once again the interaction of the legal and the commercial spheres – and the Treasurer, D. J. Black, was the private secretary to the Lord Provosts of Glasgow.[62]

The MCU's portrayal of the petite bourgeoisie as being 'ground between the upper and nether millstones of capital and labour' was compelling enough to encourage many on small fixed incomes and those who ran small businesses to become involved.[63] It is difficult to determine the strength of the Clydeside membership with any precision. However, by 1920 there were branches in Glasgow, Greenock, and Bearsden, and the league's rules stated that there had to be a minimum of 250 members in a branch. Moreover, nationally, the MCU claimed to have a membership of 9–10,000 people organised in 50 branches by mid-1919.[64] During the 40 hours strike of 1919 the Clydeside branches of the MCU played a key role. Telegrams were immediately sent to the Prime Minister and Sir Eric Geddes at the Ministry of Transport pledging assistance; 75 MCU members subsequently acted as engineers and stokers, 200 more served as stand-in porters and labourers; and a car pool was organised so that those commuting to and from the city could economise on petrol.[65]

Several conclusions can be drawn from the activities of the MCU. Firstly, like the working class, the middle class was not homogeneous but was constantly changing. Secondly, the activities of the MCU suggest there was a significant degree of lower middle-class identity on Clydeside which matched that of the industrial elites. Thirdly, Clydeside's role as the Scottish base of the MCU may indicate that both capital and labour were more organised here, and presented a greater threat to the class sandwiched between them, than in other parts of the

61. *GH*, 17 March 1919.
62. *The Bailie*, 17 April 1889, and 18 Feb. 1920.
63. It is likely that the organisation was also inspired by the anti-socialist feeling of the time. See K. D. Brown, 'The Anti-Socialist Union, 1908–49', in K. D. Brown (ed.), *Essays in Anti-Labour History* (London, 1974), pp. 234–262.
64. See *The Bailie*, 18 Feb. 1920; also *Newcastle Daily Journal*, 10 April 1919; *Brixton Free Press*, 2 May 1919.
65. *Sunday Post*, 28 Sept. 1919; *The Bailie*, 18 Feb. 1920; see also A. Nasibian, p. 80; also *Motor World*, 20 Oct. 1919.

country. And finally, this collective response to economic pressures by a significant proportion of Clydeside's small employers, underlines yet again that individualism was not the keynote of capitalism.

Collective responses to government intervention
The activities of the MCU during the 40 hours strike of 1919 illustrate that direct involvement in politics was not the only way in which capital could influence the state's relations with labour. Capital was frequently effective as a pressure group in nullifying political decisions. Well before the beginning of our period Clydeside employers used their collective strength to modify potentially profit-threatening legislation. For example, in 1795 the Glasgow Candle and Soap Makers' Society campaigned to bring about the abolition of duties on manufactured candles.[66] Employer organisation within the chambers of commerce was frequently and effectively utilised to put pressure on Members of Parliament to bring about concessions favourable to the business interest. The Scottish Chamber of Manufacturing Industries was established in 1902 specifically for this purpose. Over half of this organisation's Council of Management were Clydeside employers, and the Chamber represented many of Clydeside's most important manufacturing firms – W. H. Coats was a member. The Chamber's main purpose was to protect capital from encroaching government labour legislation, and this was made quite clear by its declaration of intent:

> The objects of the Chamber are to watch in particular the Factory and Workshops Act, and, in general, all legislative proposals affecting manufacturers' interests; also to take such steps as may be necessary to oppose such proposals where prejudicial.[67]

However, employers' associations themselves were also effective pressure groups. The Lanarkshire Coalmasters' Association petitioned against the Truck Bill in 1886, and ensured that modifications were made before the act was passed.[68] In 1899 the Scottish Provision Trade Association attacked the new Food and Drugs Bill, which specified a minimum percentage of butter in butter substitutes. When the bill appeared in 1900, most of the amendments which the Association had called for were granted.[69] In engineering the NWETEA was involved in the fight to abolish sugar bounties. Moreover, its minutes also reveal

---

66. Glasgow Candle and Soap Makers' Society, Minute Book (TD 818/1).
67. *Glasgow Post Office Directory*, 1919–20, p. 180.
68. Lanarkshire Coalmasters' Association Minute Book 1, 22 Feb. 1886.
69. M. Moss, *One Hundred Years of Provisioning in Scotland* (Glasgow, 1989), p. 12.

that the capitalist network was used to the fullest: 'personal influence was being brought to bear upon the Magistrates and Police Court Judges ...'[70] In an effort to safeguard the general interest of the Scottish lead trade, the Scottish Lead Manufacturers' Association formed a committee in 1918 to monitor the Non-Ferrous Metal Industry Bill – then being presented to Parliament.[71] In 1903 the Scottish Coal Exporters' Association began a determined protest against the imposition of Coal Export Duty. In this campaign the SCEA was joined by the Lanarkshire Coalmasters' Association, the Fife and Clackmannan Coalmasters' Association, and several English masters' associations. The result was the complete repeal of Coal Export Duty in 1906.[72] And in 1919 the National Farmers' Union of Scotland, the Scottish Chamber of Agriculture and the Highland Agricultural Society all registered their displeasure at plans to include agricultural labour within the 48-Hour Week Bill. A letter from the NFUS to the Ministry of Labour in October 1919 remarked how 'the introduction of departmental interference as regards working hours will be to the serious detriment of production of food in Great Britain'. The government subsequently decided to exclude farm workers from the bill.[73]

Employer collective pressure, therefore, was easily mustered, and frequently successful, as in the victorious attack on the principle of workmen's compensation. This was a thorny issue amongst employers from its inception in 1880, even although several occupations and accidents were excluded in the early act, and employers could opt out. However, many Clydeside employers looked upon the 1897 bill as being too far-ranging, and some saw it as 'an experiment in Socialist legislation'.[74] Determined employer resistance tempered the eventual contents of the Act. For example, in 1897 the Lanarkshire Coalmasters' Association sent a deputation to Chamberlain to push for modifications to the proposed bill – the very principle of which the LCMA thought unjust. Subsequently, the LCMA was pleased to report that amendments were made at the report stage in the employers' favour.[75]

70. NWETEA, Minute Book 2, 28 Jan. 1907, p. 280.
71. Scottish Lead Manufacturers' Association Minute Book 2, 11 Jan. 1918.
72. Scottish Coal Exporters' Association, Minute Book 1, Nov. 1903; also Directors' Report May 16, 1906. D. M. Stevenson was nominated by the Scottish Coal Exporters' Association in 1919 to give evidence before the Coal Mines Commission regarding the effect of nationalisation on exports of coal. Scottish Coal Exporters' Association, Minute Book 3, 19 May 1919.
73. Ministry of Labour Report, 1919, PRO Lab/2/740/13. See also *North British Agriculturist*, 7 Aug. 1919, p. 582.
74. *GH* 30 June 1897, p. 8.
75. Lanarkshire Coalmasters' Association Minute Book 3, 26 May and 21 July 1897.

When the more extensive 1906 Workmen's Compensation Bill appeared – which included industrial diseases – the EEF was determined to fight it every inch of the way. The EEF had its own Parliamentary Committee which closely monitored the employer interest in Westminster; and in 1906 the Home Secretary received its delegation as the first stage of a Federation campaign to ameliorate the terms of the proposed Act.[76] Fortunately for the EEF, the Clydeside MP George Younger – Member for Ayr Burghs – undertook to move any amendments submitted to him by the Federation. Younger was himself an employer – as well as being a member of the GCC, and a director of the National Bank of Scotland, Lloyds Bank, and the Mercantile Insurance Company – and, although not engaged in the engineering industry, wholeheartedly supported the EEF's stance. Consequently, despite determined opposition from the Labour Party – 'who, on more than one occasion carried amendments against the government' – three main concessions were won for the employers through Younger's efforts. Firstly, in contrast to the 1897 legislation, sub-contractors were now compelled to bear the cost of their own risks. Secondly, the employers won the right to have workmen who claimed to be suffering from industrial diseases examined by company or employers' association doctors. And thirdly, the right of Scottish workers to take their employers to court to seek damages by jury trial – a system under which, according to the EEF, 'litigation had been oppressive' – was abolished. Such a process was now only possible if legal actions were raised at common law in the High Court. This final concession was ironed out after the Parliamentary Committee of the EEF had several meetings with the Solicitor General for Scotland. Throughout, Younger was the key to the employer interest's success, and the EEF minutes record that his assistance had been 'most valuable'.[77]

The EEF was not alone in attacking Workmen's Compensation. The GCC petitioned strongly against the Bill which it thought 'too large an extension of the previous measures, considering how relatively short a time it was since the principle of compensation had been introduced'. The Chamber also believed that certain industrial diseases should be omitted from the Act's coverage.[78] And the Grocers' Federation pressurised the government into altering the legislation so that it applied only to shop assistants in premises employing three or more workers –

76. Minutes of EEF, 20 April 1906, p. 9.
77. Parliamentary Committee of the EEF Annual Report 1906, pp 2–5; also, Parliamentary Committee Annual Report 1907, p. 1. Both reports in EEF Minute Book 3, 1904–1907.
78. Report by the Directors of the GCC, Jan. 1907, p. 31.

and not two or more as had been originally planned.[79] Employer organisation pressure, therefore, helped bring about significant alterations to one of the most important pieces of labour legislation during our period.

The scope of safety legislation was also frequently curbed by capitalist lobbying. We saw in Chapter 3 how a strong employer lobby forced Lloyds to reduce their safety standards, and effective employer combination such as this was often used against government safety legislation too. In 1898, for example, the Siemens Steel Ingot Makers' Association petitioned against the Steam Engine and Boilers (Persons in Charge) Bill, which it thought 'would be very detrimental to the interest of all large users of steam power'.[80] Other associations protested against this legislation too, such as the Lanarkshire Coalmasters' Association, and the Scottish Mine Owners' Defence Association; and, again, amendments were made before the legislation passed into law.[81] In 1905 the SSIMA was petitioning again, this time against proposed safety measures affecting the operation of railway wagons. All the members were asked to provide statements regarding accidents which had occurred over the previous six years which they thought could have been avoided under the proposed act. After receiving this information, a government safety inspector visited several of the members' premises and 'very considerable modifications' were made to the new Act by the Home Office. However, even this was not good enough for the SSIMA. The Association took legal advice, and enlisted the support of the Scottish Steel Makers' Association and the North of England Iron and Steel Makers' Association. Consequently, 'very important and material modifications were made by the effort of joint association' – all for the cost of £372 legal expenses shared by three associations.[82]

Therefore, the idea of a neat correlation between increasing government intervention in industrial safety and the implementation of effective safety measures needs to be re-assessed. In many cases organised employers ensured that significant adjustments were made to legislation before it passed into law. As a final illustration, in 1904 the government proposed to pass safety legislation to protect dock workers. Immediately, the NWETEA and the CSA petitioned against the proposed legislation, and, once again, concessions were won in the employers' favour.[83]

79. *Forward*, 1 Dec. 1906, p. 2.
80. Siemens Steel Ingot Makers' Association, Minute Book 1, 25 May 1898, p. 124.
81. Lanarkshire Coalmasters' Association Minute Book 2, 24 April 1895.
82. Siemens Steel Ingot Makers' Association, Minute Book May 1901-Nov. 1906, 18 May, 1905, p. 128, 3 Aug. 1905, p. 262, 12 Oct., p. 275, 15 Feb. 1906, p. 296, 19 Oct. 1906, p. 324.
83. NWETEA, Minute Book 2, 19 Dec. 1904, p. 462.

It was a similar story with safety at sea. Shipowners had for many years been disgruntled at the Board of Trade's efforts to make the working environment at sea safer, and the initiation of a Royal Commission on Shipping in 1884 caused Clydeside shipowners to form the Clyde Steamship Owners' Association (CSOA) to ensure that they would be properly represented.[84] By 1906, defending its members against state legislation was still this organisation's principal *raison d'être*, and the retiring President reflected on the fact that there had been 13 Commissions of Inquiry concerned with ship-owning matters over a 22-year period.[85]

Clyde shipowners also cultivated close connections with politicians. At the general election of 1885 all of Glasgow's MPs, and all the candidates for election, were interviewed by the CSSOA to find out where they stood regarding shipping legislation.[86] Similarly, in 1892 a conference was held in which both shipping associations exchanged views on shipping matters with parliamentary candidates for Glasgow.[87] The CSOA also saw itself as a 'strong self-protection association' and constantly monitored any bills in the Houses of Parliament that related to the shipping interest.[88]

Small-scale capitalists also managed at times to take the sharp edge off legislation by effective lobbying. The Glasgow and West of Scotland Master Plumbers' Association (GWSMPA) joined a deputation to the House of Commons in 1897 urging the government to make it a law that all Scottish plumbers be registered.[89] Also, in 1922, the GWSMPA formed a joint propaganda committee – along with Clydeside architects and surveyors – to convince the public that private enterprise was cheaper than Glasgow Corporation's direct labour.[90] The issue of direct labour was also of vital concern to the Federation of Master Printers. The government had been contemplating setting up its own printing works since 1906, and during the war began producing food control tickets and other official paperwork. However, much to the consternation of private printers, in 1923 the government plant was still in operation, and there were plans afoot to extend it so that printing could be done for the Admiralty. This spurred the Scottish Alliance of Master Printers (SAMP) and the Federation of Master Printers into action, and all

84. *GH*, 13 Jan. 1887.
85. *GH*, 23, Jan. 1906.
86. CSSOA Minute Book 1, Annual Report 1886, pp. 69–70.
87. Ibid., Directors' Report 1892.
88. Unidentified Newspaper Cutting in CSOA, Minute Book 1, p. 2.
89. *GH*, 30 April 1897, p. 10.
90. *GH*, 9 March 1922, p. 13.

potential MPs were told in no uncertain terms that direct printing of this kind had to be curtailed. The campaign, according the SAMP, met with 'remarkable success'.[91]

Another good example of small employers successfully changing the course of political legislation is that of the Glasgow pawnbrokers. In 1900 there were around 120 pawnbrokers in the city and most of these were members of the Glasgow Pawnbrokers' Association (GPA). This organisation dated from 1851 when it came into being 'to protect its members from the numerous frauds of designing individuals'. However, one of the main services which it offered its members was the ability to protect them from damaging legislation. The GPA was dedicated to pawnbroking reform in its formative years, and in 1872 its persistent lobbying persuaded the government to bring in legislation that would regulate the pawnbroking industry. Once this was achieved, the Association continued to act as a policing agency to ensure there were no infringements of the Act – and it even enlisted female spies to help bring about convictions.[92]

Interference by local government was also successfully curtailed by effective united action. In 1901, for example, the Paisley master bakers resisted their town council's proposal to charge them for collecting their oven ashes – Greenock master bakers presented a similar united front to their local council on exactly the same issue.[93] The Greenock Master Hairdressers' Association was also active regarding legislation. The association had been established primarily to curb competition in the town by coordinating the price of haircuts and shaves. However, it also provided other services to its members – such as legal and medical advice, and mutual insurance – as well as the social dimension illustrated in the previous chapter.[94] Lobbying by the Greenock hairdressers also ensured that they were included in the 1911 Shop Hours Act – and like the Glasgow Pawnbrokers they set up a Vigilance Committee to make sure members and non-members closed their shops at the set times.[95]

The Shop Hours Act of 1911 extended the scope of earlier acts passed in 1892 and 1904, was piloted through the Commons by Churchill, and came into force on May 1, 1911. The legislation provided for a compulsory weekly half-holiday for most shop staff. In London, the Liberty

91. Maclehose Scrapbooks, Volume 201, 1922, p. 58.
92. W. Weir, *Glasgow Pawnbrokers' Association, The First Hundred Years 1851–1951* (Glasgow, no date).
93. *British Baker*, 13 Dec. 1901, p. 707.
94. *Ibid.*, 14 April 1912.
95. Minute Book of Greenock Hairdressers' Association, 3 June 1909.

and Property Defence League held a special meeting to discuss the terms of the Act, and the Federation of Grocers' Associations of the UK – which represented almost 140 organisations by 1910 – pledged to fight the implementation of what it called 'Winston's little bill'.[96] On Clydeside the bill had a mixed reception. Traders with expensive rented shops in the likes of Argyle Street, Union Street, and Renfield Street, expressed alarm at the new legislation.[97] Also, the Glasgow Grocers' and Provision Merchants' Association campaigned against the bill from 1910, and pressurised local MPs to vote against it.[98] However, many shopkeepers colluded to turn the terms of the bill to their mutual advantage. Glasgow's retail tailors and clothiers, for example, met in November 1912 to decide on the most suitable day for the weekly half-day closure.[99] The West of Scotland Wholesale Confectioners' Association persuaded Glasgow's town council to exclude their trade from the compulsory half-day holiday.[100] The Glasgow Master Boot Repairers' Association – like the Greenock hairdressers – welcomed such legislation as a way of ensuring a more even playing field, and successfully petitioned to have their trade included under the new Act.[101] And this was also the point of view of the Scottish Grocers' Federation (SGF). The SGF consistently pushed for stiffer regulation of opening hours in the grocery trade, and had welcomed the compulsory early closing of shops under the wartime Defence of the Realm Act.[102]

The Scottish Master Bakers' Association (SMBA) also represented a large number of small capitalists, and was determined to protect the baking trade from unwanted government legislation. This particular employers' association came into being in 1891 for precisely this reason. Unlike their Scottish colleagues – who baked a standard-sized loaf – English bakers were legally bound to weigh customers' bread at the point of delivery. The Master Bakers' Association (MBA) decided that the only way to end this time-wasting practice was to put pressure on the government to change the law. However, Scottish members of the MBA were deeply troubled at what they saw as 'blundering and tinkering with the bread laws' by their English counterparts, and were alarmed at the prospect of unnecessary legislation being imposed on

---

96. *Scottish Leather Trader* 22 Oct., 1910, p. 5.
97. *GH*, 2 Jan. 1911, p. 4.
98. *The Scottish Trader*, 15 Jan. 1910, p. 7; and 5 Feb. 1910, p. 9.
99. *The Tailoring World*, Nov. 1912, Number 5, p. 39.
100. *Confectioners' Union*, 15 Feb. 1913, p. 215.
101. *Shoe and Leather Trader*, 16 May 1912, p. 16.
102. *The Fingerpost*, Aug. 1921, p. 13.

the Scottish trade. It was primarily over this disagreement that the
SMBA came into being as a breakaway section of the MBA.[103]

Soon after the formation of the SMBA, more alarm over impending
government legislation resulted in the creation of an important sub-
section. This time the offending legislation arose from a government
campaign aimed at eradicating underground bakehouses. In 1891, it was
estimated that over half of London's bread was baked in underground
bakeries, and inspectors were horrified by the insanitary conditions they
found in many of these premises – some being periodically flooded by
sewage.[104] Consequently, the 1901 Factory Act stipulated that owners
of bakehouses – in Scotland and England – which were more than three
feet below pavement level had to apply to their local authority for a
certificate of fitness, or cease trading. As a result, many small Scottish
family-owned bakeries faced closure if they failed to obtain the necessary
certificate by January 1st. 1904. Once again the response by small-scale
producers was a concerted one, and to this end the Underground Bakehouse Section of the SMBA appeared in March 1903. This offered advice
on sanitary matters – drawing on the expertise of an Edinburgh-based
engineer – and was instrumental in ensuring that many small bakeries
obtained the crucial certification.[105]

The Glasgow drinks trade fought an intensive war on two fronts:
against government intervention on the one hand, and prohibitionists
on the other. To a great extent this battle was fought out within the
sphere of civic government. The drinks trade offers a prime example of
how politics and trade regulation intertwined.[106] Like the grocery trade
and many other small-scale industries, the nature of the drink industry
meant that collective action was the sensible course to follow. In 1878
around 1,000 publicans and hoteliers were members of the Glasgow
Wine and Beer Trade Association.[107] Such collaboration was further
stirred by the sustained attacks the industry had to endure from the
1880s. The Glasgow-based Scottish Licensees' Mutual Insurance Association (SLMIA) was established in 1899, and by 1905 there were 154
members. Its main function was to insure members against any legal
costs incurred in defending their licenses against attacks by the anti-drink

103. *British Baker*, Oct. 1891, p. 804.
104. *British Baker Confectioner and Purveyor*, May 1894, p. 723.
105. The sub-section also went under the name of the Master Bakers' Defence Asso-
    ciation. *British Baker*, 20 March 1903.
106. I. Sweeney, 'Local Party Politics and the Temperance Crusade: Glasgow, 1890–
    1902', *Scottish Labour History Journal*, Number 27 (1992).
107. Royal Commission on Grocers' Licenses (Scotland) 1878 [Cd. 1941], p. 251.

lobby.[108] Also in Glasgow there was the Glasgow and West of Scotland Licensed Grocers' Association (GWSLGA). It, too, was a trade defence organisation established 'to protect the rights of those holding grocers' licenses in all parliamentary, local, or licensing court proceedings'.[109]

By 1908 the situation had worsened. Stiffer drink legislation and determined attacks by the anti-drink faction had caused a 6% drop in the number of Scottish alcohol vendors over a three-year period.[110] In response to the widespread alarm which permeated the industry the Glasgow Licensed Trade Defence Association (GLTDA) was established, and immediately claimed to represent 75% of the city's drink trade.[111] The GLTDA mobilised the disparate groups involved in the trade, and by 1907 it had spent over £1000 defending its members from attacks on their licenses. However, like the GWSLGA the organisation also kept a watchful eye on any potentially damaging acts which could prove harmful to a trade which it maintained was already overburdened by too much legislation.[112]

In the other camp was the Glasgow Citizens' Vigilance Committee (GCVC). This rather shady organisation came into being in 1902 intent on enforcing stricter licensing laws and preventing drunkenness. It immediately began opposing the issue of public house licences, and attempted to block the renewal of existing ones. This was done by canvassing selected areas of the city and enlisting members of the public to testify against licensees in the licensing courts – the organisation employed a lawyer whose sole duty was to oppose the issuing of drink licences. Many of Glasgow's leading teetotalers were involved with the Committee, such as the future Lord Provost D. M. Stevenson – a founder member of the Scottish Coal Exporters' Association and the Scottish Labour Colony Association – and Sir William Bilsland of the Glasgow Master Bakers' Association.[113]

For a final example of how capital could effectively negate the intended effect of legislation we turn to the solicitor Thomas Biggart, whose role in forging employer unity on the Clyde is examined in Chapter 7. Biggart was an experienced lobbyist who had frequently

108. Scottish Licensees' Mutual Insurance Association, Minute Book 1, Jan. 1899, and Feb. 1905.

109. *Glasgow Post Office Directory* 1886–87, p. 125.

110. *GH*, 12 Sept. 1908, p. 10.

111. *GH*, 28 Jan. 1908, p. 7; 8 Jan. 1908. The SLMIA supported this new organisation and donated £100 to the cause in 1908. Scottish Licensees' Mutual Insurance Association, Minute Book 1, March 1908.

112. *GH*, 28 Jan. 1908, p. 7.

113. *GH*, 8 Jan. 1908, p. 8.

spoken up for the employer interest in the pre-war period, and when war broke out his knowledge and advice were eagerly sought by several government bodies. One of his most important services to Clydeside capital, though, was his involvement in the employers' crusade to recoup a significant amount of Excess Profit Duty (EPD). This was imposed by the wartime government as part of the *quid pro quo* for labour's loss of bargaining rights. Towards the end of the war Biggart joined a three-man committee to negotiate the termination of EPD with the Chancellor of the Exchequer, and later became a member of the Board of Referees to deal with appeals from capitalists regarding EPD. So successful was Biggart in clawing a proportion of the duty back into industrialists' pockets that *The Bailie* in 1925 eulogised his achievements, declaring that this was 'the greatest repayment that has ever been made by the Treasury of this country or any other State'.[114]

114. *The Bailie*, 1 July 1925.

CHAPTER SIX

Clydeside Capital and Labour Relations

Effective trade unionism evolved slowly in Scotland. In 1892, 3.7% of the adult population in Scotland were trade unionists, compared to 4.9% south of the Border. Several reasons have been put forward to explain this. Many Scottish workers viewed trade unionism as superfluous in industries – such as engineering and shipbuilding – where the employers normally only retained a number of skilled workers when trade took a downturn.[1] Also, the growth of collective bargaining was retarded by occupational and sectarian sectionalism – as well as by an inward-looking nationalism.[2] Employer hostility was also significant and this will be examined in the next chapter. However, collective bargaining did strengthen in Scotland over time, and this was certainly the case on Clydeside where employers and workers increasingly realised the benefits of negotiation as opposed to outright conflict.[3]

The heavy industries

The Clydeside engineering industry was a bastion of highly skilled craft labour for most of our period – 60% of the total workforce in this industry were classed as skilled in 1914. However, even when workers had high levels of skill, effective trade unionism could still be problematic.[4] In the early 1860s, workers in the main British shipbuilding regions managed to increase their wages by picking off employers one at a time. However, in 1865 – during a downturn in trade – the situation was reversed, and this was especially so on the Clyde. Here, the bosses combined to defeat the workers over the issue of a nine-hour day, and by 1866 membership of the Boilermakers' Society had collapsed. The situation was so bad that two years later its Glasgow branch – which was now the strongest in the country – could only muster 41 members.

1. S. G. Checkland, *The Upas Tree, Glasgow 1875–1975* (1976), p. 15.
2. W. Knox, 'Class Work And Trade Unionism in Scotland', p. 112.
3. A. J. McIvor, 'Were Clydeside employers more autocratic?', in W. Kenefick and A. J. McIvor (eds), *Roots of Red Clydeside* (Edinburgh, 1996), p. 40.
4. W. Knox, *Industrial Nation* (Edinburgh, 1999), p. 206.

By the beginning of our period, then, only 10% of Clyde shipyard workers were unionised.[5]

In contrast the employers managed to sustain a united front. Between 1872 and 1876 the Iron Trades Employers' Association – formed in 1872 – successfully organised a campaign to increase working hours by insuring its members against the financial costs of industrial action.[6] In 1876 a strike by 400 shipyard riveters resulted in a lockout, in which any unfinished work was completed by scab labour and apprentices.[7] The following year the shipbuilding employers felt confident enough to resist their shipwrights' demands for a pay increase, and, according to the union, 'assumed an offensively dignified position'. However, to make sure that this position was maintained, the employers set up their own Vigilance Committee to prevent any backsliding in the ranks.[8] The ensuing employer victory was soon followed by victory over the iron-workers too – despite the fact that their union had a reported strike fund of around £45,000.[9] Organised capital, therefore, seemed to hold all the cards at this time, and the engineering workers' failure to hold on to the 51-hour week during the 1878 recession was mainly due to strong employer unity.[10] By 1880, though, things seemed to be improving, and membership of the Amalgamated Society of Engineers (ASE) now stood at 54,000 across Britain.[11] But on the Clyde the employers still retained the upper hand. The CSA remained intolerant of negotiation and frequently used scab labour to maintain control – indeed, it was only in the latter years of the decade that the Boilermakers' Society was grudgingly recognised by the major Clyde employers.[12] Clearly, then, from the mid-1860s to 1880 the organised employers were in the driving seat and the stick was being used much more than the carrot.

Throughout the 1890s, though, collective bargaining began to replace older confrontational methods of labour control, and this was a strategy

5. *Ibid.*, p. 117. Disgruntlement with the Boilermakers' Society following this defeat led to the formation of a breakaway Scottish union. W. H. Fraser. *A History of British Trade Unionism*, 1700–1998 (Basingstoke, 1999), p. 60.
6. A. J. McIvor, *Organised Capital*, p. 44.
7. *GH*, 4 Feb. 1876.
8. Monthly Report of Associated Ironmoulders of Scotland, Jan. - Feb. 1877, p. 39. SRA TD/389/24–27
9. *GH*, 15 Oct. and 15, 18, and 10 Nov. 1877.
10. W. Knox, *Industrial Nation*, p. 120; W. H. Fraser, *A History of British Trade Unionism*, p. 61.
11. W. H. Fraser, *A History of British Trade Unionism*, p. 73.
12. J. Foster, 'Class', in A. Cooke *et al.* (eds), *Modern Scottish History* (East Linton, 1998), p. 223; see also letters in *Engineering*, Oct. 1880, p. 319, and *The Engineer*, 7 June 1886, p. 29.

that also called for a high level of employer unity. The Glasgow District Engineers' and Boilermakers' Association was established in 1892 when the Clyde engineering employers split from the shipbuilders, and, with the formation of the Engineering Employers' Federation (EEF) in 1896, became the NWETEA. The EEF was the first nationwide employers' association for engineering employers, and from its inception was dedicated to ensuring that its members retained their right to manage in the face of trade union interference – and especially locally organised trade union interference.[13] This was achieved by a combination of two strategies. On the one hand, older authoritarian methods of labour control and surveillance were retained. For example, the NWETEA could quickly organise a lockout if the situation required it; secret payments were made to a strike-breaking organisation called the National Free Labour Association; and the names of blacklisted workers were routinely circulated amongst the member firms.[14] However, on the other hand the NWETEA blunted the strike weapon by fostering a network of procedural agreements that encompassed most of Clydeside engineering's workforce. Within these agreements labour disputes that could not be settled at the workplace had to be passed up through various tiers of negotiation – while work continued. Graph 6.1 gives some idea of the breadth of this system regarding wage negotiation.

A good example of heavy-handed tactics being used by the engineering employers was the lockout of 1898. This dispute arose over the Amalgamated Society of Engineer' (ASE) demand for an eight-hour day, but quickly centred on the issue of the engineering employers' right to manage. One hundred and eighty firms were initially involved in the EEF's crusade. However, by the end of the dispute over 700 companies supported the employers' campaign, and 76 (11%) of these were Clydeside firms.[15] As the lockout progressed, some of the smaller Clydeside

13. W. H. Fraser, *A History of British Trade Unionism*, p. 86.
14. NWETEA Private Letter Book 1, Letter of Thomas Biggart to James Robertson, 10. Oct. 1896. For an account of the activities of the National Free Labour Association see G. Alderman 'The National Free Labour Association: Working Class Opposition to New Unionism in Britain', in W. J. Mommsen and H. G. Husung (eds), *The Development of Trade Unionism in Great Britain and Germany 1880–1914* (London, 1985), pp. 302–311.
15. EEF booklet entitled 'List of the Federated Engineering and Shipbuilding Employers who Resisted the Demand for a 48 Hour Week'. Modern Records Centre MSS 237/4/5/1. The only significant employer on the river to refuse to join the lockout was Fairfields. This company maintained that the dispute was purely in aid of a 'minority of London Masters' who were using the NWETEA to fight their battles. Fairfields was expelled from the Association for this breach of discipline but was allowed to rejoin two years later. NWETEA Minute Book 2, April 1897 and 14 Jan. 1900.

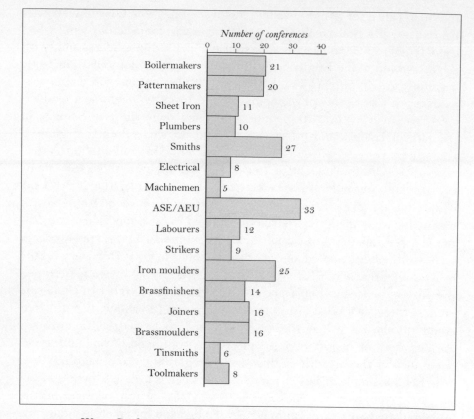

Number of conferences

Boilermakers	21
Patternmakers	20
Sheet Iron	11
Plumbers	10
Smiths	27
Electrical	8
Machinemen	5
ASE/AEU	33
Labourers	12
Strikers	9
Iron moulders	25
Brassfinishers	14
Joiners	16
Brassmoulders	16
Tinsmiths	6
Toolmakers	8

GRAPH 6.1. Wage Conferences Affecting Clydeside Engineering Employees, 1892–1924. *Source*: *EEF Wage Movements, 1889–1924.*

companies began to suffer serious financial hardship. Ultimately, though, the financial muscle of the NWETEA proved strong enough to sustain the fight, and a fund of £50,000 was made available to help the smaller companies. This was supplemented by donations from non-member employers, who, although not affected by the industrial action, all identified with the plight of those who were.[16] The effectiveness of employer

16. Glasgow Federated Shipbuilding and Engineering Employers, Letter Book. Letter from Biggart to Fullerton, Hodgart and Barclay Ltd., 9 Nov. 1897. During the 1897–98 dispute the Association had depended upon funds from outside sympathisers to give it the financial stamina to defeat the engineers. The Federation, however, thought this too unreliable a method of developing a fighting fund, and in 1913 a Subsidy Scheme was initiated. Every member paid a levy, and during disputes firms were paid out of the fund once their operatives had struck for a minimum of 14 days. The name of the scheme was changed to the 'Indemnity Fund' in 1924. Letter from EEF (London) to J. H. Carruthers, Polmadie Iron Works. UGD/333/1/6/1.

collectivism, then, should not be gauged solely by the numerical strength of their employers' association, as overall employer solidarity – sustained through the hidden capitalist network – was an important factor too. In the years after the lockout there is little evidence of any fading away of employer unity. In 1907, during a dispute involving Clyde boiler-makers, the close connection between the NWETEA and the CSA was put to good effect once again, and the assistance of fellow employers in the north-east of England was mustered to help ensure a speedy employer victory.[17]

The lockout cost the ASE £658,000 and pushed the union to the verge of bankruptcy.[18] More importantly, the terms of settlement which followed the 1897 victory gave the engineering employers virtual *carte blanche* to enforce control over shop-floor practices and to end trade union restrictions once and for all. However, no major assault took place; but the reasons the employers drew back from the brink were more to do with market pragmatism than through any failure of resolve. Most engineering and shipbuilding companies produced bespoke capital goods, and this – combined with the abundant pools of skilled labour at the employers' disposal – acted as a disincentive to any radical break with tried and tested craft-centred production – production that depended upon the apprenticeship system.[19] The management of William Weir's, for example – which was one of the most authoritarian employers in the region – found that despite extensive modernisation and re-tool-ing, it still had to employ highly skilled engineers to complete its specification-built orders.[20]

It was a similar story in shipbuilding. The Clyde shipbuilders were an effective fighting force over this period. In the lockout of 1877, for example, employer unity held fast for a crucial eight weeks – by which time the men were forced to go back on the masters' terms. Shortly after this dispute the CSA became involved in another lockout of iron-workers. Here again, employer unity won the day – with the assistance of the shipbuilders in the North of England – and a comment in *The Times* summed up the power of inter-regional employer unity:

Great employers like great Monarchs are entitled to enter into

17. NWETEA Minute Book 2, 3 Oct. 1906, pp. 178 and 182.
18. W. H. Fraser, *A History of British Trade Unionism*, p. 86.
19. See, for example, E. H. Lorenz, *Economic Decline in Britain: The Shipbuilding Industry, 1890–1917* (Oxford, 1991), *passim*. For a view highlighing the waning of employer unity in the aftermath of the lockout, see A. McKinlay and J. Zeitlin, 'The Meaning of Managerial Prerogative: Industrial Relations and the Organisation of Work in British Engineering, 1880–1939', *Business History* 31 (1989), pp. 32–47.
20. A. McKinlay, *Employers and Skilled Workers*, p. 38.

alliances for the protection of their interests; and if so, a great
league on the Clyde, extended to the Wear, the Tyne, the Humber,
and the Thames, is simply a choice in policy which the employers
may resort to.[21]

During the 1902 dispute a similar alliance was put into play – during
which the Clyde shipbuilders displayed a distinctively harder attitude
towards trade unionism than their English colleagues. The balance of
power, then, was firmly with the employers; and this power was further
enhanced in 1907 when the Shipbuilding Trades' Agreement delegated
a disciplining role to the Boilermakers' Society, thus providing the bosses
with an agency that could control any worker agitation at site level.[22]
A downturn in the trade cycle in the early years of the twentieth
century, combined with a weakening of trade union bargaining power,
caused the number of trades disputes to fall.[23] However, despite having
the upper hand, the Clyde shipbuilders – like the engineers – remained
committed to tried and tested labour-intensive production methods that
called for highly skilled labour, and it was not really until the mid-1920s,
and the acceptance of the multiple punch, that craft-based methods of
building ships were seriously challenged.[24]
With the Clydeside employers' long tradition of success at controlling
a weak labour movement, labour's enhanced bargaining power during
the First World War came as a shock.[25] The employers were suddenly
faced with wage demands on an unprecedented scale. In 1916, for
example, the Scottish Brassfounders' Union asked for a 100% increase
on pre-war rates.[26] Demands such as this were submitted to the Committee of Production which – to the consternation of the employers –
largely marginalised them. In 1917, for example, the Scottish Employers'
Federation of Iron and Steel Founders (SEFISF) complained bitterly to
the Ministry of Munitions that it had not been consulted over a decision
to grant engineers and iron moulders a 13% wage increase. The Ministry
did not even bother to reply.[27] That same year many of the workers at
Glenfield and Kennedy's works in Kilmarnock – where company paternalism had long ensured untroubled labour relations – decided to take a

21. *The Times*, 30 May 1877, p. 6.
22. R. Price, *Masters, Unions and Men* (London, 1980), p. 205.
23. W. H. Fraser, *A History of British Trade Unionism*, p. 105.
24. W. Knox, *Industrial Nation*, p. 210.
25. W. H. Fraser, *A History of British Trade Unionism*, p. 134.
26. Kilmarnock and District Engineering Employers' Association, Minute Book 2,
    Feb. 1916.
27. Scottish Employers' Federation of Iron and Steel Founders, Minute Book 2, Oct.
    1917, p. 332.

week's rest period. The trade union argued that this should be classed as a holiday and that the company should pay overtime rates to those who continued to work. The Committee of Production agreed with this demand.[28]

However, despite such attacks on managerial prerogative the employers still managed to retain a sufficient degree of control over labour relations. For example, when the Ministry of War Act abolished leaving certificates in 1917, the NWETEA simply told its members to resort to a system of circulating inquiry notes before employing any new workers.[29] Moreover, although wage advances were conceded, most were classed as war wages on the understanding that they would be revised after the war – and this was generally the case. Finally, the experiences of war production bolstered employer unity, and many employers' associations increased their membership during and after the war. For example, six Clydeside firms joined the SEFISF in 1917 alone and numerous others contacted the Federation for advice. The first steps were also taken towards forming a federation of English and Scottish ironfounders.[30] The shipbuilders Browns and Inglis – already members of the CSA – joined the West of Scotland Iron and Steel Founders' Association in 1918, along with William Weir's.[31] And 11 Ayrshire iron founders joined the Kilmarnock and District Engineering Employers' Association in 1920 – leaving only four Ayrshire foundries unaffiliated.[32] With such strengthening of solidarity, organised Clydeside capital found itself in a strong position to stamp out many of the workers' wartime gains when the post-war boom came to an end.

Mining

Trade unionism in coal mining was also difficult to achieve and sustain. In the 1860s worker organisation in the Scottish coal field had been practically smashed. And the workers remained difficult to organise effectively – due in some measure to sectarian rivalry. However, from the 1900s the situation gradually changed and membership of the Lanarkshire Miners' Union increased from 30,000 to 40,000 between 1900 and 1914.[33] By this time there were almost 600,000 miners in the Miners'

28. Ibid., 31 Aug. 1916.
29. Scottish Coppersmiths' Employers' Association Minute Book 2, 27 Sept. 1917, p. 173.
30. Ibid., 7 Nov. 1917.
31. West of Scotland Iron and Steel Founders' Association, Minute Book 2, 25 Sept. 1918.
32. Kilmarnock and District Engineering Employers' Association, Minute Book 2, 22 Oct. 1920.
33. W. Knox, *Industrial Nation*, pp. 116, 159 and 161.

Federation, and coal mining now had a higher density of trade unionists than any other industry.

Organisation amongst the employers tended to follow the same pattern. In the earlier part of the period, labour relations in the pits tended to be dealt with at company level, where paternalism – frequently involving the provision of company housing – normally ensured that managerial prerogative was sustained.[34] However, increasing organisation amongst the miners persuaded the employers that a collective response was necessary. The formation of the Lanarkshire Coalmasters' Association (LCA) in 1887 – initially encompassing 48 member firms and 69 collieries – was a direct response to trade union growth.[35] The main issue facing the LCA in the late 1880s was the employers' demand to move to a system of sliding-scale payment – normally a successful form of procedural control. Despite workers' resistance this was achieved in 1887, although it had to be abandoned two years later when low prices made it unworkable. Throughout the 1890s the LCA – assisted by its strong links with other Scottish masters' associations – regulated the wages paid throughout the Lanarkshire coalfield. In 1898 it amalgamated with the Airdrie and Slamannan Association – which meant that 80% of the total coal output of the Lanarkshire field was now produced by LCA member firms.[36] In general, though, the organised employers remained lukewarm to the idea of collective bargaining, and this was a characteristic of Scottish mine owners in general. During the strike of 1894, for example, only 30,000 of the 70,000 strikers were members of a trade union – although workshop organisation in Scottish coal mining was an important factor.[37] However, in 1899 the LCA recognised the Lanarkshire Miners' County Union, and this indicates that a more accommodating attitude towards collective bargaining was beginning to form.

The need to keep up with increasing workforce organisation, then, was of paramount concern to the employers. Consequently, in 1909, following the expansion of the Miners' Federation into a national body, the LCA sought closer affiliation with its English counterparts, and its minutes record that the decision was taken because 'the time has come when a strong combination of the colliery owners should be made to

---

34. See R. D. Corrins, William Baird and Company, Ph.D. thesis, University of Strathclyde (1974), pp. 360–373; also J. L. Carvel, *The Coltness Iron Company* (Edinburgh, 1948), pp. 55–64.
35. LCA Minute Book 1, 19 Jan., 1887.
36. LCA Minute Book 3, 16 Nov. 1898.
37. W. Knox, *Industrial Nation*, p. 157.

meet any concerted action on the part of the Miners' Federation'.[38] The fighting stance of the LCA was maintained up until the First World War, and in 1912 the Association's members was still resorting to the frequent use of the bloc – the non-employment of striking workers.[39]

Like many organised employers, the LCA faced a serious labour shortage during the war when a large number of miners signed up for armed service – a loss of manpower that was only halted in 1916 when the government put an end to recruitment of miners. In the early stages of the war the LCA pleaded unsuccessfully with the government to suspend the eight-hour day, which the miners had won in 1908.[40] Moreover, like the metal trades' employers, the mine owners also operated in disrupted markets, and eventually saw the government taking full control of the industry in 1917.[41]

In general, worker radicalism in mining over the 1910–1920 period was more apparent at the national level – where it was directed towards the broader question of ownership – than at the local level.[42] The Sankey Commission's reports of 1919 largely condemned private ownership, recommended nationalisation or joint control, and upheld the miners' claims for a seven-hour day, a curtailment of profits, and a backdated pay award.[43] During the intense propaganda campaign orchestrated by the Miners' Association of Great Britain (MAGB), 300 MPs signed a memorial condemning the idea of nationalisation. This campaign successfully convinced Lloyd George that nationalisation should be avoided for the time being.[44] National employer unity in coalmining, therefore, successfully 'put nationalisation to sleep'.[45]

The LCA was completely in step with the MAGB's stance throughout this campaign and in the general strike of miners that followed. Lanarkshire mine owners rejected the idea of joint control, and resolved that if changes had to be made, then nationalisation was the only

38. LCA Minute Book 5, 3 Aug. 1909, p. 39.
39. LCA Minute Book 8, 29 Oct. 1913.
40. LCA Minute Book 10, 20 Jan. 1915, p. 4. The Glasgow Chamber of Commerce also sent a letter to the Prime Minister asking him to suspend the Act.
41. For the State's involvement with the wartime coal industry, see B. Supple, *The History of the British Coal Industry, Volume 4, 1913–1946* (Oxford, 1987), pp. 70–116. For the South Wales miners' strike that precipitated state control, see C. Wrigley, *David Lloyd George and the British Labour Movement* (London, 1976), pp. 122–128.
42. H. Gospel, 'Markets, institutions, and the development of national collective bargaining in Britain: a comment on Adams', *Economic History Review*, 51, 3 August 1998, p. 592.
43. B. Supple, *A History of the British Coal Industry*, p. 130.
44. *Ibid.*, p. 138.
45. *Ibid.*, p. 147.

option.[46] By this time the LCA had 50 members, and its propaganda committee petitioned local MPs and drummed up public support for the employers' cause. In line with other MAGB district associations, the Lanarkshire association resolved that miners' wages should be reduced when government control of the industry ceased – as guaranteed profits to the owners would stop on that date. The result was a four month national coal strike. During this dispute the Lanarkshire masters' propaganda committee was again active, and advertisements were placed in newspapers to publicise the coalmasters' position – much of this paid for by the MAGB.[47] Voluntary scab labour was also used by the LCA during the dispute, and a donation of £100 was made to the National Free Labour Association in April 1922.[48]

Throughout the period, therefore, employers in the Lanarkshire coal-field effectively used their collective strength to ensure that managerial prerogative was maintained. Compared to the engineers and ship-builders, though, the coalmasters had greater difficulty making procedural control an effective management strategy. In coalmining, as in engineering and shipbuilding, employer combination did not put a stop to trade union growth. However, the organised employers managed to retain their control of the workplace, and increasing trade union strength was not allowed to undermine this.

Building

As in most Scottish industries, trade unionism in the building trade was patchy. It was also undermined by sectarianism, sectionalism, and by demarcation issues – for example, between masons and bricklayers.[49] However, in several of the skilled trades the workers were well organised and had long-established procedural agreements with the employers.

The Glasgow Master Masons' Association (GMMA) held its first annual conference with the workers in 1887.[50] Industrial relations prior to this had been volatile. The union managed to win a nine-hour day in 40 Scottish towns by 1870, and two years later the Glasgow workers

---

46. LCA Minute Book 12, 24 March 1919, p. 37.
47. Ibid., 16 Jan. 1921, p. 75.
48. Ibid., 22 April 1921, p. 188. This continued the LCA's long association with non-union labour agencies, as in 1897 it had been a member of the Free Labour Protection Association. A. Renfrew, 'Mechanisation and the Miner: Work, Safety and Labour Relations in the Scottish Coal Industry', Ph.D. thesis, University of Strathclyde (1997), p. 219.
49. W. Knox, *Industrial Nation*, p. 159.
50. See H. Clegg *et al.*, *A History of British Trade Unions Since 1889*, Volume 1 (Oxford, 1964), p. 155.

demanded weekly pay.[51] During the four-week strike that followed, Edinburgh employers locked out their own workers in support of their fellow employers in Glasgow. This ploy put extra pressure on the Glasgow branch of the men's union and helped ensure that the employers won the day.[52] In 1878 there was a two-month unofficial stoppage during the slump caused by the collapse of the Glasgow Bank, and this also ended with the men going back on the employers' terms.[53] And another strike in 1883 was again sparked off by the men's demand for weekly pay. In the aftermath of this dispute, though, the employers began to realise that collective bargaining was a less troublesome method of labour control than open conflict, and annual conferences with the workers' representatives were established four years later.[54]

Once again this is indicative of the turning away from hire-and-fire management that was apparent by the beginning of the century. This was recognised by a contributor to *Engineering* in 1901 who said 'the growing movement towards organisation among employers and workmen both affords the perfect machinery which should be installed in place of the old order'.[55] However, the old order died slowly, and not all the building trade employers' associations could boast such a smooth transition to rational collective bargaining as the master masons.

The Glasgow Master Painters' Association was formed in 1860 specifically 'to resist the demands of the operatives'.[56] The aftermath of the 1860 strike saw the initiation of annual conferences between employers and workers at which working rules were negotiated, and peaceful conditions existed until 1874. However, that year the workers attempted to break out of procedural control by approaching individual masters for a pay rise – and not the employers' association as dictated in the procedure. Industrial action was avoided in this instance, and a compromise deal was struck.[57] However, when the workers attempted similar divide-and-rule tactics two years later it backfired. The resolve of the masters was stiffened, the help of non-association employers was enlisted, the strength of the association doubled, and the subsequent

51. W. Knox, *Industrial Nation*, p. 120.
52. *The Builder*, 6 July 1872, p. 522.
53. Royal Commission on Labour, 1893 Digest of Evidence, Volume 2, p. 67.
54. Minutes of Glasgow Master Masons' Association (GMMA), Book 1, April 1887.
55. *Engineering*, Volume 20, 1901, p. 924.
56. There was already a master painters' association in Greenock. *The Scottish Decorators' Quarterly Review*, June 1956, p. 130. The Glasgow bricklayers until 1885 had settled all their disputes by arbitration. In that year, though, the there was an 11-week strike involving the importation of blackleg workers from England. Minutes of Glasgow Trades Council, June 1885, p. 36.
57. See *GH*, 1 May 1875, p. 5; and 4 May, p. 5.

strike collapsed.[58] The next major dispute occurred in the spring of 1880 – in response to a wage reduction – but by this time the masters' association was affiliated to the recently formed Scottish Master Painters' Association – established in 1878 – and moral and financial assistance was quickly enlisted from other parts of Scotland. However, despite this, the strike lasted three months and severely tested the masters' resolve.[59]

Compared to the master masons, then, unity among Glasgow master painters was difficult and there was no simple progress from hostility to accommodation. Despite the implementation of collective bargaining machinery, significant tensions occasionally surfaced which were only resolved by open conflict. This was apparent to the Secretary of the Association in 1905 when he recommended in a general meeting that 'provision should be made for strengthening the GMPA financially and otherwise so as to put it on an equal footing with that of the workmen regarding future trials of strength'.[60] Trade unionism amongst the plumbers had a long history. There was a plumbers' trade union in Glasgow in 1865 called the APOS – although the meaning of these initials has been lost – and this organisation became incorporated within the Union of Operative Plumbers of Scotland in 1872. In 1891 the Scottish Operative Plumbers' Protection and Benefit Federal Union was formed as a breakaway from the British UOPA, which then later merged with the UOPA of Scotland.[61]

We saw in Chapters 2 and 3 that employer combination in the plumbing trade was initially motivated by a need to regulate trade. Moreover, in contrast to the painting trade, industrial relations in Clydeside plumbing were fairly harmonious. The master plumbers had established procedural control agreements in the 1860s, and a commentator in 1879 spoke of the 'time-honoured custom' whereby three months' notice was given by either side before any wage movements occurred.[62] In 1908 the Glasgow and West of Scotland Master Plumbers' Association (GWSMPA) boasted of a 'most harmonious' three year agreement which it had reached with the operatives, and peaceful labour relations existed until 1912. During that year, though, both sides were unable to resolve a dispute within the established bargaining machinery,

---

58. *The Scottish Decorators' Quarterly Review*, Nov. 1958, p. 93.
59. In the aftermath six employers were discharged from the Association for breaking ranks and a few others resigned. *Ibid.*, p. 94.
60. *GH*, 17 Feb. 1906, p. 11.
61. Research Note Mss 134, University of Warwick Business Records Centre.
62. One of the main grievances by the masters during a strike in 1879 was that this custom was not adhered to by the operatives. *GH*, 7 Jan. 1879.

and the Lord Provost – D. M. Stevenson – had to be brought in to arbitrate.[63]

The GWSMPA rejected the idea of industrial council wage bargaining and argued that a Scottish council should be set up – as the council established for the plumbing trade was made up of predominantly English members.[64] This view, though, was not shared by the trade union, and in February 1920 the peaceful industrial relations record of the Association was broken when 40 plumbers struck in four large Glasgow shops over the GWSMPA's refusal to abide by the Compensation for War Services Scheme recommended by the Industrial Council.[65] The strong employer solidarity which had been nurtured over the years for trade regulatory purposes – and the almost total representation of the GWSMPA on Clydeside – made the master plumbers an effective fighting force. The employers' association locked out over a thousand workers in 40 shops until employer control was once again restored.[66]

Effective employer combination, therefore, was essential both for conciliation and conflict – both of which were effective labour control practices – and unity amongst building trade employers remained a valuable insurance policy long after collective bargaining had been established. In 1902, for example, at a meeting to discuss the formation of the Employers' Council, the Vice President of the GMMA told representatives of Clydeside's building trade employers that 'it would be better to be combined so as to be able to fight against the combination that is so strong against us'.[67] This foreshadowed events two years later when the master masons' cherished conciliation procedure finally broke down, and the employers were obliged to enlist the assistance of other organisations to strengthen their hand. The Secretary of the GMWA was asked if his organisation would 'endeavour to reduce as far as possible their working staff, especially those members employing masons ... [as] they were not fighting for themselves, but for all connected with the building trade'. The master wrights immediately gave their full support.[68]

63. By this time the Association had 175 members in Glasgow and 60 throughout Clydeside. D. M. Stevenson awarded half of what the trade union had demanded, but commented that the operatives had not been working to their full capacity. *GH*, 23 Aug. 1912, p. 8.
64. *GH*, 3 April 1920, p. 9.
65. *GH*, 26 Feb. 1920, p. 10. The scheme involved apprentices being paid nine tenths of the journeyman's rate. The government was to pay one-third of this.
66. *GH*, 1 March 1920, p. 10.
67. Glasgow Master Wrights' Association (GMWA), Minute Book No. 2 Dec. 1902.
68. Ibid., 11 Aug. 1904.

The Glasgow Master Wrights' Association further exemplifies the dual nature of the role which employers' organisations performed. It helped re-organise the Clydeside building industry by whipping up enthusiasm for better regulation of the trade. However, at the same time the Association also ensured that its members' right to manage remained sacrosanct. In 1905, for example, inquiry notes modelled on those used by the Engineering Employers' Federation were adopted – illustrating once again the widespread influence of the EEF. Moreover, that same year a dispute arose over the signing of a new bye law, and at a special meeting of the GMWA every master was urged to lay off his workers in stages until the workers who had refused to sign were forced back to work: 'This fight must be won and the only way to do so speedily is to put the men on the street.' [69] Consequently, 136 men found themselves on the street by the end of May, more and more followed, and by September the strike was over.[70] The network of employer connections was played to the full and other organisations gave their support, including the Scottish Furniture Manufacturers' Association.[71] After this employer victory more Clydeside joinery firms saw the benefits of employer combination, and membership of the GMWA increased considerably. By 1906 the Association had clearly seen the benefit of tying workers to agreements, and that year a rigid disputes procedure was set in place for the Glasgow joinery trade.[72]

The war gave further impetus to the implementation of comprehensive methods of procedural control in the Clydeside building trade. In 1916 representatives of building trade employers' associations gave their wholehearted support to Committee of Production wage bargaining.[73] This collaboration led to further meetings and to the eventual formation of a joint wages board for employers and operatives in 1919. Moreover, the GMWA – which had set up an organisational fund in 1916 – played a leading role in the setting up of the Scottish National Federation of Building Trades Employers in 1918.[74] However, it would be wrong to see the employers being forced into an extension of collective bargaining by wartime government pressure, as their determination to take the initiative in this area was evident in the pre-war years.

69. Ibid., 1 May 1905.
70. Ibid., 30 May 1905.
71. GMWA Minute Book 2, 4 Sept. 1905.
72. *GH*, 4 Dec. 1906.
73. GMWA Minute Book 4, 13 Dec. 1913, pp. 216–217.
74. With the setting up of the National Industrial Council for the Building Trades of Great Britain, the Scottish body returned ten members. *Plumbing Trade Journal*, July 1918, p. 26.

We saw in Chapter 2 that the main impetus behind the formation of an employers' association for the Clydeside slating trade in 1873 was the need to stand up to labour militancy. Like most of the employers' associations throughout the period the Glasgow Master Slaters' Association frequently had to resort to confrontational methods. The worst case was in 1908 during a strike over the issue of allowances for working outside the Glasgow boundary. Several weeks into the dispute the GMSA discovered that the slaters' trade union – which had 365 members in Glasgow at this time – had only six weeks' financial reserves left. Despite this heartening news, the Association took no chances: three local employers' associations were approached for assistance, and an advertisement for scab labour was placed in the *Slate Trade Gazette*. Subsequently, 24 blacklegs arrived at St Enoch's Station to be met by 2–300 pickets; only three of the blacklegs were placed in jobs, and the rest returned to England. During this seven month dispute GMSA members helped each other complete vital contracts, and by mid-July the strike was settled in the employers' favour – despite a few concessions.[75]

However, the long dispute took its toll on the GMSA. Membership fell from 101 to 80.[76] One of the reasons for this was the growing disgruntlement amongst the employers at the extent of undercutting in the trade (Chapter 3). However, an inability to pay subscriptions on top of the costs incurred by the strike was an important factor too. A successful recruitment campaign in early 1913, though, orchestrated by the GMWA, increased the organisation's strength, and by the end of 1918 – at which point its records end – the Association was still playing a vital role in regulating both commercial and industrial relations in the Clydeside slating trade.

All of these Clydeside building trade employers' associations, then, ensured that the balance of power lay with the employers throughout the period, which further supports the notion that employer control was maintained in two ways: by strengthening procedural control through conciliation channels on the one hand; and by ensuring that employer unity was strong enough to herd workers back into conciliation agreements when the situation demanded.[77]

75. See GMSA Minute Book 4, 15 May 1908–15 July 1908; see also *GH*, 16 May 1908, p. 13; 21 May 1908, p. 13; 25 June 1908, p. 3; and 3 July 1908, p. 5.
76. GMSA Minute Book 4, 2 Feb. 1909.
77. R. Price, *Masters, Unions and Men*, p. 266.

Furniture

The Clydeside furniture industry depended on skilled craft labour as it produced goods for a high-quality market. There were already substantial trading links between the SFMA member firms and Clyde shipbuilding companies that commissioned good-quality furnishings. Consequently, when the EEF hammered home its right to manage in 1897–98, this acted as an example to the furniture employers. Like the engineers, the furniture makers were also experiencing a pincer movement: intensifying competition on the one hand, and trade union interference on the other. In April 1898, therefore, following a wage claim by the Scottish Cabinet Makers' Union, notices announcing new working conditions were posted in all the SFMA's members' factories. These stipulated that restrictions on output would no longer be tolerated, that limitations on overtime working were to be put into force, that the employers alone would decide on the best method of payment, and that they would retain the right to employ non-trade union labour. The posting of these notices provoked a bitter 10-month strike and lockout. During this contest the SFMA received financial and moral support from the NWETEA, while the Glasgow Master Wrights' Association and the Dundee Master Joiners' Association pledged not to employ any strikers; similar pledges were received from employers in Manchester and London.

To help break the deadlock the employers conceded that the minimum wage would be held at the pre-strike level, and that overtime would be restricted to 10 hours a week. They also allowed that there would be some limitations on the amount of piece work. However, there were to be no restrictions on output, and the employers were to retain the right to employ non-trade union labour. Moreover, a comprehensive disputes procedure was brought into force which forbade any stoppage of work while grievances were under discussion.[78] The trade union tried to have the clause regarding the employment of non-union workers rescinded – in 1906 and in 1913 – but the employers doggedly refused to concede this valuable point.[79]

In 1919 the SFMA faced demands for a 40-hour week. The Association, however, was only prepared to concede a 47-hour week and prepared itself for a showdown on this issue. Once again 'substantial support' was pledged by non-federated firms. However, in this instance the workers' resolve caved in after only four days. The inter-war depression stifled what was left of trade union militancy, and this, combined with the introduction of a sliding scale in early 1922, resulted

78. SFMA Minute Book 1, 28 July 1898, 10 Aug. 1898.
79. Ibid., Minute Book 2, 1 Dec. 1905; 17th AGM, 25 Nov. 1913.

in untroubled industrial relations throughout the 1920s. Overall, the main legacy of the 1898 furniture lockout – and the main benefit to the employers – was the initiation of procedural control, and this was reinforced as the period progressed.[80] By the end of our period the SFMA's collective agreement with the Scottish Furnishing Trades Advisory Committee affected over 3,000 workers. This agreement bound the workers to sliding-scale payment and to a rigid disputes procedure.[81]

The formalisation of industrial relations in the furniture industry, then, ensured that the employers still had control of the point of production by the end of our period. By this time, though, the nature of the furniture market was changing, as the introduction of hire-purchase schemes stimulated a demand for cheaper furniture. This, coinciding with increased competition from England and abroad, led to the demise of high-quality furniture making in the West of Scotland.[82]

Baking

Intensifying competition from the 1870s to meet Clydeside's demand for bread and confectionery compelled the employers to shake off trade union restrictions, and by 1877 collective bargaining in Glasgow had collapsed.[83] The spread of machine baking accelerated in the 1880s and 1890s, and this further whittled away the master bakers' traditional reliance on craft labour; and especially so in the large bread factories. *The Northern Millar and Baker* realised how much the industry was changing, but reasoned that the stripping away of craft autonomy was beneficial to the employer: 'The subdivision of labour is, as is well known, the true secret of power ...'[84] By this time Glasgow was the leading centre of British machine baking, and it was here that employer opposition to craft interference was strongest. The Clydeside employers certainly demanded hard work. In 1884, for example, Glasgow bakers struck in an attempt to reduce the working week from

80. *GH*, 25 Feb. 1910. The regularisation of industrial relations began to be resented by the rank-and-file in the pre-World War One period. SFMA Minute Book 2, 1913, p. 99.

81. Although there is no evidence of the employers using collective action to increase the pace of production, the President of the SFMA confessed to the Board of Trade in 1923 that many of its members used piece working to this end. Collective Agreement between SFMA and the Scottish Furnishing Trades Advisory Committee 1923. Ministry of Labour Report, PRO 65553, 1926.

82. Board of Trade Industrial Survey of the South West of Scotland, 1932, p. 97.

83. I. McKay, 'Bondage in the Bakehouse? The Strange Case of the Journeymen Bakers 1840–1880.' R. Harrison and J. Zeitlin (eds), *Divisions of Labour* (Sussex, 1985) p. 71.

84. *The Northern Millar and Baker*, 1 Oct. 1885, p. 13.

80 hours.[85] Further, around the same time it was normal for the Glasgow machine bakeries to pay overtime only once every worker had produced 35 dozen loaves a day.[86]

In 1889 there was a major dispute in the baking trade over the issue of Sunday working and early starts in the factory bakeries – during which the workers were given the support of the Church of Scotland.[87] Early starts and the introduction of machinery were seen by the trade union as the root cause of the industry's problems, and the secretary made this quite clear at a mass meeting in Glasgow. 'The trade', he maintained, 'had been reduced from a state when employers and employed had been able to work together for the general good, until all had been changed by the introduction of the factories and that more terrible curse, early men.' [88] The union insisted that 5.00 a.m. should be the earliest starting time; whereas the employers maintained that normal trading – which necessitated the delivery of early bread – would be impossible without retaining a significant number of early workers.[89] During the strike 11 Glasgow employers successfully faced up to trade union demands for an alteration of working hours.[90]

Moreover, although a representative told the Royal Commission on Labour that the union was able pick off the organised employers at its leisure after the dispute, evidence suggests that this was not entirely the case.[91] The Glasgow factory bakers remained a tightly unified section of the Scottish Master Bakers' Association (SMBA), and in December 1889 a union official was still lamenting that 'the system of early men had not been overcome' – that year the Glasgow Master Bakers' Association (GMBA) was organised enough to regulate the price of bread in the city.[92] In 1892 the union was still trying to win an eight-hour day, and complained about the lack of control it exercised over bakery apprentices. In 1896 the union asked the employers to set up boards of arbitration to regulate wages – to which the employers agreed. Clearly, therefore, there was no evaporation of employer resolve in the baking trade by this time.

85. T. Johnston, *History of the Working Classes in Scotland* (Glasgow, 1929), p. 329.
86. *GH*, 27 April 1886, p. 3.
87. W. Knox, *Industrial Nation*, pp. 171–172.
88. *GH*, 24 Aug. 1889, p. 6.
89. *Ibid.*, p. 8.
90. *GH*, 23 Sept. 1889, p. 8. The companies were Bilslands, Stevenson, McFarlane Lang, Thomsons, Milne, Gray Dunn, Sprout and Archibald, Beattie, Muir, Dunlop, and Thomson.
91. Royal Commission on Labour 1894, Group C, Vol. 2, p. 205.
92. *GH*, 18 Dec. 1889, p. 8; 23 Dec. 1889, p. 11.

The determination of the Glasgow bakers to dictate how they managed their companies continued. Their persistent refusal to become involved with an Industrial Council for the bakery trade resulted in the SMBA's withdrawal from the Council in March 1922.[93] In an attempt to arrive at a national agreement for the whole of Scotland in line with the Industrial Council, the trade union declared a national strike. This was meant to force the hands of the 30 Glasgow firms trying to forge a local agreement with their workers. However, the GMBA saw this as part of the general leftist trend of labour relations: 'Some of the Communists and Bolsheviks in the ranks have been spoiling for a fight and they won't be happy until they get one'.[94] The ensuing battle saw this determined group of Clydeside employers pulling off another conclusive victory. The GMBA rejected arbitration, enlisted blackleg labour, and ensured that supplies of bread were brought in from firms outwith the strike area. James MacFarlane, the President of the GMBA, told the Board of Trade's Chief Conciliation Officer that there was 'an abundant supply of good men' willing to work on the Association's terms.[95] This was certainly the case, as Bilslands – one of the most trenchantly anti-trade union employers in Glasgow – accommodated blackleg workers within its Hydepark factory during the strike.[96]

Later in a private interview MacFarlane commented on how the state of technology decreed that employers must take and maintain firm control of the production process:

> He and his colleagues had come to the conclusion that it was imperative in the interests of their industry that a proper settlement of working conditions be arrived at ... With the plant now available it was now possible to bake bread practically continuously, and it was a waste of machinery to let it stand 16 hours out of 24.[97]

Consequently, despite financial support from fellow trade unionists all over Scotland – and from over the Border – the union found that its financial resources were exhausted by early July, and the strike collapsed.[98] The workers were forced to accept that early men would

93. *GH*, 7 April 1922, p. 7.
94. *GH*, 19 May 1922, p. 34.
95. Letter dated 2 June 1922, from James MacFarlane to Sir D. J. Shakleton. PRO LAB 2/901/3
96. Bilslands' Minute Book 2, 16 June 1922. The total cost to the company of housing these workers amounted to just over £195.
97. Ministry of Labour Report, June 1, 1922. Private interview between Sir A. Shakleton and James MacFarlane. PRO LAB 2/901/3.
98. Ministry of Labour Report, 6 July 1922. PRO LAB 2/901/3.

FIGURE 9. Lord Provost Bilsland.

FIGURE 10. William Beattie.

start work at 2.30 a.m., and the employers even managed to secure an agreement that female labour could be employed in certain bakery departments.[99] It should also be noted that there was no caving in of employer unity after this victory. In 1937 a government inquiry into night baking heard that although most Scottish bakers abided by the 1922 dictates of the Industrial Council, the Glasgow employers were still insisting that the many men began work early in the morning, and that night baking was continued.[100]

Printing

The skill of the operative printer had been diluted from the 1890s with the introduction of linotype in newspaper production and monotype in the book trade.[101] However, despite this degree of deskilling, labour relations in the West of Scotland printing trade were an uneasy stand-off by the turn of the century. The formation of the Scottish Alliance of Master Printers in 1913 proved timely for the Glasgow employers as in 1912 the Glasgow Typographical Association began pushing for a reduction of the working week from 50 to 48 hours – plus a wage increase. There had been unrest in the printing trade for the previous couple of years, and on Clydeside a dispute in November 1912 lasted for five weeks and affected 400 workers.[102] By 1913, though, the employers believed they were in a strong enough position to withstand a long fight, and support from other parts of Scotland increased their confidence even further. Consequently, they resolved to take the issue to the point of a lockout.[103] The first lockout in the history of the British printing trade, therefore, began in Glasgow in January 1913 and affected around 2,000 workers. The result was a compromise. Several companies could not afford to join the lockout and this thinned the employers' ranks.[104] Consequently, the workers' demand that the employers did not allow any more women learners into certain branches of the trade was conceded.[105] Moreover, the masters also had to ensure that no

 99. *GH*, 9 June 1922, p. 10.
100. *GH*, 6 April 1937, p. 8.
101. W. Knox, *Industrial Nation*, p. 148.
102. BOT Trade Disputes Record Book, PRO Lab/34/29, p. 64.
103. Annual Report of Glasgow Master Printers' Association, Feb. 1912; also, Circular Letter to members of Glasgow Master Printers' Association, dated 12 Dec. 1912. In 1913 there were 64 master printers in the Glasgow area who were full members of the alliance, compared to 39 in Edinburgh; these included Collins, one of the largest employers in the printing trade.
104. *GH*, 28 Jan. 1913, p. 9.
105. For an account of the struggle of women in the Scottish printing industry, see S. Reynolds, *Britannica's Typesetters* (Edinburgh, 1989).

Glasgow employee would be asked to work more than nine hours' overtime.[106] After the dispute a Permanent Conciliation Committee was set up to deal with any future labour problems.

So, despite having potentially one of the strongest employer organis-ations in Scotland, the master printers failed to defeat male craft intransigence. The failure to ensure that women would be allowed to enter the printing trade had serious repercussions during the war. Wartime labour shortages – combined with the trade union's point-blank refusal to allow women to take over the jobs of the called-up men – almost brought the printing industry to its knees. So serious was the situation in the West of Scotland that an advisory committee was established in 1916 to investigate labour scarcity in the region's printing industry. But this was not just a Clydeside problem as over half the printing machines in Scotland stood idle because of a lack of skilled operators.[107] A letter from the Secretary of the Scottish Printers' Alliance to the Ministry of Labour testifies to how strong a hold the trade union had on the employers' right to manage:

> The Trades Union concerned object to any expansion of women working in the printing and bookbinding trades in Scotland ... There are certain processes in both trades which would be suitable for women, but so long as the Trade Unions take up their present attitude on the question there seems little prospect of the expansion you seem to contemplate.[108]

So frustrated were the employers that the Printers' Provident Association attempted to set up an alternative trade union in 1918. This, the Printing Trades Alliance, was based on the collectivist ideology of the Whitley Report. One of its slogans was 'With Unrestricted Output and No Strikes, Better Wages Can Be Assured'. Moreover, its publicity handout trumpeted the message that membership would entail 'No Fines, No Levies, No Strife ... The Ultimate Submission to Arbitration of All Disputes'.[109]

The Scottish Printers' Alliance grew in strength in the post-war

---

106. BOT Trade Dispute Record Book 1913, PRO Lab/34/29, p. 65.

107. Master Printers' Federation Circular, June 1916. Also British Association for the Advancement of Science, Paper entitled 'Women in Industry'. The Board of Trade set up local advisory committees in principal towns to deal with the employment of women workers. One was established in George Street in Glasgow. *GH*, 4 May 1916, p. 8.

108. Reply to Director of Ministry of Labour from Secretary A. S. Calder, dated 3 Feb. 1919.

109. Publicity leaflet entitled *What is the Printing Trades Alliance?*

period and most of Scotland's printing firms were members by
1920.[110] The Glasgow district was the largest covered by the Alliance
and constituted all the major firms on Clydeside.[111] The Alliance maintained its determination to adhere to a 50-hour working week in the
immediate post-war period. However, it was wrongfooted by events in
1919 when the National Federation conceded a 48-hour week. Subsequently, the Scottish employers felt compelled to adopt a 48-hour
week from early March 1919.[112]

Therefore, despite strong organisation the master printers were much
more reactive to industrial militancy than their counterparts in engineering, shipbuilding, baking, and the furniture industry. Even the
introduction of a Joint Industrial Council did nothing to ease the conflict
between capital and labour. Indeed, in 1922, the trade union – in what
was to be the first case of its kind – rejected an industrial council award
and threatened a general stoppage. By this time, however, the industry
was in depression with over 44,000 unemployed in the trade nationwide.[113]

Clydeside capital and unskilled workers

Effective trade unionism amongst unskilled workers was hard to achieve
because of their lack of bargaining power and lower wages. At the
beginning of our period there were sporadic attempts by unskilled
workers on Clydeside to organise; these included carters, dockers, marine
stokers, and causeway layers.[114] However, it was only with the initiation
of the Workers' Union in the 1890s that an effective agency through
which the collective bargaining of the unskilled could be achieved came
on the scene. Women workers were at a particular disadvantage. Women
tended to be marginalised into poorly paid occupations, such as domestic
service and sweated trades. This – combined with opposition from
unionised males – meant they were poorly represented within the trade
union movement. In 1901, for example, when women made up 30% of
the labour force, they constituted only 7.5% of the total number of trade
unionists.[115] Clearly, therefore, as Gordon observes, employers' and

110. AGM of Federation of Master Printers, 1920, p. 18.
111. Scottish Alliance, Estimate of Branch Expenditure 1919.
112. The Glasgow printers' working week fell from 54 hours in 1877 to 52.5 in 1891,
     to 50 in 1901, then, in 1919, to 48.
113. The secretary of the UK Federation commented 'we are suffering from a general
     strike on the part of the customers.' Federation pamphlet entitled 'The Present
     Position of the Printing Industry', May 1921, p. 5.
114. W. Knox, *Industrial Nation*, p. 117.
115. J. Hinton, *Labour and Socialism* (Brighton, 1986), p. 31.

workers' attitudes to women highlight the deficiencies of class models that concentrate upon divisions between skilled and unskilled workers and marginalise or ignore gender factors.[116] In general, then, capitalists who employed a predominantly unskilled workforce did not face the same labour relations problems as those who had to deal with workers who were classed as skilled.

Agriculture

Clydeside farmers were relatively untroubled by demands from organised labour in the pre-war years – either from unskilled labourers or skilled ploughmen. In 1893, for example, Lord Burleigh of Alloa chaired a meeting of farmers to discuss whether a half-day holiday should be conceded to the workers. The general feeling at the meeting was that although such a move might prevent some workers leaving the land for urban industry, the fact that there was no agitation whatsoever from the ploughmen for more leisure time meant the concession was largely unnecessary.[117] Collective bargaining in Scottish agriculture came relatively late. A Scottish Ploughman's Union appeared in the 1880s, but this represented skilled males and was not of immediate relevance to general farmhands.[118] It was not until the pre-First World War period, and the appearance of the Scottish Farm Servants' Union (SFSU), that any significant challenge to the employers materialised. One of the main concerns of the SFSU in its formative years was to secure more leisure time for its members, and in 1913 the union had talks with the Scottish Chamber of Agriculture on this subject – the Chamber subsequently undertook to circulate its affiliated associations to gauge their reaction.[119]

Although the National Farmers' Union of Scotland (NFUS) did not become involved in industrial relations on an industry-wide basis, collective bargaining did develop at branch level. The decision to delegate industrial relations questions to county branches was a rational one taken only a year after the organisation's launch, the idea being that county branches would be best able to deal with the varied regional peculiarities of agricultural work.[120] In June 1915, therefore, the Kilmarnock branch of the NFUS formally met with the SFSU to discuss a wage demand. Similarly, the Kilwinning branch negotiated war

116. E. Gordon, *Women and the Labour Movement in Scotland, 1850–1915* (Oxford, 1991), p. 291.
117. *Scottish Farmer*, 29 July 1893, p. 596; and 29 Dec. 1894, p. 1036.
118. J. P. D. Dunbabin, *Rural Discontent in 19th Century Britain* (London, 1974), pp. 132–150.
119. *The Scottish Farm Servant*, Nov. 1913, p. 10.
120. *North British Agriculturist (NBA)*, 4 March 1915.

bonuses, dinner breaks, and overtime payments with the Ayrshire district representatives of the union the same year. And a request for a pay rise to counter the increased cost of wartime food by Dunbartonshire farm workers was also dealt with at branch level in negotiations between the employers' association and the trade union.[121]

Nationally, the attitude of the NFUS was gradualist, and its policy in 1917 was 'to get the farm labourer to go along with the farmer and not be in an antagonistic position'.[122] By 1919 the valuable experience which the NFUS gained at local level led to a national conference with the SFSU; and this, the first ever national collective bargaining conference in Scottish agriculture, was hailed as 'significant of the change which has come over the industry'.[123] However, despite this precedent, by 1920 the NFUS was still being condemned for its failure to become fully committed to agricultural industrial relations.[124]

This lack of commitment was a reflection of the fact that the autonomy of Clydeside farmers at the point of production had not been seriously challenged, a principal reason being the difficulty of establishing trade unionism within an industry characterised by dispersed work sites and strong paternalist control through the provision of tied housing. A further important factor was the high number of low-paid women in the industry.

A recent study of women in English agriculture finds that by 1900 'women had largely passed from view as casual farm labourers. The state had intervened, they had been disciplined and now they were seen to have returned to the domestic sphere'.[125] This, though, was not the case in Scotland where a different ideology persisted. Scottish farming was regarded as being more technologically advanced, less dependent on unskilled labour, and more reliant on skilled horsemen, than English agriculture.[126] However, paradoxically, Scottish farmers also employed more female workers. The five censuses between 1881 and 1921 show that, on average, women made up 21% of Clydeside's agricultural workforce – compared to an English average of only 6%.[127] Consequently,

121. *Scottish Farm Servant*, June 1915, p. 401.
122. *NBA*, 29 Nov. 1917, p. 726.
123. *NBA*, March 1919, p. 268; Dec. 1919, p. 112.
124. *NBA*, 15 Jan. 1920, p. 37.
125. K. Sayer, *Women of the Fields* (Manchester 1995), p. 124.
126. A Board of Trade Survey conducted in 1907 bears this out. Of 18,400 Scottish male farm servants, 62% were classed as skilled horsemen, compared to 32% in England, and only 11% were labourers, compared to 43% of the English labour force. R. Anthony, *EHR* p. 559.
127. *GH*, 3 Sept. 1922, p. 8.

notwithstanding the number of skilled ploughmen, Scottish farming depended more upon the unskilled labour of women than was the case over the Border. Moreover, census enumeration greatly under-represented the number of women who actually worked in agriculture, because a great deal of farm labour was casual or part-time. For example, a farm on the outskirts of Paisley in 1912 used casual labour from the immediate Paisley area, Renfrew, Barrhead, and from the shipbuilding centre of Govan. Many of the workers were dockers, shipyard labourers and masons' labourers. But the farm also employed a large number of shipyard labourers' wives, as well as Irish girls who had settled in Paisley to work in the jam factories.[128]

Industrial relations in Clydeside agricultural labour, then, were generally calm over the 1870–1920 period. Whereas urban employers tended to organise in direct proportion to the threat posed by unionised skilled males, the farmers faced an entirely different set of circumstances. The unorganised nature of the farming labour force meant there was little pressure on farmers to form a defensive alliance, although the formation of the Scottish Farm Servants' Union in 1912 may have made membership of the National Farmers' Union of Scotland an attractive option for many.

Tailoring and clothing

The clothing trade provides a good example of an industry in which skilled status was generally reserved for men. Tailoring was the most prestigious branch of this industry. Here, workshops were graded into three classes, and the wages that tailors were paid were in proportion to the amount of hand stitching required – the more machinery that was used, the lower the wages. In the earlier part of our period most operative tailors were male and were members of trade unions. Therefore, the two principal employers' associations that represented the clothing trade – the United Kingdom Association of Master Tailors and Foremen Cutters, and the National Federation of Merchant Tailors – were designed to deal with skilled males.[129]

As in the baking industry, the 1880s and 1890s brought technological change to the clothing trade, and this reinforced employer determination to ensure control of the production process. Technology also undermined male domination of the trade. The mass production of sewing

128. *NBA*, Dec. 1912, p. 814.
129. The *Sartorial Gazette* stated that master tailors – many of whom were employers of sweated labour – had no place in the Merchants' Association. To be classed as a merchant tailor one had to deal directly with the public and be an employer of labour. *Ibid.*, p. 146.

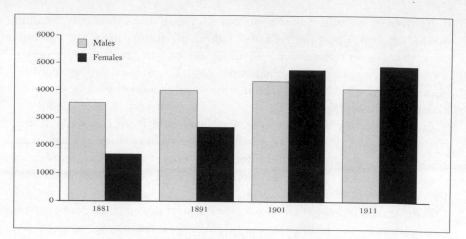

GRAPH 6.2. Male and Female Tailors in Glasgow, 1881–1911. *Source*: Census of Scotland 1881–1911.

machines peaked in the 1890s, and from the 1880s more and more women were employed in the clothing industry.[130] Graph 6.2 shows the increase in the number of female tailors in Glasgow over the 1881–1911 period.

Moreover, this was happening all over Scotland and provoked discontent amongst the male workers. For example, in 1901 sixteen Kilmarnock tailors struck for five months over the introduction of women who were paid less than the standard rate – the men were eventually replaced. Similarly, in Edinburgh in 1902, 32 men were locked out after striking in protest at the employment of women – who were again paid at a lower rate than the men.[131] In 1908 operative tailors in conference spoke of worrying changes taking place in the trade. The main concern was that employers were introducing the division of labour system into the higher reaches of tailoring, and not just in the low-quality sector. They also lamented that whereas previously they had only male blacklegs to contend with, more and more women were now being used as strike breakers.[132]

It was in the lower-quality wholesale clothing end of the business

---

130. A. Godley, 'The Development of the UK Clothing Industry, 1850–1950: Output and Productivity Growth', *Business History* 37 (1995), p. 50.

131. Board of Trade Detailed Statement of Labour Disputes, 1901, p. 80; and 1902, p. 94. PRO Lab 34/1 and Lab 34/2.

132. *GH*, 27 Feb. 1908, p. 18. This unrest must be kept in perspective, as during the volatile 1911–1913 period 50 tailoring disputes were reported to the Board of Trade but none of these there were on Clydeside. BOT Labour Disputes, PRO Lab 34/29–31.

that sweating was most apparent. This was a persistent characteristic of the clothing and shirt-making trades throughout the period, and a House of Lords Committee heard how wages in these industries were held down because of this.[133] By the end of our period the wholesale clothing industry had its own trade board – the Wholesale Bespoke and Tailoring Trade Board for GB – and the industry itself was made up of two sections: ready-made tailoring, and wholesale bespoke.[134] Both activities were performed in factories using power-driven machinery. Notwithstanding the dominance of women in this industry, though, a strict division of labour still ensured that men were streamed into the highest-paid skilled processes, such as band-knife cutting, and pressing.[135] However, in contrast to tailoring, women were not employed in sufficient numbers – nor were organised enough – to stimulate employer combination amongst clothing trade employers.

Comprehensive employer organisation in the clothing industry dates only from the initiation of its trade board. In 1910 the Scottish Wholesale Clothing Association was established 'to deal with all matters affecting members arising out of the Trade Boards Act of 1909'.[136] Similarly, employers in other female-dominated textile and clothing trades – such as shirt manufacture and drapery – formed organisations around this time specifically to deal with the imposition of Trade Boards. The minutes of the inaugural meeting of the Glasgow Shirt Manufacturers' Association illustrate how this unaccustomed collectivism amongst the employers was stirred up: 'While not opposing the inclusion of the shirt trade under the Trade Boards Act, the meeting recognises that there should be common action among the employers in the trade for the protection of their interests'[137]

Clearly, then, employers in the female-dominated clothing trade only felt compelled to organise collectively when minimum wage legislation threatened their profits. Moreover, a deep hostility to paying women workers any more than their sex deserved persisted, and during the war the Scottish Wholesale Clothing Association was adamant that it

133. Fourth Report of the House of Lords Committee on the Sweating System 1889 (331), D. McLaughlin's evidence.
134. The President of the Scottish Wholesale Clothing Association was one of the two Scottish members of the board. *The Bailie*, 17 Nov. 1920, p. 4.
135. Paper Relating to the Suitability of the Wholesale Clothing Trade for the Employment of Disabled Ex-servicemen. SRA TD 967/5/3. During the war many skilled male jobs in the clothing industry were taken over by women. For example, by 1916 a third of band-knife cutters were women. SRA TD 967/5/3.
136. Rules of the Scottish Wholesale Clothing Association, SRA TDA 967/5/2.
137. Minutes of Glasgow Shirt Manufacturers' Association, 3 April 1913, p. 2. SRA TDA 967/6/1.

would not pay its female substitute labour the wage rates recommended
by the Home Office.[138]

However, although national collective bargaining tended to be thrust
upon the clothing industry by the state, employer organisation ensured
capitalist supremacy was maintained. A good example of this was the
West of Scotland Textile Association (WSTA). As the war drew to a
close, the 10 companies which made up this Association, together with
seven Clydeside trades unions, helped set up the Joint Industrial Council
for the textile trade. However, despite taking part in this new negotiating machinery, the WSTA still insisted that its members retained
the right to employ non-trade union labour.[139]

Building and engineering

There were a large number of unskilled workers in the Clydeside building
trade, and as late as 1932 they made up half the total labour force.[140]
As the period progressed, unskilled workers became increasingly
unionised. In 1873 – during the first significant phase of trade union
growth – the National Labourers' Union caused some alarm on Clydeside
when its membership increased by around 500 a week.[141] This upsurge,
though, was not sustained, and in general trade unionism remained the
preserve of skilled building trade craftsmen until the 1890s. This skilled
status was jealously guarded. In 1882, for example, some operative
slaters complained to the Glasgow Master Slaters' Association that
several 'so-called slaters' employed by one company were not actually
time-served men but 'labourers and halflins [apprentices]'. Also, the
following year, several slaters went on strike when a labourer had been
found working on scaffolding – the preserve of the skilled slater.[142]

The appearance of the Workers' Union in the 1890s forced building
trade employers to pay more attention to the demands of the unskilled.[143]

138. The Wholesale Clothing Trade of the United Kingdom, Minute Book, Jan.
     1910–Nov. 1913; 2 Dec. 1915.
139. West of Scotland Textile Association Minutes, 5 March 1918; 25 March 1918.
     TDA 967/7/1/1.
140. Board of Trade Industrial Survey of the South West of Scotland 1932, p. 98. In
     contrast to retailing and farming, though, female participation was minimal in
     this industry – only 60–100 women were employed in the building trade in the
     whole of Clydeside by the end of our period. Ibid., p. 100.
141. *GH*, 22 Feb. 1873.
142. Glasgow Master Slaters' Association Minute Book 1, 4 March 1882; and 1 May
     1883.
143. A. J. McIvor finds a similar reaction among building employers in the North West
     of England during this period to the demands of unskilled labour. A. J. McIvor,
     Organised Capital, p. 138.

The Secretary of the Glasgow Master Masons' Association (GMMA) told the Royal Commission on Labour in 1896 that labourers were much harder to deal with than skilled men as the Workers' Union organised all labourers in Glasgow, and not just those in the masons' trade.[144] The Workers' Union originated in an idea by Tom Mann to create a general engineering union, and by 1914 its membership nationwide stood at 143,000.[145] By this time the Union claimed to represent all of Glasgow's building trade labourers, and the GMMA was forced to hold a special meeting to decide how to deal with this growing menace. So confident was the Association of its own strength – and of the support it could rely on from other building trade employers' associations – that the decision was made not to recognise either the union or its claim for a wage increase. This provoked an immediate strike of 3000 Clydeside building trade labourers which lasted a week. Four masters' associations were directly affected – the master masons, bricklayers, plasterers, and slaters – but when the Glasgow Master Plasterers' Association gave in to the union's demands, the others soon followed.[146] This, though, did not result in an erosion of employer resolve to withstand the claims of the unskilled. The following year the GMSA confidently refused to concede any claims by slaters' labourers for wage rises as its members thought that such a rise would 'place the labourers on the same footing as the journeymen for allowances and general conditions'.[147] A disdainful attitude towards unskilled labour, then, was a main factor in employer reluctance to concede collective bargaining rights.

The Workers' Union caused concern amongst engineering employers too, and many firms from the 1890s came under increasing pressure to recognise the bargaining rights of labourers. In March 1913, for example, Denny's, the Dumbarton shipbuilder, informed the NWETEA that most of its labourers had joined the Workers' Union, and that they were refusing to work with the dozen or so men who had not. The company refused to concede the trade union's demand for a closed shop, and this provoked a three-week strike of around 200 labourers. In the end Denny's determination won through, and the labourers were forced to return to work alongside their non-union workmates.[148]

Two years later, though, wartime labour conditions greatly enhanced the bargaining power of the unskilled, and the engineering employers

144. Royal Commission on Labour 1894, Group C, Vol. 2, p. 305.
145. W. H. Fraser, *A History of British Trade Unionism*, p. 119.
146. GMMA, Minute Book 6, pp. 255–259. See also Ministry of Labour File PRO LAB 69/16; and *GH*, 9 May 1913.
147. GMSA Minute Book 5, 29 Jan. 1915.
148. NWETEA Minute Book 5, March 1913, p. 68.

came under more pressure. At Glenfield and Kennedy's works in Kilmarnock in 1915 the labourers who operated electric cranes joined the Workers' Union and demanded a shilling an hour increase.[149] In 1916 the National Amalgamated Union of Labour and the National Union of General Workers pushed for a 2d wage rise on behalf of their Clydeside members.[150] However, throughout the period the official line of the EEF and the NWETEA was that trade unionism amongst the unskilled should not be recognised, and the members were told to deal with such demands on a plant-by-plant basis only.[151] This dictate was generally adhered to, and only at the very end of our period did a dispute between the Workers' Union and the NWETEA get as far as an EEF central conference.[152]

Dock labour

Establishing effective trade unionism amongst the shifting casual labour force in the docks was difficult.[153] However, in the years leading up to the First World War, employers of dock labour on the Clyde had to deal with an increasingly organised workforce. As we saw in Chapters 2 and 3, the Clyde Steamship Owners' Association (CSOA) and the Clyde Sailing Ship Owners' Association came into being as trade regulatory bodies. However, during this period they were also called upon to address the problem of increasing labour militancy.

The shipowners had got used to dealing with a drifting, unorganised workforce in which casualism was rife, and trade unionism sparse. However, strengthening trade unionism on the one hand, and the initiation of labour legislation on the other, began to make their mark. The passage of the 1906 Trades Disputes Act was a particularly sore point for employers, and in 1923 the President of the CSOA had this to say about it:

> Nothing in recent years has done so much to undermine the sanctity of contracts as the Trades Disputes Act which permits tortuous acts to be committed by trade unions and their members with impunity.[154]

The Clyde shipping associations were also dissatisfied with the implementation of the Miners' Eight Hours Act in 1908, as they were

149. EEF Kilmarnock District Minute Book, Jan. 1909-Nov. 1917; 23 Sept. 1915.
150. West of Scotland Iron and Steel Founders' Association, Minute Book 3, 13 Sept. 1916.
151. NWETEA Minute Book 5, Aug. 1912, p. 46.
152. *EEF Decisions of Central Conference* (London, 1926), p. 336.
153. W. Kenefick, 'A Struggle for Control: The Importance of the Great Unrest at Glasgow Harbour, 1911 to 1912', in W. Kenefick and A. J. McIvor (eds), *Roots of Red Clydeside?*, pp. 129–152.
154. Directors' Report of Clyde Steamship Owners' Association (CSOA), 1923.

convinced that this would entail more expensive ships' coal. Also, the Workmen's Compensation Act became a 'source of considerable friction' for the shipowners as they believed that it would lead to a spate of fictitious claims by workers.[155] Clearly, therefore, the shipowners were uncomfortable at what they saw as infringements of traditional methods of hiring and firing labour.

In July 1911 the Shipping Federation organised a meeting between the two Clydeside dock employers' associations to try and get them involved in concerted action against labour militancy.[156] The unrest on the waterfront continued, and by the following year both associations were convinced that 'professional agitators' were behind the trouble.[157] During war, though, the situation in the dock became intolerable when the tight labour market strengthened the hand of dock labour even more. Bad time keeping became a serious problem and – according to the employers – drinking at work became more prevalent.[158] The Ministry of Munitions also complained that turn-around rates for ore ships in Glasgow were unduly slow, and 120 soldiers were sent to the Glasgow docks to speed things up.

The volatile situation on the waterfront did not improve in the immediate post-war period. By this time the Clyde Harbour Workers' Union had amalgamated with the Scottish Union of Dock Labourers, which meant that the employers were faced with a much more organised workforce. There was a strike at Glasgow harbour in 1919, and after this the employers once again complained about the poor quality of labour in the docks.[159] However, the most galling factor was that unskilled labour had managed to secure significant concessions to which they thought only the skilled were entitled. This position was summed up by the President of the CSOA, Major R. J. Dunlop, in 1924:

Men, so very often highly skilled, are often paid less than comparatively unskilled men engaged on such work as dock and railway labour, and in municipalities. The latter men on the grounds of cost of living and sometimes without any good reason at all, press for and often secure increases of wages. The labourer is extracting wages of which relatively he is not worthy. The skilled workers with tightened belt, and the staple industries of the country bled white, are carrying the labourer on their backs.[160]

155. *Journal of Commerce*, 9 Feb. 1910, p. 3.
156. CSOA Minute Book 2, 4 July 1911, p. 348.
157. *GH*, 10 Dec. 1912.
158. CSOA Directors' Report 1916.
159. Presidential Address CSOA, Directors' Report 1919.
160. Presidential Address CSOA, Directors' Report 1924.

FIGURE 11. Major R. J. Dunlop.

CHAPTER SEVEN

How Authoritarian was
Clydeside Capital?

We have seen how many Clydeside capitalists worked together throughout the 1870–1920 period for various reasons: for example, to regulate
trade, to protect themselves against organised labour by lockouts or by
creating collective bargaining agreements, or to organise social events.
This level of capitalist unity broadly fits in with what we already know
about employer combination in the rest of Britain – although more
regional case studies need to be carried out. Clydeside capital also seems
to have been fairly typical in that many small businesses evolved into
larger-scale enterprises over the period, and there was a general movement towards the introduction of new technology. However, the one
thing that makes Clydeside employers stands out from those in other
parts of Britain is that they have gone down in history as being
particularly hostile towards organised labour. Let us turn first to look
at how this reputation came about, before turning to examine whether
it is wholly justified.

Clydeside capital in historiography
Within Marxist writing the notion of Clydeside employer authoritarianism looms large. J. Foster, in his book *Class Struggle and the Industrial
Revolution* (1974), argued that employer hegemony was so effective in
the North of England that it diverted the potential leadership of the
working class from the path of revolution.[1] Regarding Scotland, he says
capitalism had a distinctive stamp due to factors such as high levels of
labour migration, a volatile business cycle, less investment in machinery,
and an emphasis on labour-intensive production methods.[2] Moreover,
in contrast to the situation in Edinburgh – where labour relations were
quite passive – Clydeside employers in the 1860s and '70s habitually
resorted to the lockout and limited the freedom of many workers by
ensuring that they owned the houses in which they lived.[3]

1. J. Foster, *Class Struggle and the Industrial Revolution* (London, 1974).
2. J. Foster, 'A Proletarian Nation? Occupation and Class Since 1914', in T. Dickson
   and J. Treble (eds), *People and Society in Scotland, 1914–1990* (Edinburgh, 1992),
   pp. 209–210.
3. *Ibid.*, p. 217.

It was for reasons such as these, according to Foster, that the Clydeside working class remained resistant to socialist ideology up to the First World War. Consequently, when the war brought full employment, authoritarian labour control methods became obsolete and ineffective, and this helped precipitate the outpouring of class consciousness known as Red Clydeside. A direct link is being suggested between employer authoritarianism and the growth of working-class consciousness. For Melling, Scottish labour relations diverged from the British norm from the 1850s; collective bargaining was less highly developed there than in England; and capitalists were more inclined to use company welfarism as a way of destroying trade unionism.[4] Marxist accounts of Clydeside's industrialisation, therefore, are permeated by a notion that a distinctively acrimonious form of capital/labour relations evolved on the Clyde because of the distinctive nature of capitalism there.

However, it is not just Marxist historians who subscribe to the idea of tyrannical Clydeside employers. McIvor and Paterson have argued that industrial capital on Clydeside came down much harder on labour during the 1910–1914 period than employers elsewhere.[5] Reid contrasts Clyde shipbuilders with those in the North-East of England and says: 'broadly speaking, the west of Scotland employers were more authoritarian and more anti-union, keen to seize any opportunity to weaken or even destroy trade unionism'.[6] It has also been suggested that the roots of confrontational labour relations in Scotland lie in the country's distinctive religious and education systems – the idea being that Scottish Calvinism bred a particularly hardened type of employer.[7] Historical precedent has also been cited as a factor. Fraser's account of the Clydeside cotton masters' ruthless assault on trade unionism in the 1830s

4. J. Melling, 'Scottish industrialists and the changing character of class relations on the Clyde, *c.* 1880–1918', in T. Dickson (ed.), *Capital and Class in Scotland* (Edinburgh, 1982); see also J. Melling, 'Non-Commissioned Officers: British Employers and their Supervisory Workers, 1880–1920', *Social History 5* (1980), pp. 183–221.

5. A. J. McIvor and H. Paterson, 'Combating the Left: Victimisation and Anti-Labour Activities on Clydeside, 1900–1939, in R. Duncan and A. J. McIvor (eds), *Militant Workers* (Edinburgh, 1992), pp. 129–154; see also A. J. McIvor, in W. Kenefick and A. J. McIvor (eds), *Roots of Red Clydeside, 1910–1914?*, pp. 41–65. More recently N. Kirk has cited Melling and Foster's models of Clydeside employer anti-trade unionism. N. Kirk, *Change, Continuity and Class: Labour in British Society, 1850–1920* (Manchester, 1998), pp. 168–169.

6. A. Reid, 'Employers' Strategies and Craft Production', in S. Toliday and J Zeitlin (eds), *The Power to Manage?* (London, 1991), p. 38. The evidence for this assertion appears to be strong only for the post-1900 period.

7. See, for example, S. and O. Checkland, *Industry and Ethos, Scotland 1832–1914* (London, 1984), pp. 174–179.

and 1840s suggests that the example they set may have established a model for subsequent generations of Clydeside employers to follow.[8] Let us turn now to examine to what extent Clydeside employers were authoritarian – in the sense that they opposed the principle of collective bargaining.

Evidence of Clydeside employer authoritarianism

The testimony of several witnesses to the 1897 Royal Commission on Labour gives us the chance to compare some Clydeside employers with those in other parts of the country. Much of this evidence suggests that there was indeed a harsher employer regime in the West of Scotland. Perhaps the most famous witness was the founder of the Labour Party, Keir Hardie. Hardie told the Royal Commission that in the Ayrshire coal-mining industry a third of the miners were Irish, and that this tended to devalue labour.[9] The comments of the representative of Scottish chemical workers, George Mitchell, broadly support what Hardie said. According to Mitchell there had been two unsuccessful attempts to form a union among Scottish chemical workers, but these had failed because, he maintained, 'some 75% of the working population was of a floating character'.[10] The evidence, then, points to the fact that the local employers had an over-supply of workers to choose from.

The Glasgow area, Lancashire, and London were the three main destinations for Irish immigrants, and their impact upon the Clydeside labour market was intensified by the fact that most of them were young men; a Greenock sugar manufacturer maintained that 'the alternative to using Irish labour was to import Germans or give up the trade'.[11] Moreover, as well as Irish migrants there was also a steady stream of workers from over the Highland Line and from the lowland farming areas. The Scottish Poor Law was harsher than its English equivalent and tended to encourage labour mobility. Consequently, as lowland farming moved to capitalist production and many areas of the Highlands were cleared for sheep grazing, the Scottish central belt received a large number of migrants seeking employment.[12] It could well have been the

---

8. W. H. Fraser, 'The Glasgow Cotton Spinners', in E. Lythe and J. Butt, *Scottish Themes* (Edinburgh, 1976), p. 83. See also his *Conflict and Class: Scottish Workers, 1700–1838* (Edinburgh, 1988).
9. Royal Commission on Labour (RCL) [c6884-IX], K. Hardie's evidence, p. 206.
10. RCL [c6795 III], George Mitchell's evidence, p. 3.
11. Ibid., p. 286. R. Trainor finds that young males were similarly represented among the Black Country's immigrants. R. Trainor, *Black Country Elites* (Oxford, 1993), p. 31.
12. Although there had been a long tradition of seasonal migration into the region.

case, then, that an abundance of labour helped shape employer attitudes to collective bargaining, and this is borne out by other witnesses. The Royal Commission heard the General Secretary of the Association of Blastfurnacemen, William Snow, relate how his union had met with dogged resistance from Scottish masters over its demands for an eight-hour day and time-and-a-half on Sundays. He also said that the union was fully recognised by employers in England, and that working conditions in the Scottish industry 'ought to be a standing disgrace to men who call themselves Christians'.[13]

Some testimony given to the Royal Commission on Labour allows us an insight into the state of the Clydeside chemical industry – an industry almost devoid of records. A chemical worker called Steele from the east of England was interviewed directly after a Scottish chemical worker, Mitchell. Mitchell was asked if there was a good understanding between the employers and the workers and said that there was no understanding whatever. In contrast, Steele, who represented the Tyneside National Labourers' Union, related that his union had over 4,000 members and was recognised by most of the employers in his region. Further, according to Mitchell most chemical workers in Scotland worked an 84-hour week and were paid between 13/6 and 17/– a week. When Steele was asked to respond to this he remarked that the pay and the working hours were much better on Tyneside, and that even the old men who are brought in to sweep up were paid more than the Scottish workers.[14] The working conditions were also reported to have been much worse north of the Border to the extent that 'On Saturday, being pay day, you will find that the furnaces are in a great number of cases out, for the simple reason that the men's exhaustion is so great that they generally get drunk immediately after getting their pay'.[15] Although we have to allow for some distortion here, it does appear that the Clydeside chemical employers were a hard-nosed bunch. Moreover, the evidence is borne out to some extent by the reports of government inspectors who visited chemical works in Rutherglen, Glasgow, and Falkirk in 1893. At all three sites the inspectors found

13. RCL [c.6795 III], William Snow's evidence, p. 278
14. RCL [c.6894–XII], George Mitchell's evidence, p. 19, and T. Steele's evidence [c.6894–IX], p. 3. Mitchell's evidence is refuted to some extent by government statistics for 1880 and 1890. These show that the average number of hours worked in Glasgow was 57 at both dates – one of the lowest averages for chemical workers in the whole of the UK. Only vitriol workers in St. Helens, according to these figures, worked 84 hours a week. Board of Trade Returns of Average Number of Hours Worked 1890 [375], pp. 24–25.
15. RCL, George Mitchell's evidence [c.6894–XII], p. 19, and T. Steele's evidence [c.6894–IX], p. 3.

that the workers' habitual inhalation of noxious fumes had left them with perforated septums, and that many of them had no septums left at all. They also noted that on average the workers were being paid less than those at four comparable works in England.[16]

The Royal Commission on Labour also heard that Clydeside coal-masters were ruthless in their dealings with labour. In 1894 the only trade union in the Lanarkshire coalfield was the Blantyre Miners' Association – reputed to have over 10,000 members.[17] However, its spokesman said that the employers ignored its very existence, vicitmised union representatives, and blacklisted any agitators. According to this witness, things were so bad that a recent strike in Blantyre involving around 30,000 men had resulted in the employers calling out the cavalry. When pressed to explain why it was so difficult to organise workers in Lanarkshire, the witness simply blamed 'the memory of class hatred'.[18] An appeal by some of the region's miners printed in *The Engineer* in 1886 supports this view: 'The miners of Lanarkshire would desire to draw the attention of His Majesty's Government to the long continued and increasingly depressed conditions of Scottish mines' labour, arising they aver from landlords and capitalists placing illegal burdens upon labour'.[19] Keir Hardie also condemned working conditions in the West of Scotland coal industry. Hardie had been President of the Ayrshire Miners' Union – formed in 1880. In its early years the Union had only managed to recruit 11% of the local workforce, and Hardie blamed this poor performance on 'terrorism exercised by the employers over those who take an active part in Trades Union work'.[20] Hardie also told the Royal Commission that working conditions were dire in the Scottish coalfields – although his evidence was contested by the Inspector of Mines for West Scotland who was also interviewed.[21] A Larkhall miner told of how the employers gained an unfair advantage over the workers through providing company housing; and this witness also remarked on the increasing strength of the Lanarkshire Coal-masters' Association (LCA), whose object, he said, was to combine the employers against the workmen and 'to raise a fund for the purpose of

16. Report on the Conditions of Labour in Chemical Works 1893 [c. 7235], p 50. According to this evidence no women were employed at any of the works.
17. RCL, W. Small's evidence, p. 74.
18. Ibid., p. 82.
19. *The Engineer*, Feb. 19 1886, p. 158.
20. RCL, Keir Hardie's evidence, p. 196.
21. The Inspector did concede, however, that in Scotland the workers did their own timbering, and that this had been the cause of many accidents. RCL, J. M. Ronaldson's evidence, p. 206.

fighting workmen if they go on strike'.[22] Industrial relations, then, were in a primitive state compared to many other coalmining areas, and not just those in England. During the coal dispute in 1894 the West of Scotland pits were quickest to come out on strike. The coal mines in the east of the country, though, worked on for some time as effective conciliation procedures had been in place there for some time.[23] Once again, then, the evidence does suggest a particularly hardened attitude to labour amongst certain Clydeside capitalists.

In 1880 the coal company Merry and Cunningham brought in a batch of Welsh ironworkers to break a strike at their Ayrshire iron works.[24] That same year a strike by miners caused many Clydeside ironmasters to extinguish their furnaces rather than give way to the workers' demands. The strikers were eventually forced back to work on the masters' terms.[25] Also, whereas conciliation agreements were set up in Cleveland in 1879, West Cumberland in 1889, and Barrow-in-Furness in 1888, it was not until 1900 that such an agreement between Scottish blastfurnacemen and their employers came into being.[26]

In the earlier part of our period coalmasters and ironmasters tended to be one and the same. However, as the period progressed the region's dependence on iron ore declined as steel production increased. The steel industry also tended to evolve quite distinctly from coal and iron production. This divergence occurred as hardened attitudes to collective bargaining were changing, and by the early twentieth century Clydeside steel producers were not as distinctively hostile to the principle of skilled trade unionism as the ironmasters had been. However, their attitudes to the unskilled workers were different. The Siemens Steel Ingot Makers' Association refused to include unskilled labour in sliding-scale agreements until 1905, and in 1914 the organisation fully supported its Clydeside members' efforts to resist their unskilled workers' demand for a pay rise – the Clydeside bosses also completely refused to go to arbitration on this issue.[27] Attitudes towards unskilled labour took longest to change.

22. RCL, Mr. Smellie's evidence, pp. 44–55. In 1886 striking miners at William Dixon's pits were evicted from their homes because of 'the leading part they played in certain labour movements', *The Engineer*, 1886, p. 158.
23. *Labour Gazette*, June-Sept. 1894.
24. *Engineering*, 6 Feb. 1880, p. 119.
25. *Engineering*, 10 Sept. and 17 Sept. 1880, pp. 214 and 234.
26. Report on Collective Agreements Between Employers and Workpeople in the United Kingdom 1910 [Cd.5366], p. 70. The Scottish Manufactured Iron Trade Conciliation and Arbitration Board was set up to regulate ironworkers; West of Scotland Iron and Steel Dressers got a similar scheme in 1900.
27. Steel Ingot Makers' Association Minute Book 4, 20 March 1914, pp. 65 and 239.

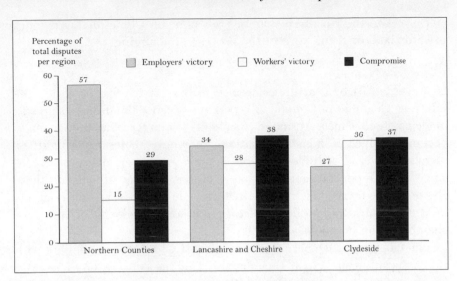

GRAPH 7.1. Outcome of coal mining disputes in three regions: 1901–1903; 1911–1913; and 1918–1920. *Source*: Board of Trade Record Books of Labour Disputes.

In general, though, the evidence suggests that by the twentieth century the principle of collective bargaining had been accepted by many Clydeside employers – although it is not being suggested that 1900 was a watershed. For example, in 1913 the Summerlee Coal and Iron Company decided that it would only employ union labour and several other LCA companies had already conceded the closed shop. Supervisors were also by this time allowed to join a trade union, and the practice of contracting had largely been abolished.[28] There is also evidence in the Board of Trade's Labour Disputes Record Books that West of Scotland coalmasters were no longer the tyrants they had once been.

As the graph shows, over the three periods examined there were 189 labour disputes in the Northern Counties of England, 142 on Clydeside, and 64 in Lancashire and Cheshire. Clearly, the mine owners in the Northern Counties were much more successful in their dealings with labour at this time – indeed these employers won more than 20% more disputes than their Clydeside counterparts. Moreover, the replacement of striking workers by blacklegs and the fining of miners after disputes were practices common amongst the North of England employers but not on Clydeside – there were 23 reported instances of fining of

28. A. Renfrew, 'Mechanisation and the Miner: Safety and Labour Relations in the Scottish Coal Industry c. 1890–1930', unpublished Ph.D. thesis, University of Strathclyde (1997), pp. 227–228.

employees in the Northern Counties but none on Clydeside.[29] Attitudes towards labour, then, were in the process of changing.

Chambers of Commerce

However, anti-labour attitudes seemed to have lasted longer within the Glasgow Chamber of Commerce – perhaps because the directorship was made up of older men. Although chambers of commerce did not normally become involved in industrial relations, they nevertheless reflected their members' overall attitudes towards labour. Moreover, many of Clydeside's most important employers' associations became affiliated to these chambers. If there was a distinctive attitude towards labour relations in this region, one would expect to see some evidence of it in the chambers' minute books.

The Glasgow Chamber of Commerce (GCC) refused to affiliate with the Association of British Chambers of Commerce (ABCC). The main reason for the formation of the ABCC was to achieve greater leverage for the business interest in Parliament. By 1900 the ABCC represented 90 chambers throughout Britain and had 50 Members of Parliament fighting for the commercial and industrial interests in the House of Commons.[30] The Glasgow chamber, though, remained aloof; and two years after the national body came into being the Directors of the Glasgow chamber decided not to become involved as they reasoned 'the independent action of this chamber would, or at least might be, interfered with were they to join the Association'.[31] The Chamber kept its distance until 1912.

One possible reason for this reluctance to join the national body was that the majority of ABCC members were not engaged in national and international commerce to the same extent as those of the Glasgow chamber.[32] Glasgow was also the first chamber of commerce to be established on the British mainland, and the prestige of being first in the field may have sustained the Chamber's determination to remain independent. Also, the GCC had a good track record of protecting the interests of its members because of its links to the corridors of power, and this may also have proved to be a disincentive to affiliate with the ABCC.

However, an underlying reason may have been that the ABCC was

29. Board of Trade Record Books of Labour Disputes.
30. R. Ilerisic and P. F. B. Liddle, *Parliament of Commerce* (London, 1960), p. 26.
31. Minutes of Glasgow Chamber of Commerce (GCC), 13 May 1862.
32. Many of the chambers in the ABCC were really chambers of trade representing small retailers rather than chambers of commerce. W. Grant and D. Marsh, *The CBI* (London, 1977), p. 71.

out of step with the Glasgow chamber's attitude to labour relations. In 1871, for example, when the Trades Unions Bill was being framed, the ABCC declared it was in favour of 'giving legal status to associations of workmen united together for the purpose of legitimate joint action in the arrangement of wages'.[33] This accommodating tone was in sharp contrast to that of the Glasgow Chamber of Commerce which trumpeted that the proposed bill 'was wrong in principle and would offer facilities for the evasion of the law'.[34] In a similar way, when the ABCC had little complaint regarding the Factory Acts, the GCC strongly petitioned against the Factory Acts Amendments Bill in 1874.[35]

There is further evidence that the Glasgow chamber had a particular dislike of interference in capitalist production in its statement to the 1886 Royal Commission on the Depression of Trade and Industry. The Commission circulated all of Britain's chambers of commerce for their views on falling prices, foreign competition, taxation, trade union restrictions, etc., etc. The GCC emerged as being most in favour of curtailing the power of organised labour, and this was further accentuated by the fact that it was the only chamber to return a comprehensive written statement:

> It appears to the Directors that manufacturers have vainly endeavoured to secure prosperity by cheapened production, and have extensively afforded employment both to skilled and unskilled labour, the wages of which in many cases absorb so large a proportion of the price as to leave no adequate return for capital invested. I am also to add that, with the exception of shipbuilding, workmen generally, both skilled and unskilled, are in full employment with good wages, which wages have at present a purchasing power that has never been exceeded or even equalled at any previous time. And lastly, I am requested to state that certain of the directors of the chamber entertain a strong opinion that, as regards competition in manufacturing with foreign countries, the operation of the provision of the Factory Acts of this country require careful consideration and revision.[36]

This distinctive lack of patience with interference in the pursuit of profit was also evident in the GCC's opposition to the 1906 Workmen's Compensation Act – which again the ABCC had no substantial

33. W. Grant and D. Marsh, *Parliament of Commerce*, p. 157.
34. Minutes of GCC, 13 March 1871, p. 23.
35. Minutes of GCC, 13 April 1874.
36. Royal Commission on the Depression of Trade and Industry [c. 4621], Appendix A, pp. 73–81 and 84.

complaints with.[37] Moreover, that same year, the President of the GCC
lamented that British employers had to put up with trade union restrictions, such as the control of apprentices, demarcation agreements, the
coercion of non-union labour, and passive resistance to the introduction
of labour-saving machinery.[38]

In contrast to the intolerant attitude towards organised labour of the
GCC, down the Clyde at Greenock the situation was much more
quiescent. There are several reasons why the Greenock Chamber of
Commerce was less hostile to collective bargaining. Firstly, the
Greenock chamber was not as powerful and influential as its Glasgow counterpart – from which it separated in 1813. In 1889, for
example, the trade depression was inflicting financial hardship on the
Greenock chamber; in contrast the Glasgow chamber never seemed to
have any shortage of funds.[39] Also, although there were 221 members
in 1898, the Directors were still concerned that more were needed in
order to increase the Greenock chamber's strength and influence.[40]
With such a lack of confidence it was unlikely that the Greenock chamber would become involved in labour relations issues. Secondly, unlike
the Glasgow Chamber, the Greenock Chamber of Commerce became a
member of the ABCC and would have been subsequently obliged to
follow the more accommodating attitude to labour adopted by the
national body. Further, whereas many of the prime movers in the GCC
were large-scale manufacturers, there was a different balance in the
Greenock chamber. Only 22% of the members there were involved in
engineering and shipbuilding; 22% were in the sugar trade; but the
majority, 52%, were connected to the shipping industry.[41] In
general, then, most of the members of the Greenock Chamber of
Commerce did not have to face the same level of interference from
skilled craft labour as those in the GCC. Given all these factors, it is
understandable that the anti-labour ethos which permeated the Glasgow
Chamber of Commerce was not replicated in a similar body 20 miles
downriver.

In 1912 the GCC suddenly abandoned its 50 years' autonomy and
joined the ABCC. Its records reveal no reasons for this *volte face*. However, the labour unrest in the region and strengthening socialism were
no doubt important stimuli. Another factor, though, may have been that

37. W. Grant and D. Marsh, *Parliament of Commerce*, p. 157. Also, Report by the
    Directors of the GCC, 1907, p. 31.
38. Report by the Directors of the GCC, 1906, p. 78.
39. Minutes of Greenock Chamber of Commerce, Jan. 1889, p. 194.
40. Ibid., Directors' Report 1898, p. 10.
41. Ibid., Directors' Report 1901, p. 12.

the ABCC had recently begun to show more concern over the power of trade unions, and this brought it more into line with the Glasgow chamber's historically intolerant approach. In 1908, for example, the ABCC was disgruntled at the passage of legislation that gave the miners an eight hour day, and at the introduction of National Insurance three years later. In 1912, then, representatives from the GCC took part in an ABCC deputation to Westminster, demanding that trade unions be held financially responsible for wanton damage, that secret ballots be enforced before disputes, and that unions be prevented from intimidating non-union workers.[42]

In the years following the end of the First World War paranoia over increasing labour militancy on Clydeside peaked, and a principal reason for this was the panic caused by the Russian Revolution.[43] The editorial in the GCC's *Journal* sounded the alarm bell:

> There is a growing distrust of parliamentary government, and even in trade unionism – a blind and impatient desire for 'direct action' in the shape of local general strikes and the actual taking over of the means of production.[44]

And an even more aggressive response was apparent in an article which appeared in the journal two months later:

> If labour thinks it gains the strength by a great combined movement, capital must also be conceded the right to bring into existence the community of interests which it believes to be necessitated by the march of events. No question is involved of an anti-labour alliance ... but when great undertakings believe that better results can be secured from concerted effort, it must be remembered that the same view prevails from another stand-point.[45]

The following year the President's address further testified to the serious situation which Clydeside capital thought it was in: 'Sinister influences are at work in our midst, teaching dangerous, perilous, and pernicious doctrines, which, if they should be adopted, must wreck not only the Government, but our great commercial fabric'.[46]

42. W. Grant and D. Marsh, *Parliament of Commerce*, p. 162.
43. For a detailed account of the response by Clydeside workers and capitalists to the Russian Revolution, see A. Nassibian, 'Attitudes on Clydeside Towards the Russian Revolution, 1917–1924', unpublished M. Litt. thesis, University of Strathclyde (1977).
44. *Monthly Journal of the Glasgow Chamber of Commerce*, Feb. 1919.
45. *Ibid.*, April 1919, p. 89.
46. *Ibid.*, Nov. 1920, p. 253.

A definite intolerance of organised labour amongst capitalists represented by the Glasgow Chamber of Commerce can be traced throughout
the period, and this was not replicated to the same extent in any other
British region. Of course, we should not overstate the case. In general,
the GCC – like chambers of commerce everywhere – did not concern
itself to a great extent with industrial relations. This was normally left
to the employers' associations or to individual employers. However, an
acute sensitivity towards interference with capitalist production, combined with strong links to industries historically resistant to trade
unionism, and the fact that powerful labour relations-oriented employers'
associations were affiliated members, meant any shock waves from
Clydeside's volatile industrial relations were felt within these corridors
of employer power.

There is some statistical evidence suggesting that Clydeside employers were more reluctant to engage in collective bargaining than
those elsewhere. An analysis of strikes and lockouts conducted by the
Glasgow Labour History Workshop found that 40% of disputes on
Clydeside over the 1910–1914 period involved the use of blackleg labour,
and that this figure was more than twice the rate of labour replacement
in England.[47] Conclusions based on a comparison between Clydeside
and the whole of England have to be treated with care. However, there
has also been an attempt to use statistics gleaned from the Board of
Trade Annual Reports of Strikes and Lock-outs, and this also shows
there was a tendency for Clydeside employers to be more hostile in
their initial response to strikes than those in Yorkshire and Lancashire.[48]
The evidence also shows, though, that Clydeside bosses were also 13%
less likely than their colleagues in the North-East of England to respond
to strikes in an initially authoritarian way. We can only conclude, then,
that there was a tendency among Clydeside employers during this period
to be *slightly* more hostile towards organised labour than those in some
other areas. Overall, though, it is the employers of the North-East of
England who – according to this research – are most deserving of the
label 'authoritarian.'

Clydeside wage rates

If the Clydeside employers were as ruthless in their attitudes to labour
as some have suggested, then this should have been reflected in a lower

47. A. J. McIvor and H. Paterson, 'Combating the Left', in R. Duncan and A. J. McIvor
    (eds), *Militant Workers* (London, 1992).
48. R. Devlin, 'Strike Patterns and Employers' Responses in Comparative Perspective',
    in W. Kenefick and A. J. McIvor (eds), *Roots of Red Clydeside?* (Edinburgh, 1996),
    pp. 81–97.

regional wage. Research carried out on wage variations across Britain shows that Clydeside was a low-wage region in 1850; that by 1870 it lay near the national average; but that by the early years of the twentieth century it was one of the highest-wage areas in Britain.[49] Therefore, although the main evidence here is drawn from the wages of agricultural workers and skilled builders, it does suggest that the notion of the Clydeside autocratic employer is a myth. It has also been noted that in 1900 fitters' and turners' wages on the Clyde were second only to London and Cardiff, which also indicates that by this time employer authoritarianism was not being reflected in low wages.[50]

However, craft workers on the Clyde were not paid higher-than-average rates throughout the whole period. In 1880 *Engineering* reported that low wages had forced delegates from Clydeside engineering shops to form the Glasgow and District Wages Committee. A memorial issued by the men stated that

> The workmen employed in the engineering trades are, when compared with other classes of skilled artisans, very poorly paid. If compared with their brethren in other competing ports such as Hartlepool and Hull, and other places, they are paid three to eight shillings less of wages. If the employers on the Thames, Tyne, Wear, Tees, Humber, and Mersey, are able to pay so much higher wages, surely the Clyde district employers are able to pay at least equal rates of wages.[51]

This evidence is supported by a letter from an employer in *The Engineer* written six years later complaining of the unfair cost advantages enjoyed by employers in areas where trade unionism was relatively weak:

> A marine engine fitter on the Thames must have about 36/– a week, the same man on the Clyde would have 24/– a week, yet the London master must compete with the Clyde master. A locomotive fitter at Manchester must have about 34/– a week, the same man in Glasgow would have about 26/– and no overtime; yet the Manchester master must compete with the Glasgow master. Cannot A. C. and his brother members [referring to a previous letter] perceive how gradually, but surely, the engineering business is going from the South and Midland counties, where wages are high and trade

49. E. H. Hunt, *Regional Wage Variations in Britain, 1850–1914* (Oxford, 1973), p. 53.
50. K. Burgess, 'Authority relations and the division of labour in British Industry, with special reference to Clydeside, c. 1860–1930', *Social History* 11 (1986), p. 210.
51. *Engineering*, 5 Nov. 1880, p. 405.

unionism strong, to the North where wages are low, unionism weak, and Liberalism rampant? [52]

Government statistics provide more evidence that Clydeside was not a high-wage area in the 1880–1900 period. In 1885 the average wage in Glasgow's engineering and machinery works was £60 a year compared to £80 a year in London, £77 in Sheffield, and £68 in Manchester.[53] In shipbuilding the difference was even greater. Here, the London area led the field with an average annual wage of £112. However, the average wage on the Clyde was only £68 a year – below the national average shipbuilding wage of £76.[54] By 1906, though, the situation had changed, and the wages of most Clydeside shipbuilding trades were above the national average.[55] There was a similar pattern in iron manufacturing, although Clydeside did not fall below the national average here. Of seven districts assessed, the average yearly wage in Scotland was £74 – only £1 above the national average. In contrast, the average wage in Cleveland, Derby, and North Staffordshire, was £80.[56]

There was a similar pattern regarding unskilled workers, although by the 1900s the differential between Scottish skilled and unskilled workers' wages was wider than south of the Border. In 1906, the difference in wages between craftsmen and labourers in Glasgow and Greenock was distinctively wide – and this had also been the case in 1886 regarding the differential between skilled and unskilled building workers in central Scotland.[57]

If Clydeside was a high-wage area, then, it was craftsmen's wages in certain trades that were pulling the average up. In the 1890s members of the Glasgow Master Painters' Association paid their workers above the industry's norm.[58] However, at the same time the wages of unskilled chemical workers and other unskilled workers – especially women workers – were much lower than in comparable regions, and this was especially so in bleaching and printing works.[59] Female labour also got

52. *The Engineer*, 8 Jan. 1886, p. 29.
53. General Report on the Wages of the Manual Labouring Classes in the UK 1893 [c–6889], p. xxxviii. The Clydeside average was even lower at £54 a year.
54. *Ibid.* [c–6889], p. xi.
55. Board of Trade Inquiry into Earnings and Hours of Labour in the UK 1906, Metal Engineering and Shipbuilding [Cd.5814], p. xxxii.
56. Ibid. [c–6455], p. xxxvi.
57. Ibid., p. 51, fn. 7.
58. *The Scottish Decorators' Quarterly Review*, Volume 36, Number 4 (1958), p. 96.
59. Board of Trade Report on Earnings and Hours of Labour in the Textile Trades 1906 [Cd. 4545], p. 225.

a raw deal from the Clydeside farmers. Throughout our period Clydeside was the highest-paid farming district in the whole of the United Kingdom. Moreover, according to the General Secretary of the Scottish Farm Servants' Union, low wages were not the main reason that farm workers were leaving the land in favour of urban employment in the years after the war. This, he maintained, was more to do with disgruntlement over tied housing and the labour hiring system.[60] However, a lot of farm labour was female casual labour and not recorded in census or wage statistics. Clydeside agriculture depended to a great extent on women workers, and the big disparity between their wages and those of men led to many women forsaking farm work for urban employment after the war. Moreover, so strong was the reaction against low-paid farming work that even the doubling of women's wages by many farmers failed to stop the exodus.[61]

Shipbuilding and engineering employers

Unity amongst Clyde shipbuilders was strong throughout the period, and this combined strength was bolstered by enlisting the help of Northern England employers from time to time. This was the case in 1902, and this dispute suggests that the Clyde employers were more hostile towards the principle of trade unionism. The Federation of Shipbuilding Associations was formed in 1897, and the 1902 dispute – when the North-East of England yards asked their Clyde counterparts for help – was the organisation's first real test of solidarity. After some negotiation the CSA made an unequivocal declaration:

This Association will join the North East Coast Associations in intimating to the various shipyard trades a reduction of wages equivalent to the last advances given ... on the understanding that should any section of workmen in any of the Districts resist the reduction, so far as to bring about a strike, that the parties to this movement for a reduction will lock out the particular trade concerned in order to make the settlement a general one.[62]

The Clyde bosses came up with a plan that would result in the complete elimination of the Boilermakers' Society. However, the North-East of England employers were not prepared to go to such lengths

60. *Scottish Journal of Agriculture* No. 2, 1919, p. 501.
61. *GH*, 14 Oct. 1920, p. 10.
62. NWETEA, Minute Book, 2, 5 Oct. 1902, p. 293.
63. A. J. Reid, 'Employers' strategies and craft production', in S. Toliday and J. Zeitlin (eds), *The Power to Manage?* (London, 1991), p. 38, see also J. Lovell, 'Employers and Craft Unionism: A Programme of Action for British Shipbuilders', *Business History* 34, No. 4 (1992), pp. 38–58.

and the scheme fell through.[63] Moreover, during a dispute in 1906 the Clyde masters persistently refused their trade union's request for arbitration.[64] This dislike of outside interference was characteristic of the Clyde engineering and shipbuilding employers, and a columnist in the *Glasgow Herald* in 1910 commented on it:

> Shipbuilding and engineering employers have always acted on the principle that outside arbitration is not permissible in their respective industries ... They do not object to arbitration as a principle, but they contend that no outsider can possibly know the many complexities which exist in the relations of capital and labour.[65]

By this time members of the CSA were paying the highest wages in British engineering and shipbuilding – illustrating yet again that to equate low wages with employer authoritarianism is questionable. The evidence does suggest, though, that this 'great league on the Clyde', as *The Times* called it in 1877, was consistently more enthusiastic about hammering the unions than shipbuilders in the North-East of England.[66]

However, although trade unionism was only slowly acknowledged by the Clyde shipbuilders, as the period progressed the CSA increasingly used its influence to build up effective collective bargaining procedures, and this brought the situation more into line with the rest of the UK. The acceptance by the Clyde shipbuilders of the Shipbuilding Trades Agreement in 1907 also illustrates that the CSA had by this time decided that conciliation was preferable to open conflict.[67] However, collective strength remained important to the shipbuilders, and in 1919 the CSA joined a scheme initiated by the Shipbuilders' Employers' Federation

64. NWETEA Minute Book 2, 3 Oct. 1906, pp. 178, 182.
65. *GH*, 12 Oct. 1910, p. 8. In a similar way the Ironmoulders' Association consistently refused to go to arbitration when conferences between it and the Federation of Ironmoulders reached deadlock. Scottish Employers' Federation of Iron and Steel Founders, Minute Book 2, p. 286. However, this was by no means a characteristic of this particular industry or of the Clydeside region, as Manchester cotton spinners and their employees were equally ambivalent towards 'inexperienced outsiders' coming in as arbitrators. See J. H. Porter, 'Wage Bargaining under Conciliation Agreements, 1860–1914', *Economic History Review* 2nd Series, 23 (1970), p. 464.
66. Not all Clyde shipbuilders were hostile to collective bargaining at this time. John Scott, for example, told the Royal Commission on the Depression of Trade and Industry in 1886 that the ASE was a 'well conducted trade union which was in many respects useful to the employers'. Third Report of the Royal Commission on the Depression of Trade and Industry 1886 [c–4797], Evidence of John Scott, p. 192.
67. Although R. Price has argued that this agreement was in the employers' favour as it placed the responsibility for ensuring worker discipline on the Boilermakers' Society. R. Price, *Masters, Unions and Men* (London, 1980), p. 205.

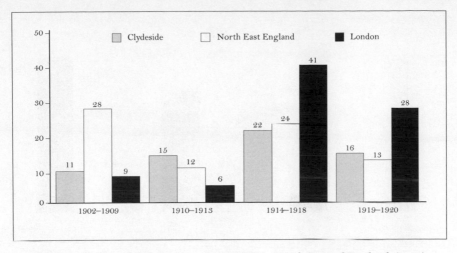

GRAPH 7.2. Number of Conferences of NWETEA, North-East of England Association, and London Association, 1902–1920. *Source: EEF Decisions of Central Conference, 1898–1925* (1926).

that aimed to bring about nationwide employer unity when dealing with the trade unions.[68]

Employer combination was also strong in the engineering industry throughout the period, and this remained the case long after the 1897–98 lock-out. The NWETEA was the northern sector of the EEF, and this allows us to see the extent to which the NWETEA members were distinguished by their opposition to organised labour. The conciliation machinery set up in the engineering industry following the 1897 lock-out involved passing disputes from the local, to the regional, and eventually to central conference level. If there was a general reluctance by the Clyde employers to deal with disputes at the first level, this should show up as more disputes passed on to central conferences. However, as Graph 7.2 shows, the Clyde employers were not distinguished in this way.[69]

Clearly, it was the London employers who recorded the most conferences. Also, EEF records show over the 1898–1924 period Clydeside employers conceded more wage demands than their counterparts in London and the North-East of England – Graph 7.3.[70]

68. Shipbuilders' Employers' Federation Unity Scheme. SRA TD241/15/5.
69. Compiled from an analysis of data in the EEF publication, *Decisions of Central Conference, 1898–1925* (London, 1926).
70. Compiled from the EEF's *Wage Movement, 1897–1925* (London, 1926). Pay demands which were not clearly stated or left to individual firms have not been recorded in either category, but have been included in the total number of demands for the respective area. It should also be noted that over the war period many wage

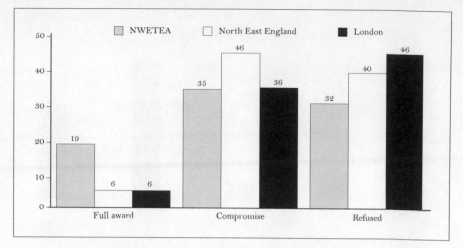

GRAPH 7.3. Results of Wage Claims NWETEA, North-East of England Association, and London Association, 1898–1924. *Source*: EEF Wage Movements 1897–1925.

Although the most common result of pay demands was a compromise – followed by outright refusal – 13 percent more pay claims were conceded in full on Clydeside than in the other two areas.

Despite this evidence, though, it would be wrong to imagine that the membership of the NWETEA was soft on labour. On the contrary, during the war it was the NWETEA that first complained to the Admiralty about workers moving between engineering shops chasing the higher wages available on government contracts, and this concern resulted in the government initiating the Munitions of War Act in 1915.[71] Lloyd George was aware that that several Clydeside bosses were keen to enforce strict control over their workers during the war. In 1915 he received a deputation of shipbuilders from the Clyde urging him to bring in prohibition – he thought this a rather ironic request coming from people who 'neither in figure or physiognomy [gave] any indication of having spent their leisure hours in the service of the Band of Hope'.[72] But this deputation was not an eccentric fringe movement of Clydeside capital, as a memorial from all the principal engineering employers' associations on the river requesting similar state intervention was sent to the government at the same time.[73]

questions were determined by the Committee of Production, and these have been omitted.

71. E. Wigham, *The Power to Manage* (London, 1973), p. 88.
72. D. Lloyd George, *War Memories* (London, 1938), p. 194.
73. Scottish Sheet Metal Workers' Employers' Association Minute Book 2, 27, Sept. 1916, p. 4–6.

However, apart from this concern at the loss of control over labour during the war, from 1900 onwards there was no characteristically intransigent attitude among Clydeside engineering employers that made them stand out from employers elsewhere.

Organised employers in action: Thomas Biggart and the shipbuilders and engineers

We turn now to a case study that highlights a neglected figure in Clydeside labour management relations. To a great extent much of the employer unity enjoyed by the shipbuilders and engineers was achieved through the activities of the solicitor Thomas Biggart, the secretary of the NWETEA.[74] Biggart's involvement with Clydeside employers began in December 1892 when he became Secretary of the newly formed Glasgow District Engineers' and Boilermakers' Association – soon to become the North West Engineering Trades Employers' Association (NWETEA). His success in handling the affairs of the engineering employers was such that when the master coppersmiths and brassfounders in the region decided to organise against the labour threat, it was Biggart to whom they entrusted the responsibility of setting up their associations. By 1920, as Table 7.1 shows, Biggart's legal firm was responsible for some of the most powerful employer organisations in Britain.[75]

Although his title was Secretary, Biggart performed his role so enthusiastically that he could be credited at times with single-handedly building up an employer front to combat the labour threat. His roving commission was first put to good effect during the 1895 engineers' lock-out, and five years later he reflected on his efforts:

> I had in mind our experience in 1895 when, for the first time, we secured the adhesion of the Clydeside Company, Fairfield Company, the London and Glasgow Company, and Messrs. Napier. None of them would join us singly, but by dint of negotiation and perseverance, we got from one or two a promise to join if some other would join, and we went round them all in this way and ultimately the consent of the whole four was obtained. I personally visited Clydebank, Fairfield, and the London and Glasgow, and I remember I

74. See T. Rodgers, 'Sir Allan Smith, the Industrial Group and the Politics of Unemployment, 1919–1924', *Business History* 18, 1 (January, 1986), pp. 100–123. There are also some references to Biggart in E. Wigham, *The Power to Manage*.

75. Compiled from Directory of Industrial Associations, 1919 [Cmd. 328]. Also records of Biggart and Lumsden, Business Records Centre Glasgow, UGD. 339. Biggart was also the employers' secretary for the Clyde Standing Committee of Shipwrights, Joiners and Employers for the Demarcation of Work. Directory of Industrial Associations, p. 27.

FIGURE 12. Thomas Biggart.

TABLE 7.1. *Employers' Association Clients of Biggart and Lumsden,*
1890–1920

Date formed (where known)	Employers' Association
1866	Clyde Shipbuilders' Association
	Dry Dock Owners and Repairers of the UK
1891	Clyde Ship Repairers' Association
	Glasgow District Engine Boiler and Ship Repairers' Association
1894	NWETEA
1897	Engineering Employers' Federation (until 1910)
1898	Mutual Insurance Company of Engineering Employers' Federation
	Scottish Coppersmiths' Employers' Association
	Repairers' Liability Insurance Committee
1907	Scottish Sheet Metal Workers Employers' Association
	Scottish Committee of Chemical Manufacturers
1908	Glasgow Master Boiler Cleaners and Steam Pipe Coverers' Association
	Gas Meter Makers' Employers' Association
1919	Clyde Ship Plumbers' Association
	Scottish Brassfounders and Finishers Employers' Association
	Scottish Bridge Builders and Structural Engineers' Association
1920	Scottish Welding Employers' Association
	Shipbuilding Employers' Federation
	Clyde Ship Riggers Employers' Association
	Scottish Rivet, Bolt and Nut Manufacturers' Association
	Foremen's Mutual Benefit Society (Honorary President, 1917–1942)
	Iron Trades Employers' Insurance Association

could not get an application from any of them until I was able to go round again and say all were prepared to join if the other would.[76]

Following the success of this exercise in employer combination, employers from Glasgow, Greenock, Belfast and Barrow decided to form a permanent organisation in the Employers' Federation of Engineering Associations – which later became the EEF. Biggart was appointed joint

76. Private Letter Book of Shipbuilding Employers' Federation, Biggart to Colonel Watts, 31 March 1900, p. 283.

secretary of the new organisation, and its headquarters was established in Glasgow. Organised employer strength was increasing, and two years later Clydeside and North-East of England shipbuilders joined forces to form the Federation of Shipbuilders' Associations.[77]

Although the EEF's first big trial of strength was its fight with the ASE in 1897/98, trouble had been brewing since 1896. That year, during a strike affecting the Clyde yards, Biggart acted as link and co-ordinator between the National Free Labour Association (NFLA) and the employers. He was well aware, though, that he had to stay in the shadows, and wrote: 'I cannot be too careful, and under no circumstances must my name in any way come in'.[78] However, his cover was almost entirely blown when a party of blacklegs failed to meet their contact at Glasgow's Queen Street Station: 'In some unexplained way they were missed at the station, then went directly to Fairfield, and, most stupidly, passed through the gates in amongst the men, until they got a foreman, showing him their registration cards as members of the NFLA'. Most of the men had to quickly return home. Biggart managed to get one of them a job as a labourer and this enabled the man to lie low for a while. But the man's patience soon ran out and he turned up one day at Inglis's shipyard looking for a job and explaining to the foreman that Mr. Biggart had sent him there.[79] After this second fiasco, Biggart was even more circumspect, and arranged that in future contingents of blacklegs would be met by an agent on their arrival in the city.

During the engineering lock-out of 1897/98 Biggart was in the thick of the action once again. His concern over potential government intervention in the dispute illustrates how he viewed the fight as one strictly between capital and labour:

> It appears to me that in the present dispute they [the Board of Trade] are making a supreme effort to 'worm' themselves in ... Unless watched, we might find ourselves unable to get clear of them with any grace, and without turning the country against us.[80]

He made sure that he was kept fully informed of the enemy's weak spots, and he found it hard to contain his glee on discovering that ASE was becoming short of funds:

77. A representative from the CSA stated that 'only by such means could they hope to get proper treatment from the workmens' organisations'. CSA Minute Book 1899–1903 (TD 241/1/7), p. 21.
78. Telegram from T. Biggart to J. Roberston, 9 Oct. 1896. TD 1059/22/1, p. 20.
79. Private Letter Book of SEF, T. Biggart to J. Robinson, 10 Oct. 1896, p. 26.
80. Ibid., T. Biggart to Colonel Dyer, 29 Oct. 1897, p. 38.

An ounce of facts is worth a load of arguments, and the diminished strike pay is the necessary fact. We must follow this up vigorously. In view of future schemes it is peculiarly important to create dissatisfaction with the present financial position of the ASE.[81]

Biggart valued effective propaganda, and a letter of introduction written by him for a Glasgow journalist intent on a London career illustrates this:

He [the journalist] was connected for a long time with one of the leading provincial newspapers, has done good work for us, and rendered good service during the time of the '97–'98 dispute. Above all what is most important, we have found him discreet ... He makes articles on labour affairs a speciality. As a consequence he likes to keep in touch with both sides. He is well 'in' with the other side.[82]

Moreover, the idea that Biggart was fighting the cause of the employer class – and not just engineering and shipbuilding employers – is further borne out by his correspondence with the Scottish Furniture Manufacturers' Association (SFMA) during their lock-out in 1898:

Our Committee have watched the sustained effort of your members to free themselves from unwarrantable trade union interference with the freedom of your employers in the management of their works ... We are asked to mention that the cheque [for £500] is, of course, sent on condition that the firm stand taken up will be maintained and carried to a successful result.[83]

These machinations and secret deals with the furniture employers were only a part of Biggart's vision of a broad employers' coalition embracing a broad range of industrial interests. In 1898 he organised a meeting of employers' association representatives from coal mining, building, boot and shoe manufacture, furniture making, cotton spinning, and shipping. The result was the formation of an employers' committee through which united action against labour could be more easily orchestrated.[84]

Biggart remained Secretary of the EEF and the Shipbuilding Employers' Federation until the national scope of these organisations outgrew their Glasgow base and they moved to London – in 1909 and

81. Ibid., T. Biggart to Colonel Dyer, 3 Sept. 1897, p. 27.
82. Ibid., T. Biggart to A. F. Yarrow, 11 April 1905, p. 51.
83. Ibid., T. Biggart to William Wylie, 6 July 1898, p. 217.
84. E. Wigham, *The Power to Manage*, pp. 75–76.

1917 respectively. However, he retained close links with the NWETEA until 1947, by which time he was 85 years old. He died two years later.[85] His office in West George Street in Glasgow, therefore, was effectively centre of an employer network that stretched throughout the UK. Allan Smith – later Sir Allan – was trained by the firm, and with Biggart's assistance became assistant secretary to the EEF before rising to Secretary based at the Federation's new London office in 1910 – and eventually Chairman of the EEF's managing committee.[86] Andrew Duncan – who, like Smith and Biggart, received a knighthood – also received his training at Biggart and Lumsden. Duncan took up the post of Secretary to the Shipbuilding Employers' Association when it moved to London. He then became Secretary to the Shipbuilding Advisory Committee, was Coal Controller during the First World War, and entered government during the Second World War.[87] Finally, another employee, A. W. Hunter, became Secretary of the Scottish National Farmers' Union in 1916 – Scotland's first employers' association for farmers. Under Hunter's guidance the membership of the NFUS soared from 2,000 to almost 20,000.[88]

Most theories of collective action do not really account for the actions of leading individuals. Thomas Biggart's motivation was clearly class-based, and the employer class identity that he drummed up took the form of a strong network that involved capitalists in industries far removed from engineering and shipbuilding. To an extent, then, the determination of Clydeside and British engineering and shipbuilding employers to face up to and keep pace with organised labour during this period was the result of one man's zealous class-based crusade.

Printing

Several Clydeside employers' associations provided the dynamic for the setting up of national organisations. Early unity amongst the ship-builders and engineers on the Clyde led – with the help of Thomas Biggart – to the creation of the EEF, and it was the efforts of the Scottish Welding Employers' Association that brought about a National Organisation of Welding Employers in 1921.[89] It was a similar story in printing. Here labour relations were fraught throughout the period,

85. *The Bailie*, 1 July 1925, p. 3. *Ibid.*, p. 47.
86. T. Rodgers, 'Sir Allan Smith', p. 101.
87. *The Bailie*, 5 Nov. 1919, p. 3. Also, E. Wigham, *The Power to Manage*, p. 47.
88. *The Bailie*, 3 Aug. 1935, p. 3.
89. For a concise account of the struggle between the Clyde shipbuilders and the Boilermakers' Society over welding in the 1930s, see J. McGoldrick's chapter in T. Dickson (ed.), *Capital and Class in Scotland* (Edinburgh, 1982), pp. 142–182.

and despite effective employer combination the workers managed to retain craft autonomy in a male-dominated industry. In an effort to combat this, Clydeside master printers were keen to draw together a national employers' movement, and in 1889 the Glasgow Master Lithographers' Association sent out circulars to test the viability of forming such an organisation:

> The question of a Federation of Masters' Associations throughout the kingdom has frequently engaged the attention of employers here, and in view of the strong position and aggressive attitude of the Amalgamated Society, it is felt that only by combination of all the Employers' Associations can the men's recurring demands be resisted.[90]

Comprehensive employer combination was finally achieved in 1913 with the Scottish Printers' Alliance, and three years later the Glasgow Master Printers' Association asked Thomas Biggart for a copy of the EEF's rules upon which they intended to base those of the new organisation.[91] However, despite a determination to deal effectively with the labour threat, the Clydeside master printers were not more authoritarian in their dealings with the trade unions than printers in other parts of the country. The first national lock-out in the printing trade began in Glasgow in 1913, but there was only one reported instance of blackleg labour being used in Clydeside in the two years preceding this dispute.[92] Moreover, during the 1918–1920 period only three of 55 British printing trade disputes occurred in Clydeside – none of which was characterised by distinctively hostile employer behaviour.[93]

Baking

Strong organisation amongst Clydeside's master bakers successfully withstood labour's challenge throughout the period. This determined stance was to a great extent necessitated by market forces and the need to utilise new technology. Factory machine baking spread quickly in the West of Scotland – a region initially more conducive to collective bargaining than London where a workshop system was prevalent.[94]

90. M. Sessions, *The Federation of Master Printers, How it Began* (London, 1950), p. 5.
91. Letter Book No. 7, Glasgow and District Printing and Kindred Trades Employers' Association. Letter from secretary to T. Biggart dated 30 Nov. 1916, p. 11; *GH*, 28 Jan. 1913, p. 9.
92. Trade Disputes Record Books PRO Lab 34/29, and Lab 34/30.
93. Trades Disputes Record Books PRO Lab 34/36, Lab 34 /37, and Lab 34/30/38.
94. I. McKay, 'Bondage in the Bakehouse? The Strange Case of the Journeymen Bakers, 1840–1880', in R. Harrison and J. Zeitlin (eds), *Divisions of Labour* (Sussex, 1985), p. 47.

However, with the intensification of competition in the 1870s the Glasgow employers launched an attack on trade unionism, and within seven years the union had collapsed.[95] With the decline of the union, conditions deteriorated and in 1887 a mass meeting of Glasgow bakers protested against conditions in the city's bread factories, and at the reduced status of the baker in general: 'One half of the men cannot earn enough to keep their body and soul together ... many of the breadmaking portion of the breadmaking class had scarcely enough to eat'. At the same time the *Dundee Weekly News* noted how conditions in the Glasgow bakery trade were 'as bad as can be'. According to its correspondent, the Glasgow machine bakeries were guilty of 'making slaves of men, and of the human frame a mechanical automaton'.[96] Around 10 years later a union spokesman told of the tyranny of the Glasgow employers, who, he maintained, hounded the men at their work like dogs.[97] There is evidence, then, that many Clydeside master bakers were distinguished by an intolerance of organised labour.[98]

Building

The Glasgow housing market was distinctive in that the city's building regulations were notoriously strict compared to those in many other parts of the country. This 'imposed on builders a cost four to eight times that imposed on their English counterparts in time and materials'.[99] Did this cause them to be harder on their workers than employers elsewhere?

Building trade employers' associations defended small businesses against labour militancy, and were effective instigators of collective bargaining agreements. The Glasgow Master Wrights' Association (GMWA), for example, played a role in the formation of the Employers' Council in 1902; helped establish the Scottish National Federation of Building Trades' Employers in 1918, and later assisted in the creation of a federation of master wrights' associations in 1923.[100] However,

95. *Ibid.*, p. 71.

96. *Northern Miller and Baker*, 1 Nov. 1887, p. 44 also 1 Feb. 1888, p. 27.

97. *British Baker*, 12 Sept. 1896.

98. See also H. Clegg *et al.*, *A History of British Trade Unions Since 1889, Volume 1* (Oxford, 1964), p. 127. However, although many of the master bakers displayed a characteristic ruthlessness whenever collective bargaining got in the way, this was not reflected in their paying lower wages. In 1907, Glasgow bakers had the highest average earnings of all Scottish bakers. *GH*, 19 June 1907, p. 11.

99. C. M. Atherton, 'The Development of the Middle Class Suburb: The West End of Glasgow', *Scottish Economic and Social History*, 11 (1991), p. 22.

100. With the setting up or the National Industrial Council for the Building Trades of Great Britain, the Scottish body returned 10 members. *Plumbing Trade Journal*, July 1918, p. 26.

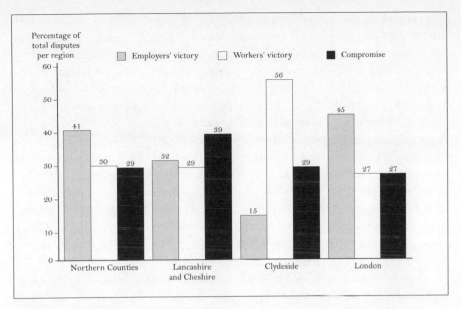

GRAPH 7.4. Outcome of disputes in the building industry, 1901–1908, 1911–1913, 1918–1920. *Source*: Board of Trade Record Books of Trade Disputes.

despite this drive to provide means of conciliation, the GMWA also retained a no-nonsense approach to strikes by resorting to lock-outs when the occasion demanded, and by supporting fellow building trade employers in other parts of the country. Exercises such as these, though, were aimed at ensuring the workers played by the rules of the game, and were not aimed at the principle of collective bargaining. This is borne out by Board of Trade statistics which illustrate that Clydeside building trade employers were not characterised by hostility towards labour.

Graph 7.4 shows that over the three periods North of England employers were 26% more successful in their confrontations with labour than those on Clydeside. Moreover, the BOT record books also reveal that scab labour was used more frequently by employers in the London area than in any other region.

Other industries
The evidence presented so far indicates that although some Clydeside employers achieved a reputation for harsh dealings with labour in the nineteenth century, as the period progressed their exceptionalism tended to fade; and a brief survey of some other industries largely presents the same picture.

Glasgow's shipowners and employers of dock labour made a

determined stand against labour radicalism during the periods of labour unrest in the pre- and post-war years. The Shipping Federation organised a meeting of Glasgow's shipowners' associations in mid-1911 to try to find a way of coming to terms with intensifying labour militancy.[101] During this meeting the Federation representative 'strongly urged the inadvisability of the Federation being beaten in any shape or form'.[102] Employer unity was made much easier by the fact that the Secretary of the Shipping Federation was also Secretary of the Clyde Shipbuilders' Association and the Clyde Sailing Ship Association – as well as four other associations concerned with shipping.[103]

In 1911 and 1912 there were serious disputes in the Clydeside docks. In Ardrossan the employers replaced 96 dockers when they struck over rates for discharging certain types of goods. There were also disputes over gang sizes and working conditions in Glasgow which resulted in 6,000 dockers being locked-out by the employers. However, this should be seen in perspective, as only 10 of the 110 dock labour disputes in Britain during this period happened on Clydeside. Moreover, in 1918 and 1919 there were 98 disputes on the British waterfront, but only two were recorded on Clydeside, both of which were settled quite amicably.

Sir George Askwith's evidence

We turn now to a particularly well informed eyewitness. The Conciliation Act of 1896 gave the Board of Trade limited powers of arbitration in industrial disputes. Consequently, by 1913 it had dealt with almost 700 trade disputes, 77% of which were settled by conciliation and arbitration. In 1911 the power of arbitration was vested in Sir George Askwith. With the establishment of the Committee of Production in 1915, he became the government's principal troubleshooter in its efforts to ensure untroubled war production. In 1917 the Committee of Production was transferred to the newly formed Ministry of Labour – which took over BOT responsibilities for conciliation, labour exchanges, and trade boards – and Askwith resigned the chair.

During his active period – between 1911 and 1917 – Askwith travelled all over the British Isles and was involved in industrial disputes across a wide range of industries. No one, therefore, was in a better position to detect regional employer traits. If Clydeside employers had been exceptionally intransigent in their relationship with organised labour,

101. Clyde Steamship Owners' Association (CSOA) Minute Book 2, 4 July 1911.
102. CSOA Minute Book 3, 2 July 1911, p. 360.
103. CSOA Minute Book 1, 9 March 1898.

FIGURE 13. G. R. Askwith, K.C.

Askwith would have been aware of it, and would have noted it. However, nowhere in Askwith's book – *Industrial Problems and Disputes* – is there any mention of distinctive employer behaviour north of the Border. On the contrary, when reflecting upon regional characteristics, he states:

> If a generalisation may be allowed, it seems to me that, on the assumption that a settlement must be effected, say at twelve o'clock, with the alternative of a fight, generally perfectly useless, Scotland will settle at five minutes before the hour and make quite sure; Lancashire will settle one minute before that hour; Yorkshire will debate so long that they may by inadvertence pass the hour and have trouble; Wales will take no note of the hour and sometimes settle and sometimes not; and Ireland say that the clock is wrong, and that if it is right they will settle or not without any regard to it. Personally I prefer the Scottish method.[104]

According to Askwith, then, by the First World War the distinctive opposition to collective bargaining on Clydeside referred to by witnesses called before the Royal Commission on Labour in 1894 had largely disappeared.

The situation by 1920

By the end of our period there were 180 local and national employers' associations operating on Clydeside. They represented the whole range of Clydeside industry from building to engineering, shipbuilding, mining and quarrying, to textile production, textile dyeing, the boot and shoe trade, clothing, food production, and agriculture – all areas where trade unionism was by this time quite well established. Most of these associations leaned towards the encouragement of collective bargaining, and only the Glasgow master bakers stand out as a particularly intolerant regime. The engineering and shipbuilding employers played a vital role in the procedural system of industrial relations that had evolved – although Biggart's influence helped ensure that they were ready to turn to more draconian measures if the situation demanded. The region was also well served by 20 trades councils and 27 conciliation and arbitration boards for particular industries, which also indicates that compromise was by now the dominant feature of labour relations in the West of Scotland.[105]

In 1918 the Wages (Temporary Regulation) Act came into force. This placed an obligation on employers to pay a standard district wage,

104. G. R. Askwith, *Industrial Problems and Disputes* (London, 1974), p. 190.
105. Directory of Industrial Associations 1919 [Cmd. 3282].

and any objections to this were heard by conciliation boards. Across the whole of the UK, 1432 complaints were heard in 1919, and only 67 (5%) of these originated on Clydeside. The Industrial Court Act of 1919 extended the provision of the 1918 Act and established a permanent conciliation and arbitration service.[106] During 1920, 841 cases were heard but only 50 (6%) came from the West of Scotland. Over these two years, then, of 2727 complaints about the standard district wage in Britain, only 117 (4%) were Clydeside cases. Of the 149 disputes reported to the Board of Trade in 1919 – involving more than 10 workers and lasting longer than a day – only six (4%) occurred on Clydeside. Similarly, in 1920, 253 disputes were recorded, but only 14 of these were in the West of Scotland. Over the 1919–1920 period, of 402 principal disputes reported to the BOT, only 5% originated on Clydeside.

Consequently – although it is difficult to draw meaningful conclusions from a comparison of one region's statistics with the rest of the country – it is reasonable to argue that Clydeside was not over-represented regarding conciliation and arbitration cases during this period. By the 1920s, then, Clydeside employers were not distinguished by an inability to deal with labour relations issues at the point of production.

106. *Labour Gazette*, Jan. 1920, pp. 6–7.

CHAPTER EIGHT

The Nature of Clydeside Capital

The steady growth of capitalist unity on the Clyde throughout this 1870–1920 period kept pace with that of organised labour, and many organisations came into being specifically to ensure that employers retained the upper hand in the capital/labour relationship. The initial dynamic for this unity came from the employers themselves, and much of this activity predated the state's cultivation and nurturing of collective bargaining channels. So, the idea of a government-induced triangular harmony involving the state, the trade unions, and the employers' associations, does not really hold true for Clydeside capital. There was a determination of engineering and shipbuilding employers' associations to resist state intervention in labour relations, and a general lack of enthusiasm for industrial council wage bargaining. Most employers' associations came into being, flourished, regulated trade, and forged conciliation channels with trade unions, independent of state involvement. Also, because in many cases their main *raison d'être* was to control the labour force, the notion that labour discipline rather than capital/labour collaboration was the guiding principle of the time seems convincing.[1]

As far as collective bargaining amongst skilled workers in the West of Scotland was concerned, it was generally the organised employers who set the agenda by moving towards the adoption of conciliation systems that gave them a high level of procedural control. This was the case in the building trade where in the 1890s the standard wage rate for the whole of the Clydeside stone mason trade was determined by the annual agreement reached between the Glasgow Master Masons' Association and the trade union; and where the Glasgow Master Wrights' Association and the Glasgow Master Slaters' Association had similar agreements with their workers by the early years of the twentieth century. Also, in furniture making the SFMA in the 1900s blunted the strike weapon by initiating a sliding-scale wage agreement and tying

---

1. J. Melling, 'The Servile State Revisited: Law and Industrial Capitalism in the early 20th Century', *Scottish Labour History Journal* 24 (1989), pp. 68–86. A. J. McIvor comes to similar conclusion regarding employers in the North-West of England. A. J. McIvor, *Organised Capital* (London, 1996).

the workers to a rigid disputes procedure. Evidence such as this is relevant to the ongoing debate regarding the extent to which it was labour and not capital that dictated the pace of collective bargaining in Britain.[2] However, the evidence from the Clyde also suggests that when unskilled workers demanded similar concessions, there was a much greater reluctance on the part of the employers to get involved. The notion that it was the trade unions – combined with state intervention – that set the pace is more convincing with regard to this type of labour.

The degree to which employer combination was used as a management strategy was dependent on various factors, and there is no single pattern that we can apply, as the range of circumstances and experiences was wide. The example of Clydeside's factory bakers illustrates how employer attitudes to collective bargaining could at times be determined by the market. The determination of these employers to control how and when their product was made was driven by the extraordinary demand for early morning bread from Clydeside consumers. This, combined with intensifying competition in which the freshness of the product was more important than the price, hardened employers' attitudes to labour's demands for later starting times and the non-employment of casual labour. The best way to resist these demands was through solid employer combination. The same could be said of the furniture manufacturers who felt increasingly frustrated by trade union interference, and in 1889 this pushed them to enforce their right to manage by collectively locking out their workers. In this case, though, there was a degree of encouragement from the region's engineering employers, and it was amongst the engineering and shipbuilding employers that united action on the Clyde became most highly developed. This was due to the unsettled nature of a market that compelled employers to hire and fire workers as the demand for their products rose and fell – especially in shipbuilding – and this largely nullified company welfarism as a labour control tool. Consequently, faced with a skilled and unionised workforce, combination was the most logical course for the employers to follow. However, some engineering companies do not fit this pattern. The locomotive manufacturers, for example, dealt quite effectively with labour relations issues throughout the period and did not have to depend

---

2. T. Adams, 'Markets and institutional forces in industrial relations: the development of national collective bargaining, 1910–1920', *Economic History Review* 50 (1997). See the exchange between Gospel and Adams in *Economic History Review* 51, 3 August (1998), pp. 591–605; J. Waddington, *The Politics of Bargaining* (London, 1995); J. Melling 'Managing the labour problem: the British worker question and the decline of manufacturing industry', *Labour History Review* 57, 3, Winter 1992, pp. 100–109.

on fellow-employers to help them do so. Moreover, in small towns like Kilmarnock where the engineering employers managed to retain a long-term workforce, effective company paternalism ensured that non-confrontational labour relations existed right up until the First World War – although several of the Kilmarnock employers were also members of the NWETEA. A principal reason for this success was that paternalism was an easier card to play in small towns than in Glasgow, and the extent of paternalism in the Paisley thread industry bears this out.[3]

However, despite the pitfalls of over-generalisation, the notion that labour management policy was chiefly determined by the market is a persuasive one, as many firms involved in less hostile markets were able to cultivate company welfarism as a way of controlling the workers.[4] Templetons the carpet manufacturer, for example, had its own Savings Bank and Mutual Benefit Society, and by the 1920s its Welfare Department was giving grants to older female employees to help them prepare for retirement.[5] For such a company, then, combination with other firms was not required to ensure peaceful labour relations. Once again, though, there is no single pattern, as Bislands' the bakers ensured that trade unionism was kept at bay by investing heavily in company welfare, while at the same time being an active member of the Glasgow Master Bakers' Association – although trade regulation was the main attraction of membership. However, as well as normally requiring a long-term workforce, paternalism was usually only effectively deployed in industries where poorly organised unskilled or semi-skilled workers were in the majority, such as in thread production. Moreover, when it was implemented in engineering and shipbuilding, it was normally aimed at managers, foremen and other key workers. In general, though, as the period progressed and trade unionism strengthened and expanded, paternalism tended to diminish as employer combination spread.

Employers' attitudes to skilled and unskilled workers were markedly different, and generally, the more skilled and unionised the workforce, the more there was a need for employer combination. Tailoring was initially dominated by organised skilled male labour, and this made employer combination a necessary tactic for the small-scale firms involved in this industry. On the other hand the majority of workers in the clothing trade were women, thus comprehensive employer

3. W. Knox, *Hanging By a Thread* (Preston, 1995).
4. H. Gospel, *Markets, Firms and the Management of Labour in Modern Britain* (London, 1992), p. 6.
5. J. N. Bartlett, *Carpeting the Millions* (Edinburgh, no date), p. 120.

combination only came into being here when a Trade Board was set up. There were wide differences in employer attitudes towards the skilled and the unskilled in the West of Scotland, and there could be several reasons for this. Many of the principal industries produced goods that demanded high levels of skill. Skill, therefore, was held in high esteem, and this was reinforced by the fact that many employers represented by the employers' associations were themselves skilled craftsmen – especially in the building trade where artisans frequently crossed and re-crossed the line separating employers from employees. Further, many employers were members of Trades Guilds, and these organisations were steeped in the iconography and ritual of craftsmanship – as was Freemasonry. These factors, combined with a high degree of sectarianism in the region, and the sheer number of unskilled workers available to Clydeside employers, sustained a greater respect for skilled than for unskilled labour.

This was especially so where female labour was concerned. When a predominantly female labour force was employed, Clydeside capitalists generally did not have to combine for labour relations reasons. For example, the vast majority of the 6000 workers in the dyeing and calico printing industry of the Vale of Leven were women. However, although the main companies had a degree of trade combination directed at regulating the market – through the Society of Master Calico Printers – labour relations were effectively handled by individual firms at plant level. Women also dominated the Paisley thread industry, but here again employer paternalism kept the workforce under control for most of the period – although the effectiveness of this strategy was wearing thin by the First World War.[6] Women were also viewed by many Clydeside employers as being weaker, less reliable, and less intelligent than their male counterparts: a representative of the Scottish Grocers' Federation remarked in 1921 that 'the relative value of women's work as compared to that of men's is generally reckoned to be in the proportion of three fifths to one'.[7] A consequence of the strong male-centred work ethic was that the dividing line between skilled and unskilled work was especially blurred where women's work was concerned – as women's work was generally classed as unskilled

6. W. Knox and H. Corr, 'Striking women: Cotton workers and industrial unrest *c1907–1914*', *in* W. Kenefick and A. J. McIvor (eds), *Roots of Red Clydeside, 1910–1914?* (Edinburgh, 1996), pp. 107–129. This view of paternalism in the Paisley thread industry has been contested. See C. M. M. MacDonald, 'Weak Roots and Branches: Class, Gender and the Geography of Industrial Protest', *Scottish Labour History* 33 (1998), pp. 6–31.

7. *Fingerpost*, Aug. 1921, p. 33.

regardless of the amount of ingenuity required.[8] Many employers in the West of Scotland exploited this cheap form of labour, and this was certainly the case in agriculture where a great deal of low-paid female farm work was not recorded by the censuses. However, this strategy was replicated by urban employers too, and by the turn of the century the higher-than-average craft wages in the West of Scotland were, to a degree, subsidised by the low wages of male and female unskilled workers.

This leads on to the question of whether Clydeside employers were more authoritarian than those elsewhere. The strongest condemnation of Clydeside capital in this respect comes from Marxist writers, and there is a notion that the inflexibility of the region's bourgeoisie, and its inability to see that concession was a weapon and not a weakness, resulted in the increased class awareness of the proletariat during the Red Clydeside period.[9] Testimony presented to the Royal Commission on Labour suggests there was a distinctive intolerance of collective bargaining within certain industries in the West of Scotland in the last quarter of the nineteenth century. The Glasgow Chamber of Commerce was similarly intolerant well into the twentieth century, and its reaction to the Communist threat in the 1920s was indicative of a strong capitalist identity amongst the members.

Problems arises when we try to locate exceptionally intolerant employer behaviour at employer association level. Although EEF records of conference decisions and wage movements provide a rough means of comparing regional employer activity, if Clydeside's engineers were as autocratic as suggested by some historians, we would expect to see this reflected in more disputes being referred to central conferences, and a reluctance by the Clydeside employers to concede wage demands. This was not the case. On the contrary, Clydeside employers were less intransigent over pay claims than employers in London or the North-East of England – although higher-than-average wage levels should not be taken to indicate employer benevolence. Clydeside employers were not soft on labour. The Memorial sent to the Board of Trade in 1915 calling for a rigorous disciplining of the labour force reflected a general discontent amongst the major engineering employers on the Clyde. The markets in which the employers had operated demanded stable labour relations, which could only be maintained if they held the balance of power. The sudden upsetting of the balance during the war caused

8. E. Gordon, *Women in the Labour Movement in Scotland, 1850–1914* (Oxford, 1991).
9. J. Foster, 'Strike action and working class politics on Clydeside, 1914–1919', *International Review of Social History* 35 (1990).

alarm as the employers were forced to come to terms with their loss of control, and at the same time to bear the brunt of a strengthened labour movement's reaction to the introduction of dilution. However, the sharpening of an already strong employer class-consciousness which these circumstances brought about was not an echo of old confrontational attitudes to collective bargaining, but a defensive reaction to an extremely difficult market situation.

The tendency amongst some nineteenth century Clydeside employers to be anti-trade union may have been caused by high levels of labour migration, Clydeside's relatively late industrialisation – which meant that industrial relations here were fairly primitive compared to other areas – the necessity for industrialists to compete with other well-established industrial regions such as Lancashire, and the effect of volatile capital goods markets that demanded skilled craft labour. As the period progressed attitudes to collective bargaining changed, but anti-labour attitudes lingered on within the Glasgow Chamber of Commerce for some time. They may also have been perpetuated to some degree by Thomas Biggart's determination to marshal an employer force on the Clyde strong enough to match the growing power of organised labour. In his efforts to ensure that the advantage in collective bargaining lay with the employers, Biggart on many occasions went beyond the call of duty. However, even he was not out to destroy trade unionism, but was determined that the system of collective bargaining worked to the employers' benefit.

It is unlikely, then, that the labour radicalism on Clydeside during and immediately after the First World War was a reaction to a history of employer tyranny directed at skilled workers. What we can say is that the further down the skill ladder we go, the more likely we are to find employer intolerance turning into employer authoritarianism. Clydeside's building trade employers, for example, were not distinguished by any anti-trade union attitude throughout the period, and were motivated – like the printing employers and the furniture manufacturers – more by a desire to regulate collective bargaining amongst the skilled artisans than to eliminate it. However, their reaction to similar demands from unskilled workers was more intransigent, and this was generally the case with other employers of unskilled labour. It was these employers who remained most hostile to the principle of collective bargaining, as it was generally the workers in the unskilled occupations who overstocked the Clydeside labour market. It is at this level, then, that the notion of the authoritarian Clydeside employer is most credible, as it was at this level that hostility to collective bargaining took longest to die.

The extent of trade collaboration that went on in the West of Scotland provides further evidence that individualism was not the keynote of capitalism, as the compulsion to regulate competition percolated every level of the region's industrial and commercial activity – so much so that the distinction between co-operative trading and private trading sometimes became blurred. Although many West of Scotland business people never became involved with employers' organisations or price associations, the impact of market forces, coupled with threats to profits, compelled a significant number of them to indulge in non-competitive trading practices. The Clydeside evidence also suggests that employers' associations concerned with labour relations, and trade associations dealing with the regulation of the market, increased the efficiency of small firms; and this supports the argument that an economy in which small companies prevailed was more than just a transient phase in a natural progression towards a modern large-scale business structure.[10] Further, many employers' associations attracted members because of the opportunity they offered small firms to regulate competition and – the best example being the building trades employers' organisations – this illustrates that the growth of employers' associations throughout Britain at this time was not just for labour relations reasons.

However, it is also clear that Clydeside employers frequently acted out of class consciousness – Biggart's activities being an obvious example. Many employers' associations, as Olson suggests, did offer incentives from which only their members derived any benefit – such as regulation of trade.[11] However such collective action – with its stress on the attraction of selective incentives – does not adequately account for employers banding together to establish or reinforce a collective identity, or for reasons of mutual defence. Moreover, some important employer institutions – such as Clydeside's Chambers of Commerce – brought benefits to the whole of the region's business community and not just to their members. In this case, therefore, capitalist unity is best explained by reference to class or status.

The theories of Max Weber can be utilised, but only if Weber's separation of class and status is abandoned. Within such a model many Clydeside employers shared the same class because – to use Weber's terms – their 'life chances' in relation to the market were

10. M. C. Casson and M. B. Rose, Introduction to *Business History* 39 (Oct. 1997), pp. 1–8; M. C. Casson, 'Entrepreneurship and Business Culture', in J. Brown and M. B. Rose (eds), *Entrepreneurship, Networks and Modern Business* (Manchester, 1993); G. Cookson, 'Family Firms and Business Networks: Textile Engineering in Yorkshire, 1780–1830', *Business History* 39, 1 (1997).

11. M. Olson, *The Logic of Collective Action* (Oxford, 1965).

similar.[12] Status, though, was different, and was manifested at the social level: in the Trade Guilds, the Chambers of Commerce, the charities and clubs, and within Freemasonry and shared religious affiliation. A broad cross-section of capitalists were members of the Chambers of Commerce, the Merchants' House and the Trades House, and membership was generally taken up for reasons of prestige. However, there was a significant overlap between the Trades Guilds and the Chambers of Commerce, and many employers' associations oriented towards labour relations were members of the Chamber too. The boundary between the social and the economic spheres, then, was blurred at times; and this was also the case with institutions such as the Glasgow City Business Club – also affiliated to the Glasgow Chamber of Commerce – which offered its members prestige, a venue for social mixing, and an agency in which they could practise restrictive trading. Therefore, it is difficult to separate class and status.

A combination of Olson's theory and corporatism has some utility in explaining why employers organised – with Olson's model accounting for the motivation of small employers, and corporatist theory explaining the emergence of large-scale organisations. However, this also fails to take into account the fact that collective action was frequently triggered and sustained by class awareness. The evidence from the Clyde, where a hidden network of capitalist connections stretched throughout the regions and beyond, suggests that this cannot be ignored, and that at certain times the notion of a steadily unifying employer class cannot be discounted.[13]

The Clydeside evidence, then, goes some way to undermining arguments in which class is seen as unimportant to historical momentum, as it is in the collective *action* of individuals that class can be located, and collective action amongst Clydeside capitalists was very significant.[14] Moreover, just as the Scottish working class was made and re-made, so too were the employer classes on the Clyde, as the intensity of their collective action rose and fell in response to various stimuli –

12. M. Weber, *Economy and Society* (New York, 1968), p. 308.
13. M. Savage, 'Space, networks and class formation', in N. Kirk (ed.), *Social Class and Marxism* (Aldershot, 1996), pp. 58–81.
14. P. Joyce, 'Refabricating Labour History; or, From Labour History to the History of Labour', *Labour History Review* 62, 2 (1997), pp. 138–151; P. Joyce, 'The Return of History: Postmodernism and the Politics of Academic History in Britain', *Past and Present* 158, February (1998); A. J. Reid, 'Marxism and Revisionism in British Labour History', *Bulletin for the Society of the Study of Labour History*, 52, 3 (1987), pp. 46–48.

such as labour market and product market factors, and state interference
in capitalist production.[15]

Clydeside capital was also politically significant during this period.
Consequently, the notion that the business interest at this time was
defensive, divided, and politically weak, cannot be sustained.[16] Before
the recent spate of revisionist writing, Perkin stated:

> The landed class possessed a clear majority of the House of Com-
> mons until 1885, of the Cabinet until 1893, if not 1905, and of the
> House of Lords until after the Parliament Act of 1911 ... Yet neither
> contemporaries nor historians have doubted that the capitalist
> middle class were the 'real' rulers of mid-Victorian England, in the
> sense that the laws which were passed and executed by landed
> Parliaments and Governments were increasingly those demanded
> by the business men and – which is not necessarily the same people
> – their intellectual mentors.[17]

Perkin's conclusions regarding the Mid-Victorian era are applicable
to Clydeside throughout the 1870–1920 period. At this time in the West
of Scotland a quarter of constituency MPs had business interests, and a
significant number were large employers of labour. Moreover, on many
occasions employer unity effectively took the edge off government legislation. The Chambers of Commerce always had the ear of parliamentary
politicians and were consequently able to act as effective political pressure
groups. Their determined and sustained monitoring of commercial legislation was important in legitimising capitalist production, and ensured
that the capitalist network of influence extended throughout the social,
economic and political spheres. Therefore, the idea that Chambers of
Commerce placed businessmen 'in a stronger position than other economic groups' is substantiated by the Clydeside evidence.[18] Employer
political power was strong at the local level too, and it was here that
employers were best able to influence political decisions by playing the
network of capitalist connections to the full. Their close involvement
with Glasgow's civic government was replicated in Greenock, Lanarkshire, and Paisley, where 60% of town councillors were employers.

15. W. Knox, *Industrial Nation* (Edinburgh, 1999), p. 17.
16. J. Turner (ed.), *Businessmen and Politics* (1984), p. 7; H. Phelps Brown, *The Origins
    of Trade Union Power* (Oxford 1986), pp. 119–123.
17. H. Perkin, *The Origins of English Society, 1780–1880* (London, 1969), p. 272.
18. R. Milliband, *The State in Capitalist Society* (London, 1979), p. 52. See also E. Gordon
    and R. Trainor, 'Employers and policymaking: Scotland and Northern Ireland,
    1880–1939', in *Conflict, Identity and Economic Development: Ireland and Scotland,
    1600–1939* (Preston, 1995).

Our period closes in 1920. The ensuing Depression would see labour losing many of its wartime gains, and the terms of settlement that were to follow the 1922 engineering lock-out would place the employers in a position to organise production and payment systems to their best advantage. There was now a recognisable employer movement in Britain, and many Clydeside capitalists were represented by the Federation of British Industry (FBI) and the National Confederation of Employers' Organisations (NCEO). Moreover, trade regulation associations and employers' organisations concerned primarily with labour relations continued to blossom and expand across a wide range of industries. Over the previous 50 years the region had produced capital goods for the home market, the Empire, and the world, and the region's industrial reputation was now well established. Clydeside capital was much more than this, though, and throughout the period the economy of the West of Scotland was underpinned by a dense and complex network of trading connections, alliances, and tacit agreements, all held together by a shared identity that set apart those who employed labour from those who did not.

Bibliography

1. PRIMARY SOURCES ARRANGED BY ARCHIVE

Strathclyde University Archives
Minute Books of Bilsland and Co., 1917–1924

Strathclyde Regional Archives, Glasgow
Clyde and East Coast of Scotland Ship Repairers' Association, Minimum Schedule Prices for Steamers, TD 241/10/8
Clyde Master Sailmakers' Association, Rules and Regulations 1906, TD 11/10/2
Clyde Shipbuilders and Engineers' Association Rules and Regulations 1866, TD 241/3/1
Clyde Shipbuilders and Engineers' Association Rules and Regulations 1906, TD 241/3/3
Clydesdale Merchants and Tradesmen's Society, Membership Role 1923, TD402/49
Collective Agreement Between Shipbuilding Employers' Federation and 17 Trade Unions, TD 241/10/6
Engineering and Allied Employers' National Federation, Decisions of Central Conference 1898–1921, TD 1059/10/1
Engineering Employers' Association Kilmarnock and District, Minute Books 1 and 2, TD 1059/1/1&2
Glasgow and District Master Slaters' Association, Minute Books 1–5, 1873–1918, TD 200
Glasgow and West of Scotland Master Plumbers' Association, Rules and Regulations 1912, TD 241/8/3
Glasgow Candle and Soap Makers' Society, Regulations, TD 818/7
Glasgow District Printing and Allied Trades Employers' Association, Letter Book 7, TD 175/6/2
Glasgow Federated Engineering and Shipbuilding Employers, Private Letter Book 1, TD 1059/22/2/1
Kincaid and Company Works Masonic Club Register of Members, TD 131/9/2
Kincaid and Company Works Masonic Club Minutes 1918–1925. TD 131/9/1.
Matters of Historical Interest Regarding Some West of Scotland Engineering Firms Concerned with Industrial Relations 1865–1893, TD 1059/10/11/5
McKie and Baxter, Letter Book 1, TD 827
National Federation of Iron and Steel Manufacturers, Minutes, 1918–1922, TD 171/2/1
National Federation of Master Painters in Scotland, Glasgow Branch Information, TD 1064
NWETEA Register of Members' Voting Power, Wage Returns and Levies 1890–1929, TD 1059/5/1&2
NWETEA, Minute Books 2–5 1897–1920, TD 1059
Old Glasgow Club, Volume 1, Session 1906–08
Research note on Glasgow Town Councillors 1833–1912, I. Sweeney, AGN 994.

Scottish Candle and Soap Makers' Society, Minute Book, TD 818/1

Scottish Coppersmiths' Employers' Association, Minute Book 2, 1911–1919, TD 1059/12

Scottish Employers' Federation of Iron and Steel Founders, Minute Book 2, 1908–1918, TD 1059/13/1&2

Scottish Sheet Metal Workers' Association Minute Books 1, 2, and 3, 1907–1920, TD 1059/11

Scottish Sheet Metal Workers Employers' Association Rules and Regulations 1914, TD 241/10/4

Shipbuilders' Employers' Federation. Scheme to Ensure More Unity When Dealing with the Trade Unions, TD241/15/5.

Trust of Andrew Bryann, TD 733/8

Trust of J. William Lindsay, TD 733/43

Trust of T. M. Stevenson, TD 974/196/1.

United Collieries Active Service Roll, 1914–1919, TD 666

West of Scotland Iron and Steel Founders' Association Minute Book 3, 1910–1919, TD 1059/14

Wholesale Clothing Manufacturers' Association, Records 1914–1923, TD 967. This collection includes the Minutes of Glasgow Shirt Manufacturers' Association, the West of Scotland Textile Association. The West of Scotland Wholesale Clothing Association, and the Scottish Carpet Manufacturers' Association

Glasgow University Archives

Adam Smith Club of Glasgow, Membership Book 1868–1892, MU-i–42

Civic Society of Glasgow Membership List 1899–1900, MU29–626

Constitution and Rules of the Conservative Club of Glasgow 1899, MU22-e9

Constitution and Rules of the Imperial Union Club of Glasgow, 1899 MU22- e9

Glasgow Athenaeum Seventy-First Annual Report, MU22-f15

Incorporation of Hammermen Annual Dinner at the Grosvenor Hotel, Glasgow September 1910, Toast List, MU22-e3

Report of the Glasgow Houses of Shelter for Females 1906–1907, p. 3, MU22-e8

Scottish Christian Social Union 4th Annual Report 1905, Mu22-c7

Scottish Labour Colony Association Annual Report 1900, MU22-e8

Business Records Centre, Glasgow University

Alexander Ferguson and Company, Private Ledger, UGD 258

Ayrshire Employers' Mutual Insurance Association Articles of Association, UGD 162/2/1

City Business Club of Glasgow Minute Book 1, 1912–1923, UGD/146/2/3

Clyde Sailing Ship Owners' Association, Minute Book 1, 1885–1892, TD 925/1/1

Clyde Ship Riggers Employers' Association, Minute Book 1, 1920–1922, UGD 339/220

Clyde Steamship Owners' Association Minutes 1884–1923, TD 925/1/1

Coal Merchants' Association of Scotland, Minute Book 1, 1909–1917, Minute Book 2, 1917–1920, TD 1367/1/1 & 2

Conciliation Board for Wages in Mining, Minute Book 1, 1900–1904, UGD/160/1

Glasgow and West of Scotland Metal Merchants' Association, Minute Book 1, UGD 290

Glasgow District Engine Boiler and Ship Repairers' Association, Minute Book 1, 1891–1897, UGD 339/236

Glasgow Master Boilers and Pipe Coverers' Association, Minute Book 2, 1924–1940, UGD 339/2/40

Glasgow Master Masons' Association Minute Books 1–8 1876–1923, Uncatalogued

Glasgow Shipowners and Dock Labour Employers' Organisation, 9th Annual Report, 1922, UGD 176/1/17/13

Joint Industrial Council for the Carpet Trade, Minutes of Council 1920, UGD 265.

Lanarkshire Coalmasters' Association, Minute Book 1, 1886–1893, Minute Book 2, 1893–1895, Minute Book 3, 1896–1898, Minute Book 4, 1898–1900 Minute Book 5, 1900–1905, Minute Book 7, 1909–1910, Minute Book 8, 1911–1912, Minute Book 10, 1915–1916, Minute Book 11, 1917–1918, Minute Book 12, 1918- 1920, Minute Book 13, 1920–22

Letter from EEF (London) to J. H. Carruthers Polmadie Iron Works, re: EEF Indemnity Fund, UGD/333/1/6/1

Mirilees Watson and Company, General Letter Book, UGD 62/2

National Organisation of Welding Employers Minute Book 1, 1921–24, UGD 339/2/46

Repairers Liability Insurance Committee Minute Book, 1921–1922, UGD 339/265

Rye Pickering & Co. Minute Book, 1914–1915, UGD 12/29/25

Scottish Association of Bridge Builders and Structural Engineers, Cash Book 1923, UGD 339/2/66

Scottish Building Contractors' Association Membership Book, UGD 362/2/2/3/1

Scottish Carpet Manufacturers' Association, Minutes 1920–1923 UGD 265/2/14/4

Scottish Coal Exporters' Association, Minute Book 1, 1899–1912, Minute Book 2, 1912–1918, Minute Book 3, 1918–1923, UGD/290/1–3.

Scottish Coalmasters' Association, Minute Book 1898–1895, UGD 158/1

Scottish Lead Manufacturers' Association, Minute Book 1, 1909–1913, Minute Book 2, 1913–1918, Minute Book 3, 1918–1923, UGD 299/3/1–3

Scottish Licensees' Mutual Insurance Association, Minute Book 1, 1899–1908, UGD 110/4/1

Scottish Metal Refiners' Association, Minute Book 1, 1919–1927, UGD 290/4/1

Scottish Rivet Bolt and Nut Manufacturers' Association Minute Book 1, 1920–1923, UGD 339/2/22

Scottish Welding Employers' Association, Minute Book 1, 1920–1923, UGD 339/2/75

Scottish Wine and Spirit Merchants' Benevolent Institution, Minute Book, UGD 119 5/1

United Turkey Red Federation, Trades Disputes Book, UGD 13/4/3

Gallagher Memorial Library, Glasgow

Minutes of Glasgow Trades Council, 1885–1920

Research Notes on the Amalgamated Society of Dyers

Scottish Trades Union Conference Reports, 1898–1911

Central Library, Airdrie

Minutes of Airdrie Town Council, 1873

Watt Library, Greenock

Greenock Chamber of Commerce Minutes 1883–1913

Greenock Master Hairdressers' Association Minutes 1866–1914

Greenock Master Wrights' Association Minutes 1866–1876

Greenock Seamen's Friends' Society, Annual Report 1908

National Library of Scotland, Edinburgh
Scrapbooks of J. Maclehose, ACC 8166. Volume 1, 1911, Vol. 2, 1912, Vol. 5, 1913, Vol.
12, 1914, Vol. 17, 1915, Vol. 28, 1916, Vol. 54, 1919, Vol. 48, 1918, Vol. 58, 1919,
Vol. 92, 1920, Vol. 111, 1921, Vol. 201, 1922

Modern Records Centre University of Warwick
British Manufacturers' Association, Minute Book 1, MSS/237/3/2

EEF Booklet, List of the Federated Engineering and Shipbuilding Employers who
Resisted the Demand for a 48 Hours' Week, MSS 237/4/5/1

EEF Minute Books, 1904–1907, MRC, MSS 237/1/3/1

EEF Rates of Wages Paid to Boys and Youths, MSS 237/13/1/11

Gas Meter Makers' Employers' Federation, Minute Book 1, 1908–1918, MSS 200/3

Interviews of Mr. R. T. Nugent 1916–21, MSS 200 1/3/01/4/4

Memorandum of Conference Between Representatives of the EEF and the ASE, November 1912, MSS 237/3/9/1

Research Note on Glasgow Plumbers' Trade Union, MSS–134

Scottish Plasterers' Union Glasgow District, Minute Book, 1916–1919, MSS
126/50/1/1–2

Siemens Steel Ingot Making Trades of the North of England and West of Scotland,
Minute Books 1–4, 1896–1920, MSS 238/4/2–5

Speech delivered in Glasgow by W. Rowan Thomas, Chairman of NWETEA, 1916,
MSS 200/1/3/01/19

Wholesale Clothing Trade of the United Kingdom, Minute Book, 1910–1913, and
1914–1917, MSS 232/cm/1/1/1

Public Record Office, London
Board of Trade Record Books of Trade Disputes

Building and Coalmining 1901–1903:1901, Lab 34/1, 1902, Lab 34/2, 1903, Lab 34/3

Building and Coalmining 1911–1914: 1911, Lab 34/11, 1912, Lab 34/12, 1913, Lab
34/13.

Building and Coalmining 1918–1920: 1918, Lab 34/18, 1919, Lab 34/19, 1920, Lab
34/20

Collective Agreement between Amalgamated Society of Journeymen Cloggers and
Various Glasgow Firms 1924, Lab 83/1603

Collective Agreement between Clay Tobacco Pipe Manufacturers' Association and National Union of General Workers, 1919, Lab 83/1686

Collective Agreement between Glasgow and West of Scotland Master Coopers' Association and Glasgow Journeymen's Coopers' Society, 1919, Lab 83/1876

Collective Agreement between Glasgow and West of Scotland Saddlers' Association and
Union of Saddlers and General Leather Workers, 1928, Lab 83/1423

Collective Agreement between Glasgow Master Bootmakers' Association and City of
Glasgow Operative Boot and Shoe Makers' Trade and Funeral Society, 1920, Lab
83/1588

Collective Agreement between Greenock and Port Glasgow Timber Measurers' Association and Greenock and Port Glasgow Rafters' Trade Society, 1925, Lab 83/2569

Collective Agreement between Scottish Furniture Manufacturers' Association and Scottish Furnishing Trades Advisory Committee, 1923 Lab, 83/2034

Collective Agreement between Scottish Retail Drapers' Association and National Amalgamated Union of Shop Assistants, Warehousemen, and Clerks, 1926, Lab 83/3012

Collective Agreement between Scottish Wireworkers' Manufacturers' Association and Scottish Society of Wireworkers, Lab 83/1105

Collective Agreement between Wholesale Cloth Hat and Cap Manufacturers' Association (Glasgow Branch), and United Garment Workers' Trade Union, 1917, Lab 83/5534

Collective Agreement Boot and Shoe Industry in Scotland, Lab 83/1586

Collective Agreement Building Scotland, 1921, Lab 83/2100

Metals, Textiles, Clothing, Transport and Local Authorities, 1911–1913, Lab 34/29-Lab 34/31

Metals, Textiles, Clothing, Transport, and Local Authorities, 1918–1920: 1918, Lab 34/36, 1919, Lab 34/37, 1920, Lab 34/38

Ministry of Labour File, Agreement between Scottish Building Contractors' Association and several trade unions, Lab 2/643/26

Ministry of Labour File, Arbitration between Workers' Union and Kilmarnock Yarn Spinners' Association, 1918, Lab 2/261/12

Ministry of Labour File, Chemical Employers' Federation, Lab 2/285/3

Ministry of Labour File, Clyde Sailmaking Employers' Association, Lab 2/200/1

Ministry of Labour File, Glasgow and District Umbrella Manufacturers' Association, 1919, Lab 2/556/6

Ministry of Labour File, Glasgow and West of Scotland Master Plumbers' Association, Lab 2/935/7

Ministry of Labour File, Glasgow Kilt Manufacturers' Association 1917, Lab 83/1545

Ministry of Labour File, Joint Industrial Council for Furniture Trade, 1919 Lab 2/448/10

Ministry of Labour File, Joint Industrial Council for Vehicle Building, Lab 2/267/1

Ministry of Labour File, National Association of Biscuit Manufacturers, Lab 69/34

Ministry of Labour File, National Ironfounding Employers' Federation, Lab 69/34

Ministry of Labour File, Protest of National Farmers' Union of Scotland and Highland Agricultural Society, and Scottish Chamber of Agriculture at 48 hr Day, Lab 2/740/13

Ministry of Labour File, Shirt Making Trade Board for Scotland, Lab 35/338

Ministry of Labour File, Wagon Repairers' Association, Lab 69/16

Papers relating to the Cooperative Movement's History, Organisation, and Constitution, Lab 2/740/17

Papers relating to the Electrical Trades Union Manchester, and Electrical Contractors' Association of Scotland, Lab 2/482/3

Scottish Bakers' Industrial Council, General Correspondence, Lab 2/901/3

PRIVATE COLLECTIONS

Scottish Furniture Manufacturers' Association, Merchants' House Buildings, 30 George Square, Glasgow

Glasgow Branch Minute Book 1917–1929

Scottish Furniture Manufacturers' Association Minute Books 1890–1921

Scottish Grocers' Federation, Federation House, 222/224 Queensferry Road, Edinburgh
Scottish Grocers' Federation Annual Reports, 1918–1926

Scottish Master Wrights and Builders' Association, 98 West George Street, Glasgow
Glasgow Master Wrights Association Minute Books 1885–1923

Scottish Decorators' Federation, 1, Grindlay Street Court, Edinburgh
Glasgow Master Plasterers' Association, Minute Book 1, 1896–1916, Minute Book 2, 1916–1924
Scottish Furniture Manufacturers' Association, Merchants House Buildings, 30, George Square Glasgow
Scottish Furniture Manufacturers' Association Minute Books 1889–1924

PARLIAMENTARY PAPERS

Abstract of Labour Statistics of the UK 1902–1904 [Cd. 2491]
Board of Trade Industrial Survey of the West of Scotland 1932
Board of Trade Inquiry into Earnings and Hours of Labour in the UK 1906, Metal Engineering and Shipbuilding [Cd. 5814]
Board of Trade Report on Earnings and Hours of Labour in the Textile Trades 1906 [Cd. 4545]
Board of Trade Returns of Average Number of Hours Worked 1890 [375]
Census of Scotland, 1871, 1881, 1891, 1901, 1911, 1921
Directory of Industrial Associations in the UK 1919 [Cmd. 328]
Directory of Industrial Associations in the UK, 1902 [Cd. 945XLVI 561]
Final Report of the Committee on Industry and Trade, 1929 [Cmd. 3282]
Finance Bill 1920 (Excess Profits Duty) [Cmd. 753]
First Report of the Royal Commission on the Depression of Trade and Industry, 1886 [c. 4621]
Fourth Report of the House of Lords Committee on the Sweating System, 1889 (331)
General Report on the Wages of the Manual Labouring Classes in the UK 1893 [c. 6889]
Profiteering Acts 1919 and 1920, Central Committee Interim Report on Bricks [Cmd. 959] Furniture [Cmd. 983], Laundries [Cmd. 903], Salt Trade [Cmd. 832], Boot and Shoe Trade [Cmd. 592]
Report of Collective Agreements Between Employers and Workpeople in the United Kingdom 1910 [Cd. 5366]
Report of Standard Piece Rates of Wages and Sliding Scales 1901 [Cd 144]
Report of Strikes and Lock-outs in 1901 [Cd. 1236]
Report on the Conditions of Labour in Chemical Works 1893 [c.7235]
Report on the Strikes and Lock-outs of 1888, 1889 [c.5809]
Report on the Strikes and Lock-outs of 1890, 1891 [c. 6476]
Royal Commission on Grocers' Licences (Scotland) 1877 [Cd. 1941]
Royal Commission on Labour Laws [c. 1094]
Royal Commission on Master and Servant Act 1875 [c. 1157–1]
Royal Commission on the Depression of Trade and Industry [c.4621]

Second Report on the Royal Commission on the Depression of Trade and Industry 1886 [c.4715]

Standing Committee on Trusts, Interim Report on Glass Bottles and Jars and Scientific Glassware [Cmd. 1066]

Third Report of the Royal Commission on the Depression of Trade and Industry 1886 [c–4797]

NEWSPAPERS AND JOURNALS

Newspapers

Airdrie and Coatbridge Advertiser, 1872
Brixton Free Press, May 1919
Byestander April, 1919
Christian World, May 1919
Forward, 1906–1914
Glasgow Herald, 1870–1924
Greenock Telegraph, 1920
Labour Leader, May 1919
Motor World, Oct. 1919
Newcastle Daily Journal, April 1919
Southern Press, July 1911 and April 1921
Sunday Post, Sept. 1919
The Bailie, 1906–1923
The Times, 1870–1920

Journals

Board of Trade Gazette, 1905–1920
British Baker, 1888–1892
British Baker, Confectioner and Purveyor, 1892–1922
Builder, 1870–1880
Builders' Reporter, 1890–1906
Building Industries, No. 1, 1890
Building News, 1890–1892
Building Trade, 1906–1907
Building Trades Exchange of the City of Glasgow and District, Catalogue, 1902 and 1903
Chemical Age, 1919
Confectioners' Union, 1913–1914
Engineer, 1886–1920
Engineering Magazine, 1889–
Engineering Times, 1896–1920
Farming World, 1886–1889
Fingerpost, 1918–1922
Furniture Record, 1914
Industries, 1883–1889
Iron, 1874–88
Journal of Commerce, 9, 1910
Labour Gazette, 1893–1920
Master Printers' Annual and Typographical Year Book (London, 1920)

Master Tailors' and Cutters' Gazette 1905–1915
North British Agriculturist, 1912–1920
Northern Miller and Baker, 1885–1888
Organised Help: Organ of the Charity Organisation Society, January 1897
Paper Maker and British Printing Trades' Journal, 1875–1877, and 1908–1912
Plumbing Trade Journal, 1914–1923
Railway Engineering, 1897
Sartorial Gazette, 1915–1916
Scottish Decorators' Review, 1923 and 1958
Scottish Electrician, 1901–1904
Scottish Farm Servant, 1915–1919
Scottish Farmer, 1895–1904
Scottish Ironmerchant, 1899–1920
Scottish Journal of Agriculture, 1918–1922
Scottish Leather Trader, 1880–1898
Scottish Trader, 1897–1920
Scottish Typographical Journal, July 1910
Shoe and Leather Trader, 1898–1920
Tailoring World, 1912–1913
Timber Trades Journal, 1893
Transactions of the Highland and Agricultural Society of Scotland, 1885, 1886, 1919

CONTEMPORARY WORKS

Bremner, D., *The Industries of Scotland 1868* (London, 1969)
Campbell, W., *The Cordiners of Glasgow* (Glasgow, 1883)
Campsie, J., *Glimpses of Co-operative Land* (Glasgow, 1899)
Cruickshank, J., *Sketch of the Incorporation of Masons* (Glasgow, 1879)
Dod's Parliamentary Companion, 1870–1924
Federation of British Industries, *Report of the Committee on the Organisation of Industry* (London, 1935)
Flanagan, J. A., *Wholesale Cooperation in Scotland* (Glasgow, 1920)
Glasgow Contemporaries at the Dawn of the 20th Century (Glasgow, 1900)
Glasgow Post Office Directories, 1870–1923
Goodwill, T., *History of the Glasgow Night Asylum for the Homeless* (Glasgow, 1887)
Greenock Post Office Directories, 1870–1923
History of the Incorporation of Gardeners (Glasgow, 1903)
Industries of Glasgow and the West of Scotland (Glasgow, 1901)
Lumsden, H., and Aitken, P. H., *History of the Hammermen of Glasgow* (Glasgow, 1912)
MacCarthur, J., *New Monklands Parish* (Glasgow, no date)
McLean, A. (ed.), *Local Industries of Glasgow and the West of Scotland* (Glasgow, 1901)
Murphy, W. S., *Captains of Industry* (Glasgow, 1901)
Ness, J., *The Incorporation of Bakers of Glasgow* (Glasgow, 1889)
Paisley Post Office Directories, 1870–1923
Reid, J. A., *The Incorporation of Wrights* (Glasgow, 1889)
Reid, J. M., *A History of the Merchants' House* (Glasgow, 1891)
Reid, W., *History of the United Cooperative Baking Society, 1869–1919* (Glasgow, 1920)

2. SECONDARY SOURCES

Adams, T., 'Markets and institutional forces in industrial relations: the development of national collective bargaining 1910–1920', *Economic History Review* (1997), pp. 597–605

Alderman, G., 'The National Free Labour Association: Working Class Opposition to New Unionism in Britain', in Mommsen, W. J and Husung, H. G. (eds), *The Development of Trade Unionism in Great Britain and Germany 1880–1914* (London, 1985), pp. 302–311

Alderman, G., 'The Railway Companies and the Growth of Trade Unionism in the Late 19th and Early 20th Century' *The Historical Journal* 14 (1971), pp. 129–152

Alderman, G., *The Railway Interest* (Leicester, 1973)

Allen, G. C., *Monopoly and Restrictive Practices* (London, 1968)

Anthony, R., 'The Scottish Agricultural Labour Market, 1900–1939: A Case of Institutional Intervention,' *Economic History Review*, 46, 3 (London, 1993), pp. 558–574

Askwith G. R., *Industrial Problems and Disputes* (London, 1974)

Aspinwall, B., 'Glasgow Trams and American Politics 1894–1914', *Scottish Historical Review* 56 (1977), pp. 64–84

Atherton, C. M., 'The Development of the Middle Class Suburb: The West End of Glasgow', *Scottish Economic and Social History* 11 (1991) pp. 19–39

Bagwell, P. S., *The Railwaymen* (London, 1963)

Bartlett J. N., 'Alexander Pirie and Sons of Aberdeen, and the Expansion of the British Paper Industry *c.* 1880–1914', *Business History* 42 (1988), pp. 18–34

Bartlett, J. N., *Carpeting the Millions* (Edinburgh, 1978)

Bartrip, P. W. J., and Burman, S. B., *The Wounded Soldiers of Industry* (Oxford, 1983)

Belchem, J., 'Reconstructing Labour History', *Labour History Review*, 62, 3 (1997)

Bell, T., *Pioneering Days* (London, 1941)

Benson, J., and Shaw, G. (eds), *The Evolution of Retail Systems c. 1800–1914* (Leicester, 1992)

Bentley, M., 'The Liberal Response to Socialism', in K. Brown (ed.), *Essays in Anti-Labour History* (London, 1974)

Biagini, E. F., and Reid, A. J. (eds), *Currents of Radicalism: Popular Radicalism Organised Labour and Party Politics in Britain, 1850–1914* (Cambridge, 1991)

Birchall, J., *Co-op: The People's Business* (Manchester, 1994)

Bland, S., *Take a Seat* (London, 1995)

Blankenhorn, D., 'Our Class of Workmen: The Cabinet-Makers Revisited', in Harrison, R., and Zeitlin, J. (eds), *Divisions of Labour* (Sussex, 1985)

Bolin-Hort, P., 'Managerial Strategies and Worker Responses: A New Perspective on the Decline of the Scottish Cotton Industry', *Scottish Labour History Journal* Number 29 (1994), pp. 63–81

Bolin-Hort, P., *Work, Family and the State* (Lund, 1989)

Booth, A., Melling, J., and Dartmann, C., 'Institutions and Economic Growth: The Politics of Productivity in West Germany, Sweden, and the United Kingdom 1945–1955', *Journal of Economic History*, 57, 2 (June, 1997), pp. 416–444

Boswell, J., 'The Informal Social Control of Business in Britain: 1880–1939, *Business History Review* 57 (1983) pp. 236–250

Braverman, H., *Labor and Monopoly Capital* (New York, 1974)

Bremner, D., *The Industries of Scotland* (Edinburgh, 1969)

Briggs, A., and Saville, J. (eds), *Essays in Labour History* (London, 1960)

Broadberry, S. R., and Crafts, N. F. R., 'Britain's Productivity Gap in the 1930s: Some Neglected Factors', *Journal of Economic History*, 52, 3 (September, 1992), pp. 531–559

Brown, C. G., *Religion and Society in Scotland Since 1707* (Edinburgh, 1997)

Brown, J., and Rose, M. B. (eds), *Entrepreneurship, Networks and Modern Business* (Manchester, 1993)

Brown, K. D. (ed), *Essays in Anti-labour History* (London, 1974)

Brown, K. D., 'The Anti-Socialist Union, 1908–49', in Brown, K. D. (ed.), *Essays in Anti-Labour History* (London, 1974)

Burawoy, M., *The Politics of Power* (London, 1985)

Burgess, K., 'Authority relations and the division of labour in British industry with special reference to Clydeside c. 1860–1930' *Social History* 11 (1986), pp. 211–238

Burgess, K., *The Challenge of Labour* (London, 1980)

Burnett J., 'The Baking Industry in the 19th Century', *Business History* 5 (London, 1962), pp. 98–108

Butt, J., 'The Industries of Glasgow' in Fraser, W. H., and Maver, I. (eds), *Glasgow, Volume II: 1830–1912* (Manchester, 1996)

Cage, R., *The Scottish Poor Law* (Edinburgh, 1981)

Cain, P. J., 'The British Railway Rates Problem 1894–1913, *Business History* 20 (1978), pp. 87–99

Campbell, A. B., *The Lanarkshire Miners* (Edinburgh, 1979)

Campbell, R. H., 'The Law and the Joint Stock Company in Scotland', in P. L. Payne (ed), *Studies in Scottish Business History* (London, 1967)

Campbell, R. H, *The Rise And Fall of Scottish Industry 1707–1939* (Edinburgh, 1980)

Carvel, J. L., *The Coltness Iron Company* (Edinburgh, 1948)

Casson, M. C., 'Entrepreneurship and Business Culture', in J. Brown and M. B. Rose (eds), *Entrepreneurship, Networks and Modern Business* (Manchester, 1993)

Casson, M. B., and Rose, M. B., 'Institutions and the Evolution of Modern Business: Introduction', *Business History* 39 (1997) pp. 1–9

Cathoun, C., *et al, Bourdieu: Critical Perspectives* (Cambridge, 1993)

Checkland, S. G., and O., *Industry and Ethos, Scotland 1832–1914* (London, 1984)

Checkland, S. G., *The Upas Tree: Glasgow 1875–1975* (Glasgow, 1976)

Child, J., 'Organizational Structure, Environment and Performance: The Role of Strategic Choice', *Sociology*, 6 (London, 1972), pp. 1–22

Church, R. *et al*, 'British Coal Mining Strikes 1893–1940: Dimensions, Distribution and Persistence', *British Journal of Industrial Relations*, 28, 3 (1990), pp. 329–349

Church, R., *The History of the British Coal Industry, Volume 3, 1830–1913* (Oxford, 1986)

Clark, S., *Paisley, A History* (Edinburgh, 1988)

Clayre, A. (ed), *Nature and Industrialisation* (London, 1982)

Clegg, H. *et al, A History of British Trade Unions Since 1889, Volume 1* (Oxford, 1964)

Cook, P. L. (ed), *The Effects of Mergers* (London, 1958)

Cooke, A. *et al* (eds), *Modern Scottish History* (East Linton, 1998)

Cronin, 'Strikes and Power in Britain, 1870–1920', *International Review of Social History*, 32 (1987), pp. 144–167

Crouch, C., *Class Conflict and the Industrial Relations Crisis* (London, 1977)

Cunnison, J., and Gilfillan, J. B. S., *Third Statistical Account of Scotland* (Glasgow, 1958)

Dandie, H. J., *The Story of the 'Baxters'* (Aberdeen, 1990)

Daunton, M. J., '"Gentlemanly Capitalism" and British Industry 1820–1914' *Past and Present* 122 (1989), pp. 119–158

Davidson, R., *Lord Askwith, Industrial Problems and Disputes* (Brighton, 1974)

Devine, T. M., and Finlay, R. (eds), *Scottish Elites* (Edinburgh, 1994)

Devine, T. M. (ed), *Farm Servants and Labour in Lowland Scotland 1770–1914* (Edinburgh, 1984)

Devlin R., 'Strike Patterns and Employers' Responses in Comparative Perspective', in Kenefick W, and McIvor A. J. (eds), *Roots of Red Clydeside, 1910–1914* (Edinburgh, 1996)

Dickson, T. (ed), *Capital and Class in Scotland* (Edinburgh, 1982)

Dickson, T. (ed), *Scottish Capitalism* (London, 1980)

Dickson, T., and Clarke, T., 'The Making of a Class Society: Commercialization and Working Class Resistance, 1780–1830', in Dickson, T. (ed), *Scottish Capitalism* (London, 1980)

Dickson, T., and Treble, J. (eds), *People and Society in Scotland, Volume 3, 1914–1990* (Edinburgh, 1992)

Donaldson, L., *For Positivist Organizational Theory* (London, 1996)

Dunbabin, J. P. D, *Rural Discontent in 19th Century Britain* (London, 1974)

Duncan, R. and McIvor, A. J. (eds), *Militant Workers* (London, 1992)

Duncan, R., 'Eviction, Riot and Resistance: Motherwell and the Scottish Railway Strike: December 1890–January 1891', *Scottish Labour History Review*, No. 1 (1987), pp.10–12

Duncan, R., *Steelopolis* (London, 1991)

Elbaum, B., and Lazonick, W. (eds), *The Decline of the British Economy* (Oxford, 1986)

Fitzgerald, R., and Greneir, J., *Timber: A Centenary History of the Timber Trade Federation, 1892–1992* (London, 1992)

Fitzgerald, R., *British Labour Management and Industrial Welfare 1846–1939* (London, 1988)

Foster, J., 'A Proletarian Nation? Occupation and Class Since 1914', in Dickson, T., and Treble, J. (eds), *People and Society in Scotland Volume 3, 1914–1990* (Edinburgh, 1992)

Foster, J., 'Strike Action and Working Class Politics on Clydeside 1914–1919', *International Review of Social History*, 35 (1990), pp. 33–70

Foster, J., and Woolfson, C., *The Politics of the UCS Work-In* (London, 1986)

Foster, J., *Class Struggle and the Industrial Revolution* (London, 1974)

Foster, J., 'Class', in A. Cooke *et al* (eds), *Modern Scottish History* (East Linton, 1998)

Fox, A., *A History of the National Union of Boot and Shoe Operatives, 1874–1957* (Oxford, 1958)

Fraser W. H., and Morris R. J. (eds), *People and Society in Scotland, Volume 2*, 1830–1914 (Edinburgh, 1989)

Fraser, W. H., 'The Glasgow Cotton Spinners, 1837' in Lythe E., and Butt J (eds), *Scottish Themes* (Edinburgh, 1976), pp. 80–98

Fraser, W. H., and Maver, I. (eds), *Glasgow, Volume II: 1830–1912* (Manchester, 1996)

Fraser, W. H., *Conflict and Class* (Edinburgh, 1983)

Fraser, W. H., *The Coming of the Mass Market, 1850–1914* (London, 1981)

Fraser, W. H., *A History of British Trade Unionism, 1700–1998* (London, 1999)

Friedman, A. L., *Industry and Labour* (London, 1977)

Giddens, A., *Capitalism in Modern Social Theory* (Cambridge, 1931)

Godley, A., 'The Development of the UK Clothing Industry, 1850–1950: Output and Productivity Growth.', *Business History* 37 (1995), pp. 49–61

Gordon, E., *Women in the Labour Movement in Scotland, 1850–1915* (Oxford, 1991)

Gordon, E., and Trainor, R., 'Employers and Policymaking: Scotland and Northern Ireland, 1880–1939', in Connolly, S. J. *et al* (eds), *Conflict, Identity and Economic Development, Ireland and Scotland, 1600–1939* (Preston, 1995)

Gordon, G. (ed.), *Perspectives of the Scottish City* (Aberdeen, 1985)

Gospel, H. F., 'Product Markets, Labour Markets, and Industrial Relations: The Case of Flour Milling', *Business History* 31 (1989), pp. 84–97

Gospel, H. F., 'The Development of Bargaining Structure: The Case of Electrical Contracting, 1914–1939', in Wrigley C. J. (ed.), *A History of British Industrial Relations Volume 2, 1914–1939* (Brighton, 1987)

Gospel, H. F., *Markets, Firms and the Management of Labour in Modern Britain* (London, 1992)

Gospel, H. F., 'Markets, institutions, and the development of national collective bargaining in Britain: a comment on Adams', *Economic History Review* 51, 3 (1998), pp. 591–596

Grant, W. P., and Marsh, D., 'The Representation of Retail Interests in Britain', *Political Studies*, 22 (1974), pp. 168–177

Grant, W. P., and Marsh, D., *The CBI* (London, 1977)

Grant, W. P., and Sargant, J., *Business and Politics in Britain* (London, 1987)

Gurney, P., *Co-operative Culture and the Politics of Consumption in England, 1870–1930* (Manchester, 1996)

Hannah, L., *The Rise of the Corporate Economy* (London, 1976)

Harrison, R., and Zeitlin, J. (eds), *Divisions of Labour* (Sussex, 1985)

Harvie, C., *No Gods and Precious Few Heroes* (Edinburgh, 1981)

Hinton, J., *Labour and Socialism* (Brighton, 1986)

Hinton, J., *The First Shop Stewards' Movement* (London, 1973)

Hood, J., *The History of Clydebank* (Carnforth, 1988)

Howell, D., 'Reading Alistair Reid: A Future for Labour History?', in N. Kirk (ed), *Social Class and Marxism* (Aldershot, 1996), pp. 86–102

Hunt, E. H., *Regional Wage Variations in Britain, 1850–1914* (Oxford, 1973)

Hutchison, G., and O'Neill, M., *The Springburn Experience* (Edinburgh, 1989)

Hyman, R., 'Mass Organisation, and Militancy in Britain: Constraints and Continuities', in Mommsen, W. J., and Husung, H. G. (eds), *The Development of Trade Unionism in Great Britain and Germany 1880–1914* (London, 1985), pp. 250–266

Hyman, R., *Industrial Relations: A Marxist Introduction* (London, 1975)

Ilerisic R., and Liddle, P.F.B., *Parliament of Commerce* (London, 1960)

Jefferys, J. B., *The Story of the Engineers, 1800–1945* (London, 1945)

Jervis, F. R., *The Economics of Mergers* (London, 1971)

Johnston, R., 'Clydeside Employers, 1870–1920: Individualistic or Class Conscious?', *Scottish Labour History Journal* 32 (1997), pp. 61–79

Johnston, R., '"Charity that Heals": The Scottish Labour Colony Association and Attitudes to the Able-bodied Unemployed in Glasgow, 1890–1914', *Scottish Historical Review*, 77, 203 (1998), pp. 77–95

Johnston, R., and McIvor, A. J., *Lethal Work: A History of the Asbestos Tragedy in Scotland* (East Linton, 2000)

Johnston, T., *History of the Working Classes in Scotland* (Glasgow, 1946)

Jones, G. S., *The Language of Class. Studies in English Working Class History 1832–1986* (Cambridge, 1983)

Jones, S. R. H., 'Transaction Costs and the Theory of the Firm: The Scope and Limitations of the New Institutional Approach.', *Business History* 39 (October, 1997), pp. 9–26

Joyce, P., 'Refabricating labour history; or, from labour history to the history of labour', *Labour History Review*, 62, 2 (1997), pp.147–153

Joyce, P., 'The Return of History: Postmodernism and the Politics of Academic History in Britain', *Past and Present*, 158 (1998), pp.207–235

Kenefick, W., and McIvor, A. J. (eds), *Roots of Red Clydeside, 1910–1914* (Edinburgh, 1996)

Kenefick, W., 'A Struggle for Control: The Importance of the Great Unrest at Glasgow Harbour, 1911 to 1912', in W. Kenefick and A. J. McIvor (eds), *Roots of Red Clydeside, 1910–1914* (Edinburgh, 1996)

Kinloch, J., and Butt, J., *History of the Scottish Co-operative Wholesale Society Limited* (Glasgow, 1981)

Kirby, M. W., and Rose, M. B., *Business Enterprise in Modern Britain* (London, 1994)

Kirk, N., 'Class and the "Linguistic-turn" in Chartist and Post-Chartist Historiography', in Kirk, N. (ed.), *Social Class and Marxism* (Aldershot, 1996)

Kirk, N. (ed.), *Social Class and Marxism* (Aldershot, 1996)

Kirk, N., *Change, Continuity and Class: Labour in British Society, 1850–1920* (Manchester, 1998)

Knox, W., and Corr, H., '"Striking Women": Cotton workers and industrial unrest, *c.* 1907–1914', in Kenefick, W., and McIvor, A. J. (eds), *Roots of Red Clydeside 1910–1914* (Edinburgh, 1996), pp. 107–129

Knox, W. (ed), *Scottish Labour Leaders, 1918–1939* (Edinburgh, 1984)

Knox, W., *Industrial Nation* (Edinburgh, 1999)

Knox, W., 'Class, Work and Trade Unionism in Scotland', in A. Dickson and J. H. Treble (eds), *People and Society in Scotland, Vol. 3, 1914–1990* (Edinburgh, 1992)

Knox, W., *Hanging By A Thread* (Preston, 1995)

Levitt, I., 'The Scottish Poor Law and Unemployment', in T. C. Smout (ed.), *The Search for Wealth and Stability* (London, 1979)

Lenman, B., *An Economic History of Modern Scotland* (London, 1977)

Levitt, I., *Poverty and Welfare in Scotland, 1890–1948* (Edinburgh, 1981)

Levy, H., *Monopoly and Competition* (London, 1911)

Littler, C. R., and Salaman, G., 'Recent theories of the labour process', *Sociology* 16 (1982), pp. 251–269

Littler, C. R., *The Development of the Labour Process in Capitalist Societies* (London, 1982)

Lloyd George, D., *War Memories* (London, 1938)

Lorenz, E. H, *Economic Decline in Britain: The Shipbuilding Industry, 1890–1917* (Oxford, 1991)

Lovell, J., 'Employers and Craft Unionism', *Business History* 34, 4 (1992), pp. 38–58

Lythe, E., and Butt, J. (eds), *Scottish Themes* (Edinburgh, 1976)

MacDonald, C. M. M., 'Weak Roots and Branches: Class, Gender and the Geography of Industrial Protest', *Scottish Labour History* 33 (1998), pp. 6–31

MacDougall, I., *Labour Records in Scotland* (Edinburgh, 1978)

Macrosty, H. W., *The Trust Movement in British Industry* (London, 1907)

Marsh, D., 'On Joining Interest Groups: An Empirical Consideration of the Work of Mancur Olson Jnr.', *British Journal of Political Science* 6 (1976), pp. 257–271

Marshall, W. S., *'The Billy Boys': A Concise History of Orangeism in Scotland* (Edinburgh, 1996)

Marwick, A., *Britain in the Century of Total War* (London, 1970)

Marx, K., *Capital, Vol. 1* (London, 1976)

Maver, I., *Glasgow* (Edinburgh, 2000)

Maver, I., 'Politics and Power in the Scottish City: Glasgow's Town Council in the 19th Century' in Devine, T. M., and Finlay, R. (eds), *Scottish Elites* (Edinburgh, 1994)

Maver, I., 'Glasgow's Municipal Workers and Industrial Strife', in Kenefick, W. and McIvor, A. J. (eds), *Roots of Red Clydeside 1910–1914* (Edinburgh, 1996), pp. 214–240

McCaffrey, J., 'Liberal Unionism in the West of Scotland', *Scottish Historical Review*, 149 (April 1971), p. 58.

McCraw, T. K. (ed), *The Essential Alfred Chandler* (Boston, 1988)

McCrone, D., 'Towards a Principled Society', in Dickson, A., and Treble, J. H. (eds), *People and Society in Scotland, Vol. 3, 1914–1990* (Edinburgh, 1992)

McGoldrick, J., 'Crisis and Division of Labour: Clydeside Shipbuilding in the Inter-War Period', in Dickson, T. (ed), *Capital and Class in Scotland* (Edinburgh, 1982), pp. 143–186

McCraw, T. K. (ed), *The Essential Alfred Chandler* (Boston, 1988)

McIvor, A. J., 'Were Clydeside Employers More Autocratic?', in Kenefick, W., and McIvor, A. J (eds), *Roots of Red Clydeside 1910–1914* (Edinburgh, 1996)

McIvor, A. J., *Organised Capital* (London, 1996)

McIvor, A. J., and Paterson, H., 'Combating the Left: Victimisation and Anti-Labour Activities on Clydeside, 1900–1939', in Duncan, R. and McIvor, A. J. (eds), *Militant Workers* (London, 1992)

McKay, I., 'Bondage in the Bakehouse? The Strange Case of the Journeymen Bakers, 1840–1880', in Harrison, R., and Zeitlin, J. (eds), *Divisions of Labour* (London, 1985)

McKenna, J. A., and Rodger, R. C., 'Control by Coercion: Employers' Associations and the Establishment of Industrial Order in the Building Industry of England and Wales 1860–1914', *Business History Review* 59 (1985), pp. 223–231

McKinlay A., *Making Ships, Making Men: Working for John Brown's Between the Wars* (Clydebank, 1989)

McKinlay, A., 'Philosophers in Overalls?: Craft and Class on Clydeside, *c.* 1900–1914', in Kenefick, W., and McIvor, A. J. (eds), *Roots of Red Clydeside 1910–1914* (Edinburgh, 1996)

McKinlay, A., 'The Inter-War Depression and the Effort Bargain. Shipyard Riveters and the "Workmen's Foreman"', *Scottish Economic and Social History* 9 (1989), pp. 54–67.

McKinlay, A., and Zeitlin, J., 'The Meaning of Managerial Prerogative: Industrial Relations and the Organisation of Work in British Engineering, 1880–1939', *Business History* 31 (1989), pp. 32–47

McLean, I., 'Red Clydeside After 25 Years', *Scottish Labour History Journal* 29 (1994)

McLean, I., *The Legend of Red Clydeside* (Edinburgh, 1981)

Meldrum, A. J., and Alexander, A. F., *The Story of the Scottish Grocers' Federation, 1918–1989* (Edinburgh 1993)

Melling, J., '"Non-Commissioned Officers": British Employers and their Supervisory Workers, 1880–1920', *Social History* 5 (1980), pp. 183–221

Melling, J., 'The Servile State Revisited: Law and Industrial Capitalism in the early 20th Century', *Scottish Labour History Journal* 24 (1989), pp. 68–86

Melling, J., 'Scottish Industrialists and the Changing Character of Class Relations in the Clyde Region, *c.* 1880–1918.', in Dickson, T. (ed), *Capital and Class in Scotland* (Edinburgh, 1982), pp. 61–143

Melling, J., 'Whatever Happened to Red Clydeside? Industrial Conflict and the Politics of Skill in the First World War', *International Review of Social History* 35 (1990), pp. 3–32

Melling, J., 'Employers, Industrial Housing and the Evolution of Company Welfare Policies in Britain's Heavy Industries', *International Review of Social History* 26 (1981), pp. 255–301

Melling, J., 'Managing the labour problem: the British worker question and the decline of manufacturing industry', *Labour History Review* 57, 3 (1992)

Middlemas, K., *Politics in Industrial Society* (London, 1979)

Miliband, R., *The State in Capitalist Society* (London, 1979)

Miller, W., 'Politics in the Scottish City, 1832–1982', in G. Gordon (ed), *Perspectives of the Scottish City* (Aberdeen, 1985), pp. 180–212

Mitchison, R., 'The Making of the old Scottish Poor Law', *Past and Present* 62 (1974), pp. 36–51

Moe, T. M., *The Organisation of Interests* (Chicago, 1980)

Mommsen W., and Husung, H. G., *The Development of Trade Unionism in Great Britain and Germany, 1880–1914* (London, 1985)

Morera, E., *Gramsci's Historicism* (London, 1990)

Morgan, M., and Trainor, R., 'The Dominant Classes', in Fraser, W. H., and Morris, R. J. (eds), *People and Society in Scotland Vol. 2, 1830–1914.* (London, 1989), pp. 103–138

Morgan, N. J., and Daunton, M. J., 'Landlords in Glasgow: A Study of 1900', *Business History* 25 (1983), pp. 264–286

Morrison, K., *Marx, Durkheim, Weber* (London, 1995)

Moss, M. S., and Hume, J. R., *Workshop of the British Empire. Engineering and Shipbuilding in the West of Scotland* (London, 1977)

Moss, M., *100 Years of Provisioning Scotland* (Glasgow, 1989)

Nenadic, S., 'Businessmen, the middle classes and the dominance of manufacturing in 19th century Britain', *Economic History Review* 44 (1991), pp. 66–85

Nenadic, S., 'The Small Family Firm in Victorian Britain', *Business History* 35, 4 (1993), pp. 86–115

Nettl, J. P., 'Consensus or Elite Domination: the Case of Business', *Political Studies* 13 (1965) pp. 22–44

Newby, H., 'Paternalism and Capitalism', in Scase R. (ed), *Industrial Society: Class, Cleavage and Control* (London, 1977), pp. 59–74

Olson M. Jnr, *The Logic of Collective Action* (Oxford, 1965)

Olson, M. Jnr, *The Rise and Decline of Nations* (Yale, 1982)

Payne, P. L. (ed), *Studies in Scottish Business History* (London, 1967)

Payne, P. L., *Colvilles and the Scottish Steel Industry* (Oxford, 1979)

Payne, P. L., *Growth and Contraction: Scottish Industry, c. 1880–1990* (Dundee, 1991)

Payne, P. L., 'The Emergence of the Large-scale Company in Great Britain, 1870–1914', *Economic History Review* 2nd series, 20 (1967), pp. 519–541

Pelling, H., *Popular Politics and Society in Late Victorian Britain* (London, 1979)

Perkin, H., *The Origins of Modern English Society, 1780–1880* (London, 1974)

Phelps Brown, H., *The Origins of Trade Union Power* (Oxford, 1986)

Pollard, S., 'Co-operation: from Community Building to Shopkeeping', in Briggs, A., and Saville, J. (eds), *Essays in Labour History* (London, 1960), pp. 74–113

Porter, J. H., 'Wage Bargaining under Conciliation Agreements, 1860–1914', *Economic History Review* 2nd Series, 23 (1970), pp.460–475

Postgate, R. W., *The Builders' History* (London, 1923)

Price, R., *Masters, Unions and Men* (London, 1980)

Purvis, M., 'Co-operative Retailing in Britain', in Benson, J., and Shaw, G. (eds), *The Evolution of Retail Systems, c. 1800–1914* (Leicester, 1992)

Rawlinson, G., and Robinson, A., 'The United Turkey Red Strike – December 1911', in W. Kenefick and A. J. McIvor (eds), *Roots of Red Clydeside 1910–1914* (Edinburgh, 1996), pp. 175–193

Reader, W. J., 'The United Kingdom Soapmakers' Association and the English Soap Trade', *Business History* 1 (1958–59) pp. 77–83

Reid A. J., 'The impact of the First World War on British Workers', in Wall, R., and Winter, J. (eds), *The Upheaval of War, Family, Work and Welfare in Europe, 1914–1918* (Cambridge, 1988)

Reid, A. J., 'The Division of Labour and Politics in Britain, 1880–1920', in W. Mommsen and H. G. Husung (eds), *The Development of Trade Unionism in Great Britain and Germany, 1880–1914* (London, 1985), pp.150–166

Reid, A. J., 'Marxism and revisionism in British Labour History', *Bulletin of the Society for the Study of Labour History* 52, 3 (London, 1987), pp. 38–51

Reid, A. J., 'Employers' Strategies and Craft Production', in Toliday, S. and Zeitlin, J. (eds), *The Power to Manage?* (London, 1991)

Reid, H., *The Furniture Makers* (Oxford, 1986)

Renfrew, A., 'Militant Miners?: Strike Activity and Industrial Relations in the Lanarkshire Coalfield 1910–1914', in Kenefick, W., and McIvor, A. J. (eds), *Roots of Red Clydeside 1910–1914* (Edinburgh, 1996), pp. 153–175

Reynolds, S., *Britannica's Typesetters* (Edinburgh, 1989)

Richardson, H. W., and Aldcroft, D., *Building in the British Economy Between the Wars* (London, 1968)

Riddell, J. F., *Clyde Navigation* (Edinburgh, 1979)

Rodger, R., 'Structural Instability in the Scottish Building Industry, 1820–1880', *Construction History* (1985), pp. 48–60

Rodger, R., 'Concentration and Fragmentation: Capital and Labour and the Structure of Mid-Victorian Scottish Industry', *Journal of Urban History* 14 (1988), pp. 182–195.

Rodgers, T., 'Sir Allan Smith and the Industrial Group and the Politics of Unemployment, 1919–1924' *Business History* 18, 1 (1986), pp. 100–123

Rose, L., *Rogues and Vagabonds* (London, 1988)

Rose, M. B., 'Institutions and the Evolution of Modern Business: Introduction', *Business History* 39 (1997), pp.128–151

Rubin, G. R., *War, Law and Labour* (Oxford, 1987)

Rubinstein W. D., *Elites and the Wealthy in Modern British History: Essays in Social and Economic History* (Brighton, 1987)

Rubinstein, W. D., 'The Victorian Middle Classes: Wealth Occupation and Geography', *Economic History Review*, 2nd Series, 30 (1977), pp. 602–623

Rubinstein, W. D., 'Wealth, Elites and the Class Structure of Modern Britain', *Past and Present* 76 (1977), pp. 99–127

Rubinstein, W. D., 'A Reply to M. J. Daunton', *Past and Present* 132 (1991), pp. 150–187

Salisbury, R. H. (ed), *Interest Group Politics in America* (London, 1970)

Savage, M., 'Space, networks and class formation', in N. Kirk (ed), *Social Class and Marxism* (Aldershot, 1996)

Savage, M., and Miles, A., *The Remaking of the British Working Class, 1840–1940* (London, 1994)

Saville, J., *The Consolidation of the Capitalist State* (London, 1994)

Sayer, K., *Women in the Fields* (Manchester, 1995)

Scase R. (ed), *Industrial Society: Class, Cleavage and Control* (London, 1977)

Scott, J., and Hughes, M., *The Anatomy of Scottish Capital* (London, 1980)

Scott, W. R., and Cunnison J., *The Industries of the Clyde Valley* (Oxford, 1927)

Sessions, M., *The Federation of Master Printers: How it Began* (London, 1950)

Shaw, G., 'The evolution and impact of large-scale retailing in Britain', in Benson, J., and Shaw, G. (eds), *The Evolution of Retail Systems, c. 1800–1914* (London, 1992)

Slaven, A., and Woon Kim, D., 'The Origins and Economic and Social Roles of Scotland's Business Leaders 1860–1960, in Devine, T. M., and Finlay, R. (eds), *Scottish Elites* (Edinburgh, 1994)

Slaven, A., and Checkland, S. (eds), *Directory of Business Biography Volume 1, 1860–1960* (Aberdeen, 1986)

Slaven, A., and Checkland, S. (eds), *Directory of Business Biography Volume II, 1860–1960* (Aberdeen, 1990)

Smith, A. M., *The Three United Trades of Dundee* (Dundee, 1987)

Smith, A. M., *The Nine Trades of Dundee* (Dundee, 1995)

Smout, T. C. (ed), *The Search for Wealth and Stability* (London, 1979)

Smout, T. C., *A Century of the Scottish People, 1830–1955* (London, 1987)

Soldon, N., 'Laissez-Faire as Dogma: The LPDL', in Brown, K. D. (ed), *Essays in Anti-Labour History* (London, 1974), pp. 208–234

Stenton, M., and Lees, S., *Who's Who of British Members of Parliament*, Vols 2, 3, and, 4 (Sussex, 1978)

Stevenson D., *The Origins of Freemasonry* (Cambridge, 1988)

Supple, B., *The History of the British Coal Industry, Volume 4, 1913–1946* (Oxford, 1987)

Sweeney, I., 'Local Party Politics and the Temperance Crusade: Glasgow, 1890–1902', *Scottish Labour History Journal* 27 (1992), pp.44–64

Teichova, A., *et al., Multinational Enterprises in Historical Perspective* (Cambridge, 1986)

Tolliday, S., and Zeitlin, J. (eds), *The Power To Manage?* (1991)

Trainor, R., 'Urban Elites in Victorian Britain', *Urban History Yearbook* (London, 1985), pp. 1–17

Trainor, R., *Black Country Elites* (Oxford, 1993)

Treble, J. H., 'The seasonal demand for adult labour in Glasgow, 1880–1914', *Social History* 3 (1978), pp. 43–61

Treble, J. H., *Urban Poverty in Britain, 1830–1914* (London, 1979)

Turner, J. (ed), *Businessmen and Politics* (London, 1984)

Turner, J., 'Man and Braverman', *History, Vol. 70*, 229 (1985)

Van Waarden, F., Organizational Emergence and Developments of Business Interest Associations: An Example from the Netherlands, unpublished paper presented at Business History Conference, Leiden, 18 Oct. 1997

Vichnia, J. E., 'The Management of Labor: the British and French Iron and Steel Industries, 1860–1918', *Review of Business History* 34 (1992), pp. 195–197

Waddington, J., *The Politics of Bargaining* (London, 1995)

Walker, J., *British Economic and Social History* (London, 1968)

Wall, R., and Winter, J. (eds), *The Upheaval of War: Family, Work and Welfare in Europe, 1914–1918* (Cambridge, 1988)

Weber, M., *Economy and Society* (New York, 1968)

Weir, W., *Glasgow Pawnbrokers' Association, The First Hundred Years 1851–1951* (Glasgow, No Date)

Westall, O. M., 'The competitive environment of British Business, 1850–1914', in W. Kirby and M. B. Rose (eds), *Business enterprise in Modern Britain* (London, 1994)

White, S., 'Ideology Hegemony and Political Control: The Sociology of Anti-Bolshevism in Britain 1918–1920', *Scottish Labour History Journal* 9, June (London, 1975) pp.14–27

White, S., *Britain and the Bolshevik Revolution* (New York, 1979)

Who Was Who, Volume 4 1941–50 (London, 1952)

Wiener, M. J., *English Culture and the Decline of the Industrial Spirit, 1850–1918* (London, 1992)

Wigham, E., *The Power to Manage* (London, 1973)

Williamson, O., *Markets and Hierarchies* (London, 1975)

Wilkinson, F., *The Dynamics of Labour Market Segmentation* (London, 1981)

Winstanley, M. J., *The Shopkeeper's World* (Manchester, 1983)

Winstanley, M., J., 'Concentration and competition in the retail sector, *c.* 1800–1990', in Kirby, M. W. and Rose, M. B. (eds), *Business Enterprise in Modern Britain* (London, 1994)

Wood, S. (ed), *The Degradation of Work?* (London, 1982)

Wrigley, C. J., *David Lloyd George and the British Labour Movement* (London, 1976)

Wrigley, C. J. (ed), *A History of British Industrial Relations, 1914–1939* (Brighton, 1983)

Wrigley, C. J. (ed), *A History of British Industrial Relations, 1939–1979* (Cheltenham, 1996)

Wrigley, C. J., *Cosy Co-operation under Strain: Industrial Relations in the Yorkshire Woollen Industry, 1919–1930* (York, 1987)

Yamey, B. S. (ed), *Resale Price Maintenance* (London, 1966)

Yarmie, A. H., 'Employers' Organisations in Mid-Victorian Britain', *International Review of Social History*, 25 (1980), pp. 209–235

Young, F. H., *A Century of Carpet Making, 1839–1939* (Glasgow, 1943)

Zeitlin, J., 'The Internal Politics of Employer Organisation: The Engineers' Employers' Federation, 1896–1939', in Tolliday, S., and Zeitlin, J. (eds), *The Power To Manage?* (London, 1991)

Unpublished Theses

Brown, C., Religion and the Development of an Urban Society: Glasgow, 1780–1914, Ph.D. thesis, University of Glasgow (1981)

Corrins, R. D., William Baird and Company, Coal and Iron Masters, 1830–1914, Ph.D. thesis, University of Strathclyde (London, 1974)

Cotterill, M. S., The Scottish Gas Industry up to 1914, Ph.D. thesis, University of Strathclyde (1976)

Donnachie, I., The Development of the Scottish Brewing Industry, 1750–1914, Ph.D. thesis, University of Strathclyde (1976)

Eccles, A., Shipyard Employers and Urban Townships on Clydeside, M. Phil thesis, University of Paisley (1994)

Edwards, B. W., Urban Design and Conservation in Glasgow, 1840–1910, with Particular Reference to the Old Town, Ph.D. thesis, University of Glasgow (1989)

Magrath, I. M., Wool Textile Employers' Organisations, Bradford *c.* 1914–1945, Ph.D. thesis, University of Bradford (1991)

McKinlay, A., Employers and Skilled Labour in the Inter-War Depression. Engineering and Shipbuilding on Clydeside, 1919–1939, D. Phil. thesis, University of Oxford (1986)

Melling, J., British Employers and the Development of Industrial Welfare *c.* 1880–1920, Ph.D. thesis, University of Glasgow (1980)

Nasibian, A., Attitudes on Clydeside towards the Russian Revolution, 1917–1924, M. Litt. thesis, University of Strathclyde (1977)

Nenadic, S., The Structure and Influence of the Scottish Urban Middle Class, Glasgow 1800–1870, Ph.D. thesis, University of Glasgow (1986)

Reid, A. J., The Division of Labour in the British Shipbuilding Industry, with Particular Reference to Clydeside, D.Phil. thesis, University of Cambridge (1980)

Renfrew, A., Mechanisation and the Miner: Work, Safety and Labour Relations in the Scottish Coal Industry c.1890–1939, Ph.D thesis, University of Strathclyde (1997)

Sweeney, I., The Municipal Administration of Glasgow, 1833–1912: Public Service and the Scottish Civic Identity, Ph.D. thesis, University of Strathclyde (1990)

Index